'A vehement thirst after knowledge'

'A vehement thirst after knowledge'

Four centuries of education in Shetland

JOHN J. GRAHAM

"... *people (of Foula) have a very vehement thirst and desire after knowledge*".   Zetland Presbytery Petition to SSPCK 7/6/1716

The Shetland Times Ltd.,
Lerwick.
1998.

Copyright © John J. Graham 1998.

First published by The Shetland Times Ltd., 1998.

ISBN 1 898852 41 3

All rights reserved.
No part of this publication may be reproduced, stored in a retrieval system, or transmitted, in any form, or by any means, electronic, mechanical, photocopying, recording or otherwise, without the prior written permission of the publishers.

British Library Cataloguing-in-Publication Data
A catalogue record for this book is
available from the British Library.

Printed and published by
The Shetland Times Ltd.,
Prince Alfred Street,
Lerwick, Shetland, ZE1 0EP.
1998.

Contents

LIST OF ILLUSTRATIONS viii
ACKNOWLEDGEMENTS ix
ABBREVIATIONS x

Chapter

I   BACKGROUND 1
II   CHURCH AND LOCAL ADMINISTRATION 7
III   EDUCATION BEFORE 1700 13
IV   BEGINNINGS OF ORGANISED EDUCATION 1700-1740 . . 18
    SSPCK Schools
    Lethargic Presbytery
    "Petty" Schools
    Society Schools in Orkney
V   SOCIETY SCHOOLS CONSOLIDATE 30
    Buchan of Northmavine
    Society's Ambulatory Schools
    The Remote Islands
    Negligence and Incompetence
    Society Curriculum
    Salaries
    Experiment in Practical Education
VI   LEGAL SCHOOLS — EARLY ATTEMPTS TO ESTABLISH . . 43
    Reluctant Heritors
    Thomas Gifford, Laird of Busta
    Gifford's Initiative
    Gifford's Plan Collapses
VII   BUCHAN OF WALLS 50
    A Sympathetic Heritor
    Famine and Pestilence
    Local Men as Teachers
    Problems of Ambulatory Schools
    Blast from Buchan's Trumpet
    Buchan's Grand Design
    "That Laudable End"
    "A Lasting Foundation"

        Happyhansel School
        A School for all Seasons
        A Legal Foundation at Last

VIII LEGAL SCHOOLS — THE LONG STRUGGLE 70
        Society's Ultimatum
        Commissioners of Supply Involved
        Kemp Controversy

IX MATHEWSON AND YELL 83
        Removal to Fetlar
        Teacher in the Making
        Candidate for Parochial School
        "A Sufficient Schoolhouse"
        The School Opens
        Inside the Classroom
        Discipline
        Text-books
        Sabbath Schools
        Conflict with Parish Minister
        Absences from School

X A PATCHWORK SYSTEM 106
        A Changing Society
        Educational Surveys
        Accommodation

XI SOCIETY SCHOOLS INSPECTED, 1835 118

XII SCHOOLS OF ADVANCED EDUCATION 123
        Lerwick Subscription Schools
        Moravian Teachers
        Lerwick Instruction Society
        Arthur Anderson
        Anderson Educational Institute

XIII BEGINNINGS OF STATE EDUCATION 136
        School Boards 1872-1900
        Curriculum in the Elementary School
        Discipline
        Payment by Results
        Teachers after 1872 — the Move to Professionalism
        Pupil Teachers
        Women Teachers
        Junior Students
        Security of Tenure
        The Robert Young Dismissal

XIV ANDERSON EDUCATIONAL INSTITUTE — THE
SCHOOL IN OPERATION 164
Elementary Department
Under School Board Control
Secondary Department
John Allardice (1876-1883)
National Development of Secondary Education
Anderson Institute — Secondary School for Shetland

XV SOME REMARKABLE TEACHERS 177

XVI THE TWENTIETH CENTURY 183
Lerwick — Pressure on Accommodation
Anderson Institute — Solely Secondary School
Joseph Kirton
Andrew T. Cluness

THE LONG PLATEAU 1900-1960 187
Curriculum
Side Schools
Health
School Meals
Bursaries
Control Examination
Promotion Scheme

DECADES OF CHANGE 1960-1990 192
Curricular Change
Secondary Education
Two-Tier System
Anderson High School
Barrage of Official Reports

FURTHER EDUCATION 200
Plans for Agricultural Training
Rapid Expansion
Fisheries Training

XVII RETROSPECT 205

APPENDICES:
A. Shetland Teachers and Schools (Early Days-1900) 207
B. Gifford's Country Act, 1724 230
C. Report on Society School in Sandness, 1744 233
D. Buchan's Letter on his Plans for Happyhansel 234

GLOSSARY 240

MAIN SOURCES CONSULTED 241

INDEX OF NAMES AND PLACES 244

List of Illustrations

1. AEI with teachers and pupils c. 1880.
2. AEI staff and pupils c. 1880.
3. Sandness School — Appeal Letter.
4. Andrew D. Mathewson.
5. Robert Jamieson.
6. East Yell schools.
7. Assembly school, Laxfirth, Tingwall.
8. John Ross.
9. Charles C. Beatton.
10. Thomas Gifford of Busta.
11. Happyhansel School — ruins.
12. SSPCK School, Tangwick, Eshaness.
13. Gilbert Williamson.
14. School Board letter.
15. Malcolm Gaudy.
16. Arthur Anderson.
17. Quarff bairns c. 1903.
18. John Allardice.
19. Robert Young.
20. Lerwick Parochial School c.1872 — pupils with headteacher.
21. Weisdale Public School c.1895 — pupils with headteacher.
22. AEI, 1932 — Class Six with teachers.
23. "Byre" school, Laxfirth, Nesting.
24. AEI — prospectus 1888.
25. Old Vidlin schools.
26. New Vidlin Primary School, 1996.
27. Classroom in Burra Public School, c.1910.
28. Pupils and teacher in new school, Vidlin.

Acknowledgements

SINCE I began, in the early 1960s, gathering information about Shetland schools and schooling, I have been fortunate in receiving help and encouragement from many local people. I owe them all a great debt.

I have obtained a wealth of material from Shetland Archives where I found great co-operation and assistance from Brian Smith and Angus Johnson. Not only did they respond promptly to my many requests but they kept me informed of material which they felt might be of interest. I am also indebted to the staff of Shetland Library and Shetland Museum for help on many occasions.

The original manuscript was read in whole or in part by Miss Nessie Robertson, Mr Lollie Graham, Mr Stewart Hay, Mr Brian Smith, Mr Robert J Storey, and Mr George Watt. I am grateful for their valuable comments.

My researches have trundled on for over 30 years and for her forbearance during that time I must thank Beryl, my wife.

Abbreviations

AB	Able-bodied seaman
AEI	Anderson Educational Institute
HMI	Her/His Majesty's Inspector
Ibid	in the same place
JP	Justice of the Peace
KSM	Kirk Session Minutes
MS	Manuscript
op. cit.	in the work previously mentioned
PP	Parliamentary Papers
RN	Royal Navy
SA	Shetland Archives
SED	Scottish Educational Department
SRO	Scottish Record Office
SSPCK	Society in Scotland for the Propagation of Christian Knowledge
3Rs	Reading, Writing, and Arithmetic
ZPM	Zetland Presbytery Minutes

Chapter 1
History of Education in Shetland

Background

THE DEVELOPMENT of education in any particular area will follow the overall national pattern but the rate of growth and distinctive character will be determined by local conditions — geographical, historical, economic and social. Shetland's position as Scotland's remotest county has made her, even to this day, a difficult unit to fit into any national design, and it is not surprising that the story of her educational progress does not follow closely that of most other Scottish counties.

Throughout this account there is a recurring refrain from contemporary sources of "parishes very discontiguous", "people living in extreme poverty", "heritors in straitened circumstances". A brief account of Shetland's geography, history, economy and social conditions will give some indication of the local factors which shaped its educational development.

Geography

The Shetland Isles, lying about 130 miles north of the Scottish mainland, are an archipelago of 117 islands. Thirty of these were populated in 1861, the peak period of Shetland's population, but now there are only 17. The group extends to almost 100 miles, from Unst, the northmost island, to Fair Isle at the southmost extremity, and to almost 50 miles from Foula in the west to Skerries in the east. The principal island, Mainland, is about 54 miles from north to south.

The coastline is deeply indented with long narrow voes reaching far inland and complicating communications by land, while the general terrain is dominated by hills and moorland, only one acre in every 30 being suitable for cultivation. This arable land is found mainly along the sides of voes and in some valleys, dictating the pattern of population distribution.

The areas of human settlement have thus always been scattered, with the intervening voes and hills making communication from one local community to another rather difficult, particularly before the development of roads in the late 19th century. The county is divided into 12 parishes, each of which, though relatively small in total area, presented enormous problems of accessibility to church and school. When the minister of Nesting was settled in 1847 "he had to preach in turn at Nesting, Lunnasting and Whalsay. In going to Whalsay he had to cross a dangerous sound three or four miles broad with strong tides running... As part of his parish he still retains the district of Lunnasting. This is ordinarily supplied by a missionary. But when a vacancy occurs ... and this has sometimes lasted six months, it is the duty of the parish minister to preach at Lunnasting as well as at home. He had his choice of crossing an arm of sea called Doura Voe, about four miles broad, and then walking through pathless bogs for about another four miles, or of going all the way round the head of Douro Voe. If he went the latter way, before reaching the public road he had to walk for about five miles over ground toilsome in the finest weather. It was climbing up a succession of hillocks and then descending, jumping from one peat bank to another... It may be conceived what the state of things was when in the winter the ground was very soft, and one or two burns had to be crossed."[1]

The parish of Walls included Sandness and the islands of Papa Stour, nine miles offshore, and Foula, 22 miles. The principal heritor of this parish, John Scott, in a petition to Presbytery in 1742, stated "... when the two Isles of Papa and Foula... are quite cut off from the reckoning, there are still two large Parioches remaining in this Ministry, viz: Walls and Sandness, comprehending 884 souls, and the Kirks of these Parioches are six miles of reputed measure, but indeed at least eight English miles distant one from another, and 'tis to be consider'd that there are two lofty mountains lying betwixt them taking up five reputed miles uninhabited, wild mirey ground which makes it impracticable for aged People or Children to travel betwixt these Kirks on foot, neither can any horse pass that way in the winter time, unless he be a very mettld one, and the weather dryer than ordinary."[2]

Some well-defined geographical districts were arbitrarily yoked together to form parochial units, presumably for administrative reasons but in complete violation of geographical realities. The United Parishes of Bressay, Quarff and Burra Isle may not constitute an extensive area as the crow flies but each part is separated from the other by the sea. In 1722, James Williamson was appointed minister and teacher of what must surely be the most formidable parish any clergyman could undertake — the three remote islands of Fair Isle, Foula and Skerries. To carry out his pastoral care he would have had to undertake regular journeys of 150 miles over some of the most treacherous seas anywhere. Perhaps it is not surprising Williamson found he had been given a task which the elements made impossible to carry out effectively. In 1731 the people of Foula complain he is spending only two months annually among them. This situation was one of the extreme examples of the natural obstacles which hindered the organisation of religion and education under the parochial system.

In 1733, Thomas Gifford, one of the principal merchant lairds of the early 18th century, summed up the basic problem: "The want of parochial schools has been long much complained of by the ministers, and many efforts were made to have a school in every parish by a voluntary contribution of the inhabitants, which when set up in any one place was found to be of little use to the whole, they lying so dicontiguous, and those at a distance were not capable to board their children away from home, so such as had no benefit by the school refused to pay these quotas; and hence the school broke up before it was well settled."[3]

Economy

So far as recorded evidence can establish, Shetland has always depended on agriculture and fishing as the mainstays of its economy. With only about 12,000 acres of arable land out of a total of 352,319 acres — a mere three per cent — it is obvious that agriculture can provide a livelihood for only a limited crofting population. There can be no general optimum figure for this population as it must vary according to the standards of living prevailing at various periods; but in Professor Donaldson's study of Shetland in the early years of the 17th century[4] he estimates that at this period a population of between 10,000 and 12,000 lived to a great extent off the land. The Shetlander at that time, as indeed he has done until comparatively recently, engaged in subsistence fishing but also traded fish to the Hanseatic merchants who, during the 16th and 17th centuries, operated from a dozen or so centres throughout the Islands. Fish, agricultural produce, and hosiery were sold on an open market, while the Shetlanders were supplied with hemp, lines, hooks, tar, linen-cloth, tobacco, spirits, and beer, and other luxury articles.[5]

This was a period of relative prosperity for the people of Shetland, soon to be caught up in an economic system which restricted their freedom of choice and which was based on a form of barter. The landlord had also benefited through the leasing of sites for these trading stations at the rate of one penny Sterling for every ling landed.

The British Government's Salt Tax of 1712, with its levy on the importation of foreign salt, was the final straw which compelled the continental merchants to leave Shetland. The removal of these entrepeneurs threatened the very existence of the local economy and the only hope of reviving it lay with the lairds who alone could contribute the necessary capital outlay.

During the first half of the eighteenth century the landlords appear simply to have assumed the role of the continental merchants, buying fish and produce and selling fishing equipment, liquor and general goods, without basically altering the economic relationship between buyer and seller. While they no doubt welcomed the opportunity to turn aside from the humdrum management of unproductive estates to the lure of the world of commerce, these early eighteenth century merchant lairds found trading success all too elusive. Thomas Gifford, perhaps the most successful of them, wrote in 1733: "... but the prime cost of the fish here being very dear... with the value of the salt, and cash and charges in curing them; and that foreign markets often prove very precarious, the exporters seldom make much by these goods exported; nay, when ship's freight and charges are deducted, they oftener lose than gain."[6] This view is confirmed from Gifford's Letter Books of the period, where he frequently bemoans the parlous state of his finances. In 1718 he writes: "I have the last year met with many disappointments in my small trade to Hamburgh, which is all the fund I have for paying my credit at Edinburgh, and unless something can be raised that way, the earle [of Morton] needs expect nothing from me, for I have been travelling through the greatest part of the country to gather the rents and not received above £40 Sterling, and that all in German stoyvers and double stoyvers, a coin that passes no way in the world but in the country where it is made, and in this poor place where we are content to take anything...".[7]

Gifford was Chamberlain to the Earl of Morton, who received the Earldom rents, and the above comments convey something of the essence of the economic situation at the time: tenants impoverished by the departure of the German merchants, and lairds caught in the economic trough between the prosperity of the past, on the one hand, which at least enabled tenants to pay their rents in cash and, on the other, the precarious nature of their present trading ventures.

It is important to keep this in mind when considering the educational picture during the early eighteenth century. At this time pressure was being put on heritors to fulfil their legal obligations in the establishment of parochial schools, as well as the maintenance of kirks and manses, and it is apparent that in their straitened circumstances they were unlikely to regard these obligations with any great enthusiasm.

Having committed themselves to the role of capitalists in the fishing industry, they could not readily withdraw, for they must have realised the importance of fishing to the overall local economy and ultimately themselves. The obvious response to marginal profits was to increase the turnover of fish exported; and to obtain this more fishermen had to become involved. About 1750, bigger boats carrying a crew of six were introduced to fish the deep-sea grounds, 30 to 40 miles offshore, and to ensure the maximum labour force the landlords developed a system of fishing tenures whereby occupancy of a croft involved a commitment to fish for the landlord, who exercised the right of pre-emption in securing the total catch at previously fixed prices.

Writing in the 1790s the minister of Aithsting and Sandsting claims that: "formerly the landlords in this parish were little concerned in the ling fishing. Many persons now alive remember when there was not one six-oared boat in the ministry… The landlords now find it necessary to prosecute the fishing on their own account; and to increase the number of seamen, is their great and constant endeavour. With this view, outsets were increased, greatly to the detriment of the pasture and sheep flocks. The rentalled lands were subdivided, and set on this express provision, that they should fit out a sixth share of a boat to the ling fishing and every encouragement was given to young men to marry, and settle in the country."[8] Ministers of other parishes, writing at this time, are unanimous in their condemnation of this system. For the tenants, it was a form of economic thralldom, tying them to the fragmented crofts on a lease which could be terminated abruptly if they failed to fish for the landlord, and which gave them no stimulus to improve their land or improve stock. In bad years they were thrown completely on the landlord's provision of supplies on credit, which plunged them yet more deeply into servitude, and sapped their qualities of independence and resourcefulness. At the same time, the landlords, caught in a web of their own making, found that the enhanced profits from the expanded fishings were often dissipated in the heavy burden of credit they had to extend to their tenants, particularly when the excessively subdivided crofts failed to provide subsistence for crofter and family.

These conditions continued throughout the remainder of the eighteenth century and for a large part of the nineteenth. The population increased from 15,210 in 1755 to 31,579 in 1861, an increase which inevitably stretched the economy beyond its limits and impoverished the crofting population.

The Crofters' Act of 1886, with its reduced rents, security of tenure, and compensation for improvements, considerably eased the lot of crofters. The great herring fishings at the close of the century brought a measure of increased prosperity, while the opening up of regular sea communication with the Scottish mainland brought the islands closer into touch with modern economic and social trends. In 1872 the introduction of compulsory education provided the stimulus and the means of developing native talents so long repressed and frustrated by limited opportunities.

REFERENCES

1 Russell, John, Three Years in Shetland (1873-76), 1887, pp 130-131
2 ZPM 30/6/1742, SA
3 Gifford, Thomas, Historical Description of Zetland 1733, pp 31-32, Edin. 1889
4 Donaldson, Gordon, Shetland Life under Earl Patrick, 1958, p.136
5 Gifford, Ibid., p.24
6 Gifford, Ibid., p.26
7 Old Lore Miscellany, vol.6
8 Old Statistical Account, ed. E. S. Reid Tait, p.59

Chapter 2
Church and Local Administration

THE DEMAND for education at any particular time is determined by the social pressures, beliefs and needs existing at that time. From 1560 onwards into the 19th century the Reformed Church saw education as the agent of religious and moral progress. Literacy was regarded as the key to the Scriptures and a fuller participation in church worship. People capable of reading the Bible, understanding the dictates of the Catechism and the teachings of the pulpit would, according to Calvinist theology, produce a good community.

The Scottish civil authorities, responsible for law and order and drawn exclusively in rural areas from the landowning community, welcomed the kirk's role in laying the foundation of a disciplined community, and collaborated with it in achieving this end. The Act of the Orkney and Zetland Lawting in 1612 very typically expresses the joint responsibility of civil and ecclesiastical jurisdiction when it ordains "that the saidis Magistrattis and Counsell sall assist and fortifie the ministers and sessioun of Kirk for putting to execution of all actis and statutis made be thame for maintenance of Godis glorie, the edificatioun of the Kirk and punishing of vyce…".[1]

It is to these two pillars of society in the Shetland of the 16th, 17th and 18th centuries that we have to look for the advancement of education during that period. The church, in pursuit of the declared aims of Calvinism; the civil authorities in buttressing these aims, often in their own interest, and at the same time carrying out their statutory obligations delegated to them by the State. Their combined influence on the entire social fabric was so important that we cannot hope to understand any part of it without some knowledge of the church in its local setting, and of the civil authorities responsible for local government.

The Reformation came quietly to Shetland, unattended by either doctrinal controversy or civil strife. There is little doubt that this was largely due to the moderation and diplomacy of Bishop Adam Bothwell, a man who accepted the need for reform and made the transition as smooth as possible. Another factor which may explain the absence of contention so typical of the Scottish Reformation, was the diminished state of religious life in Shetland at the time, both among clergy and people. In 1563 a General Assembly Report stated that "not only ignorance is increased, but also most abundantly all vice and horrible crimes are there committed, as the number of 600 persons convicted of incest, adultery, and fornication in Zetland beareth witness".[2] We would like to know more about such evidence of gross immorality, the courts which indicted the offenders, the basis of the charges and the punishment, if any, accorded, but it does reveal a community sadly lacking in moral discipline and, by implication, a church extremely ineffectual in its teaching.

The religious standards of the people of Fair Isle did not impress the Spaniards from *El Gran Griffen*, an Armada ship wrecked there in September, 1588. One of them describes the islanders as "very dirty people, neither Christian nor altogether heretic" and goes on to say: "It is true they confess that the doctrine which once a year is preached to them by people from another island, nine leagues off, is not good, but they say they dare not contradict it which is a pity."[3] The heresies apparent to this Spanish Catholic may have been the result of Protestant innovation or simply the doctrinal confusion of a remote community with very inadequate spiritual guidance.

Gordon Donaldson's study[4] of Court and Commissary Records of the early seventeenth century reveals evidence of the cupidity, immorality, and neglect of duties which made some, at least, of the Shetland clergy of the period unlikely leaders of spiritual or moral revolution. The Archdeacon of Tingwall and the reader of Sandsting and Aithsting were convicted of assault. James Pitcairn, minister of Northmavine, who had been accused before the Privy Council of 1589 of troubling and oppressing his parishioners "through his avaricious and indecent behaviour, evil lyffe and conversation", left evidence of his avarice in an estate at his death of almost £3000 net value. Malcolm Sinclair and Robert Swinton, ministers of Dunrossness and Walls respectively, also accumulated estates grossly disproportionate to the general economic state of their parishes. These men certainly found unexpectedly rich livings in Shetland, but some of their contemporaries appear to have found the islands less attractive. In 1592 the Archdeacon of Zetland, and the ministers of the parishes of Unst, Nesting, and Bressay, Burra and Quarff, were dismissed as non-residents, "Never ane of them remaining… his lang tyme bypast within the boundis or countrey of Zetland… nor to have servit the cure thereat be the space of dyvers yearis…".[5]

Some indication of the temper of church life in Shetland at this time can be gathered from an accusation made in 1603 by the Sheriff Court of Dunrossness against David Leslie of Cunningsburgh for keeping his cows in the kirk.[6] The Cunningsburgh kirk was no doubt derelict, or at least very seldom used for worship, but David Leslie's sacrilege speaks more eloquently of the spiritual dereliction of the time. This view is confirmed by an Act of the Lawting promulgated at Scalloway in 1615 which speaks of the "sinne and iniquitie" which have been "the cause of great desolatioun in Kirk and policie within this countrey, for laik of discipline and putting of the actis of the Kirk... to dew execution."[7]

In 1611 the Norse laws which had been administered in Orkney and Shetland, operating through Lawting courts and a corps of officials distinctively Scandinavian in character and origin, were abolished by King James VI and I. The islands were now brought under the direct jurisdiction of the King, with James Law, Bishop of Orkney and Shetland, as Sheriff and Justice of the islands. The ancient Norse laws now proscribed, Bishop Law's Head Courts introduced a series of Country Acts and appointed parish bailies to act as local law officers in enforcing them. An Act of the Head Court of Scalloway in 1612 revealed the alliance of civil and ecclesiastical authorities in the enforcement of the acts of the kirk. These legislators were earnestly seeking to suppress the lawlessness of the times, as can be gathered from the list of punishments to be meted out to offenders — ducking in the sea, placing in the stocks, together with the use of such instruments of correction as iron collars, gags, and head braces.

In 1616 the Privy Council enacted that a school should be established in every parish in Scotland "whair convenient meanes may be had for interteyning a scoole." Bishops were instructed by the Act to visit their respective parishes and arrange the setting up of schools at the expense of the parishioners. The effectiveness of this act depended to a great extent on the zeal of local bishops, presbyteries and administrators, and the new administrative regime in Orkney and Shetland under Bishop Law certainly appeared to mean business. In Aberdeenshire, the first real advances in parochial education began after 1616, largely at the instigation of local presbyteries, but it is very doubtful if a Shetland Presbytery had been erected at that time. What may be the earliest recorded reference to a Shetland Presbytery occurs in 1629, and if this presents a true picture of presbyterial status and authority in contemporary local affairs, the Lawting Act of 1612, in all its stringency, seems to have been strangely ineffective. In 1629 the Lords of the King's Privy Council report[8] that they have received information "of the great and high contempt of the ministrie and kirk discipline within the bounds of Zetland... by the presumption and boldness of lewde and dissolute persons." These persons are reputed to have opposed the clergy in their attempts to reform vice by openly defying the ordinances of the Kirk Sessions, showing contempt "in face of the presbytereis and in the presence of the magistrate." This lurid report goes on to illustrate the sort of opposition encountered by the clergy: "... vile raylings and imprecatiouns spewed out aganis the ministrie in thair faces, the upbraiding of thame in thair pulpits... the cartalling [writing letters of defiance] of thame at thair presbyteriall meetings, the threatning of thame to break thair heads, to bullett [stone] thair bodeis, to battoun [buffet] thame if they presume to use the censure of the Kirk aganis thame, the lying at wait for the ministeris awin lyffes... coming to the kirk on the Sabbath day with unlawfull weapouns to persew the ministeris of thair lyffes...".

This state of anarchy, regarded by the Privy Council as being principally due to the remoteness of the islands from the supreme seat of justice in Edinburgh and the difficulty in bringing offenders and witnesses there to trial, was bound to militate against any schemes for establishing schools which required a degree of co-operation among heritors, churchmen and parishioners.

Seventeenth Century Education Acts

The Act of 1616 set out the basis of a national scheme of education for all but it failed to establish machinery for ensuring that those responsible carried out their obligations. In 1633 an Act of Parliament which ratified that of 1616, gave additional powers to the bishops of enforcing a stent upon heritors and parishioners. But experience proved that the legislation was still lacking in safeguards and in 1646 an Act of Parliament placed the responsibility upon presbytery to ensure that a schoolhouse was provided and a salary of between 100 and 200 merks paid to the schoolmaster. Presbytery had the power to nominate 12 honest men who would levy the appropriate stent on the parish. The Act of 1696 for the Settling of Schools consolidated the main points of the previous legislation and firmed up the process of implementation. Presbyteries were now authorised to appeal to the Commissioners of Supply in the event of the heritors failing to take action to stent the heritors in proportion to their respective rentals.

The seventeenth century educational legislation identified the church, through its presbyteries, as the moving force in educational development. Unfortunately, the seventeenth century church in Shetland was an unlikely vehicle for progress on this front. It is only after 1700 when a General Assembly Commission visited Shetland to report on the Presbyterian settlement and regularise the organisation of the local presbytery that systematic records of Presbytery and Kirk Sessions began to be kept. The situation as recorded at this time enables us to obtain a retrospective view of the church in Shetland during the latter part of the seventeenth century.

Rev. John Brand, a member of this Commission, wrote that "In the matter of God and Religion the Body of the People are said to be very Ignorant.", and ascribed this state to their want of convenient schools.[9] This assessment is confirmed by the reports of presbyterial visitation of Shetland parishes during the early years of the eighteenth century, which produce evidence of the material and spiritual poverty of the church — derelict churches, lack of manses and glebes, irregular celebration of Holy Communion, immorality among the people, and a complete absence of any schools beyond the very few established privately for the education of children of ministers and gentry. John Knox could not have envisaged so little progress in any area over a century and a half after the First Book of Discipline had outlined so bravely the church of the future. It was in the field of education that realisation fell so much short of the Reformers' ideals.

The great educational scheme formulated in the First Book of Discipline was expected to be implemented from the revenues of the Roman Church. But through the misappropriation of these funds into private hands the scheme languished to such an extent that by 1700 even a central area such as Stirlingshire had little more than half its parishes with legal schools. Apart from this basic financial weakness which undermined the Reformers' programme for regeneration of the church at the parish level, conditions in the seventeenth century were extremely uncongenial for the development of a parochial system of education placing financial demands on both rich and poor. A harsh economic climate persisting in many parts at the bare subsistence level, which frequent bad years could precipitate into famine conditions, made it very difficult for heritors and tenants to make financial sacrifices for something which could make no obvious contribution to their own material well-being.

These factors inhibiting educational progress affected Shetland as much as anywhere, but her very remoteness placed additional barriers in the way. Her geographical position has tended to isolate Shetland from the mainstream of history. Peripheral, not only to the administrative centre in Scotland, but also, in a narrower context, to the Earldom and Bishopric centre of power in Kirkwall, she suffered either from neglect of centralised authorities or the rapacities of local magnates operating in an administrative vacuum. She received only a fraction of the endowments which Orkney drew from the medieval church and none for educational purposes. Whereas Orkney certainly had a grammar school in Kirkwall in 1486, there is no evidence of a school in Shetland of any reasonably permanent nature for another 200 years.

REFERENCES

1   Acts & Statutes of the Lawting, Sheriff and Justice Courts within Orkney & Zetland 1602-44, Maitland Club Miss., Vol 2, SRO
2   Acts and Proceedings of the General Assembly, Vol 1, p.162, SRO

3   Hume, Martin, Some Survivors of the Armada in Ireland, Transactions of the Royal Historical Society, New Series XI
4   Donaldson, Gordon, Shetland Life under Earl Patrick, Edinburgh 1958
5   Craven, J.B., History of the Church in Orkney, Vol 2, 1897
6   Donaldson, Gordon, ed., Court Book of Shetland 1602-1604, Edinburgh 1954, p.82
7   Barclay, R.S., The Court Books of Orkney & Shetland, 1614-15, Kirkwall 1962, p.62
8   Register of Privy Council, Vol 3, pp 202-204, SRO
9   Brand, J., A New Description of Orkney, Zetland, Pightland-Firth and Caithness, Edinburgh 1703.

Chapter 3
Education before 1700

ALTHOUGH NO form of organised education appears to have existed in Shetland prior to the eighteenth century it would be wrong to assume that Shetlanders received no form of schooling. An isolated piece of evidence from the 15th century suggests that the Shetland pre-Reformation clergy sponsored the education of at least one talented local boy regarded as a likely candidate for the church, although it was necessary to send him to school in Orkney.

A curious autobiographical fragment[1] by a Shetlander who styled himself "Pauper Olaus", relates how he left Shetland in 1432 to attend a school in Orkney, was driven across the North Sea to be wrecked on the coast of Jutland. The people there could not understand his outlandish speech and he was subjected to much scorn, but his qualities were noticed by a local clergyman who took him into his service and later sent him to the University of Erfurt. He graduated from there in 1447, entered the church and in 1472 was Canon in the Chapter of Copenhagen.

This intriguing and tantalising glimpse of the pauper boy who may well have been Shetland's first university graduate, leaves us to speculate whether Olaus was a unique example of a Shetland "lad o' pairts" of the medieval period or only one of several proteges of local clergy who found their way into the church through Kirkwall Grammar School. Lack of documentary evidence leaves such questions unanswered, but the fact that Olaus was heading for Orkney to study clearly indicates the lack of any suitable school in Shetland at the time.

Early Shetland Schools

Orkney's Grammar School in Kirkwall was in existence in 1486 when it is referred to in the Charter presented by James III declaring Kirkwall a Royal Burgh. The clergy and landowners in Shetland would have regarded it with some degree of envy. If they wanted their children educated they had to employ private tutors or go to the expense of sending them to schools on the Mainland of Scotland. In 1733 a prominent laird stated that: "Most people of condition having their children educated at Edinburgh, the gentry are as polite here as elsewhere..."[2] A school in a central location such as Scalloway or Lerwick would obviously have been seen as very desirable. These were the only two sizeable village communities in Shetland — the seat of local government at Scalloway and the growing port of Lerwick, and as such would provide able and literate men with opportunities in trade, administration and education.

Names of a few schoolmasters in Scalloway appear at intervals throughout the century, principally as witnesses to deeds: Robert Ramsay in 1634,[3] John Yeat[4] in 1659, Alexander Craig[5] in 1674 and 1680, and William Binning 1689-1694. Craig, who graduated M.A. at Aberdeen in 1669, was later minister of Unst from 1683-1697[6] and Binning, a graduate of Aberdeen in 1686, was schoolmaster in Scalloway from 1689-1694 before becoming minister of Tingwall[7]. They were following the traditional path of many divinity students and recently qualified ministers of the time who frequently accepted posts as teachers in local schools or tutors to lairds' families thus hoping to catch a patron's eye and assist their advancement towards a parish ministry. Although a tutor would be formally engaged by a particular laird it would be surprising if his employer chose to restrict his teaching to the laird's own family. Scalloway's merchants, writers, shipmasters and others with ambitions for their children would have been prepared to contribute towards the tutor's fees.

But opportunity for continuous education was not easy. Even the son of the most powerful magnate of his time, Lawrence Sinclair of Brugh, had an erratic schooling. In 1657 one of Sinclair's retainers in Scalloway wrote to him, then in Orkney, that "Your sone... gets no learmentt att all butt verrie little quich Mr Walter gives him, & his grandmother says he hes become a worse schohler nor he was, for he hes so much given to play with a pack of wicked boyes that he learns no good att all; therefor shoe would have you to take a course with him in the spring & to putt him to soome good pairtt, qher he may be taught."[8]

Attempts had been made to establish a school supported by an official assessment. In 1612 a contract[9] was drawn up between "William Umfra skulemaster at Skallowaybankis" and a group of twelve prominent landholders and ministers whereby it was agreed that 3/- Scots be paid on every last (18 merks of land). This was calculated to amount to some £160 Scots for the schoolmaster's salary. But there is no indication that a school resulted.

In the seventeenth and early part of the eighteenth centuries local courts passed legislation on a number of local issues. These were called "Country Acts" and what appears to have been a draft for one of them,[10] ordained "that every bound within the contrie sall pay 12d. for ilk merk land as ane voluntar contribution for ane yeir for setting up of any schole and mantenance of ane scholemaster, and thairby and attour ane voluntar contribution to be gadderit of ilk gentlemen and uther indwelleris within the toun or utheris not laboureris of the ground betuix and Mertimes and to be collectit be the baillie and minister of ilk parochin." The reference to "toun" would suggest that this is an attempt to establish a school in Scalloway. Again there is no clear evidence of any school emerging from this legislation.

In 1678 and 1689 Mr Walter Innes, signatory to sasines for these years, is described in the latter as "teacher of the gramer schooll at Learwick."[11] This must have had as spasmodic an existence as most local schools of the period for when the Rev. John Brand visited Shetland in 1700 as Commissioner from the General Assembly, he said: "Altho there be a Latine School at Kirkwall in Orkney, yet there is none in all this Country"[12] [Shetland], then added, "The Ministers there [in Shetland] are very desirous that... a Latine School be set up either in Lerwick or Scalloway." Brand visited Tingwall Kirk and was informed by the Elders that there was no schoolmaster in any district in the parish "save a woman at Scalloway who taught young ones to read."

The first official investigation which could have given us some insight into the state of education in Shetland, and the local attitude towards it, were the reports made in 1627 to His Majesty's Commissioners on the "State of Certain Parishes in Scotland".[13] Unfortunately, the only Shetland parish mentioned is Nesting, of which the report states: "Thair is no schoole in the pareis nor any foundation for the same nather any provisioun thair foir may goodly be had of the parochineris bot necessair it is at lest thair sould be a schoole in the countrey in sic places as is most convenient." In Orkney, where all parishes are covered, the Report reveals that apart from Kirkwall there were no schools in any of the parishes. It would appear that the situation in Nesting would have been typical of the whole of Shetland.

The comments from the Orkney parishes all testify to the clamant need for schools. The minister of Stenness, for example, states that: "for want of ane scole the youthe wanted educatione and the trawill of the minister among the pipell is almost lost giff he tak not graitt paines upon the ignorantis." Here we have the essence of Presbyterian strategy: the need for education as an essential step towards religious enlightenment. The Stenness minister is, in fact, carrying out Knox's injunction that in rural parishes the minister or reader "take cayre over the children and youthe of the parishe to instruct them in their first rudiments and especiallie in the Catechism."

Readers

Readers were laymen either appointed to parishes unable to acquire a qualified minister or in large parishes to act as assistant to the minister. Their principal duty was to read the Scriptures to the congregation before the arrival of the minister to conduct the service or, in the absence of the minister, to read a printed sermon. Readers also functioned in many areas as schoolmasters and from the sixteenth to the eighteenth centuries, when the ability in many places to read and write was a rare achievement, particularly in remote areas, they acted as session clerks and precentors. A precentor to lead the singing was an essential functionary for a church without instrumental music and a congregation largely illiterate which had to be prompted line by line through the psalm singing.

The nature of the terrain and the scattered population made the task of the Shetland minister very difficult. However energetic and conscientious, he would have found it impossible to conduct weekly services for all his parishioners and only through the assistance of a reader would any form of regular worship have been possible. Even in those parishes which had a reader the people were expected to make an effort to attend services conducted by the minister although this might involve travelling long distances over water and rough moorland. In 1708 Zetland Presbytery expressed concern that "the Reading in churches and saying of public prayers hath greatly promoted laziness, formality and ignorance through people resting upon this to the neglect and contempt of public ordinances."[14]

At the same meeting Presbytery, in considering "the great want of Schoolmasters in this remote corner which has been and still is the great cause of prevailing ignorance and also that the poverty of this Country is such that there cannot be sufficient maintenance for Readers distinct from Schoolmasters", decided that after the following Whitsunday no reader should be allowed in any parish "but such as shall at least teach an English school." In attempting, on the one hand, to limit the function of readers in the field of worship while, on the other, emphasising their educational commitments, Presbytery realised the situation did not permit any great degree of flexibility and therefore decided that "in the meantime in case schools cannot be so soon erected as might be desired all readers are hereby discharged to say or read public prayers and pronounce the blessing upon the people as they commonly do… ".

Although the foregoing suggests that readers operated in Shetland there is no precise information regarding numbers. David Moneypenny was paid a salary (unspecified) from 1680-1685 as reader and session clerk for Tingwall parish,[15] and was subsequently referred to as "ex-precentor and schoolmaster,"[16] which suggests he undertook the normal range of duties expected of a reader.

It would appear that education in Shetland during the seventeenth century fell into three general categories: church schools conducted by the reader, private tutors providing instruction for lairds' families but also including some other local children, and private adventure schools frequently conducted by women. Although there is so little documentary evidence to support the widespread existence of any or all of these, it cannot be assumed that their educational impact was negligible. The rapidity with which Shetlanders acquired the Scots tongue suggests some element of formal instruction. A visitor to a northern parish in 1630[17] writes: "All the inhabitants seldom speak other" [than Norse] "among themselves yet all of them speak the Scots tongue more promptly and more properly than they do in Scotland." By the early 17th century, Scots as the language of the religious, legal, administrative and trading establishment, would have been seen by most Shetlanders as a social necessity. The impulse to acquire Scots was certainly great but it is not clear just how they managed to attain the degree of grammatical correctness implied by the above statement without some sort of formal schooling. This may have been supplied by the church to a greater extent than is indicated by the limited source material available, but we have to wait until the eighteenth century before we have positive evidence of organised formal education in Shetland.

REFERENCES

1 *Scr. Rer. Dan. VIII*, pp 467-474
2 Gifford, Thomas, Historical Description of Zetland, 1733, London 1786
3 PRS O&S, Shetland, iii, Fo 461r, SA
4 Ibid. 2nd series, iii, Fos. 100v and 349v, SA
5 Ibid. iv, Fo 381r, SA
6 Scott, Hew, Fasti Ecclesiae Scotticanae, Edinburgh 1928.
7 Ibid.
8 Library of the Society of Antiquaries of Scotland 569\19, Xerox copy in SA
9 SRO\RD1\232\ff.256-7
10 On a loose sheet in the Court Book of Shetland 1615-1629, ed. Donaldson, Lerwick, 1991, SA
11 PRS O&S, 2nd series, iii, Fo.226v; and iv, Fo.386v, SA
12 Brand, J., A New Description of Orkney, Zetland, Pightland Firth & Caithness, Edinburgh 1703
13 Reports on the state of certain parishes in Scotland, made to his Majesty's Commissioners for Plantation of Kirks, etc... 1627, General Reg. House.
14 ZPM, 26/2/1708, SA
15 Tingwall Kirk Session Minutes, 28\6\1685, SA
16 Ibid. 21/8/1709, SA
17 Sibbald R., Description of the Islands of Orkney and Shetland, Edinburgh 1845

Chapter 4
Beginnings of Organised Education — 1700-1740

A Changing Society

THE EIGHTEENTH century brought with it profound economic and social changes to Shetland. Legislation designed to foster English and Scottish fishing enterprise in Shetland waters was squeezing out the German merchants who had contributed so much to the local economy. The Salt Tax of 1712 was the final blow and thereafter the local lairds were forced to capitalise and operate the Shetland fishings. This led to the iniquitous fishing tenures already described and the economic bondage of the Shetland crofter-fisherman.

During the opening years of the century the Presbyterian Church began to operate effectively in the islands for the first time. The visit in May 1700 of a General Assembly Commission activated a somewhat dormant church. The Commission would appear to have given the local Presbytery very positive instructions to set its house in order and to this end to conduct a series of Presbyterial visitations to every parish. The urgency of this directive is apparent in that Dunrossness was visited almost immediately, on 14th June, followed by Delting on 3rd July.[1]

On these visits ministers, kirk sessions, heritors, and heads of families were interrogated separately on questions such as frequency of celebration of the Lord's Supper, state of kirks, manses and glebes, the minister's conduct, moral state of the people, whether elders had subscribed to the Confession of Faith, and the provision of schools. But this burst of energy inspired by the Commission soon spent itself. Three years were to elapse before the next visitation and a further seven before all 12 Shetland parishes had been investigated.

Records of these visitations reveal the spiritual and material poverty of the church at this time. The Lord's Supper was celebrated infrequently, if at all, the extreme example being Delting with two sacraments in 30 years. The usual explanation given by the ministers for this situation was "the abounding sin and ignorance of the people" debarred them from participation in the Sacrament. The ministers of Dunrossness, Nesting, Yell, Sandsting, Bressay and Lerwick had no manses and most of them were without a glebe. The church at Sand had not been plenished, was without a pulpit and its windows unglazed.[2] Ignorance and illiteracy prevented the Delting minister from obtaining the requisite number of elders. The Dunrossness minister complained that his principal heritor was withholding tithes. Education was virtually non-existent, the only schools mentioned being in Fetlar, Tingwall and Lerwick. Every parish stressed the urgent need for schools and encouragement for schoolmasters.

However ramshackle the state of the early eighteenth century church in Shetland, it was at last beginning to organise itself and as the century progressed so did the church gather strength through increasingly active Presbyteries and Kirk Sessions. As it established its hold more securely on the community so did its influence extend more positively into the area of education., But it was from outside the islands, through the Edinburgh-based Society in Scotland for Propagating Christian Knowledge, that the first regularly established schools were to come.

For the greater part of the eighteenth century education in Shetland emerges as the product of the complex inter-play of three bodies — church, local heritors and the SSPCK. In the interest of orderly presentation it is necessary to deal separately with the contributions of each of these groups but in so doing it must be stressed that the progress of education in any area, and particularly in remote places, can never wholly be ascribed to the policies or efforts of single organisations. Indeed, often the energies of a single individual can either further or frustrate nationally conceived plans, and the establishment of schools in Shetland during most of the eighteenth and nineteenth centuries was achieved through a series of actions and reactions, influenced to a great extent by local conditions and personalities — a mosaic rather than a precisely formulated scheme. The single constant factor in the situation was the pressure maintained through regular General Assembly instructions to Presbyteries to do all in their powers to establish parochial schools thus furthering the Presbyterian ideal of a literate and Godfearing community. At the local level the implementation of these instructions depended on local circumstances — the enthusiasm and influence of local ministers, the attitude of heritors, collectively and individually, the economic conditions of the time, and the nature of the local terrain. A fortunate combination in one parish of an energetic minister and a sympathetic heritor could to a great extent overcome remoteness and poverty, and schools be established. But too often lethargy and self-interest at the top stifled initiative, accepted local difficulties as unsurmountable, and left the educational needs of the parish to outside agencies, principally the SSPCK.

SSPCK Schools — Early Beginnings

In 1701 a few private gentlemen of Presbyterian persuasion met in Edinburgh and formed themselves into a Society for the reformation of manners in Scotland. They were greatly concerned at the "ignorance and barbarism" prevailing in the Highlands and Islands and conceived the plan of establishing schools in the remoter area as a means of tackling this problem. The underlying objective was to influence the rising generation of Highlanders towards the Presbyterian religion and loyalty to the Government, and to break down the barriers created by the internal loyalties of the clan system and the Gaelic language. The scheme was presented to the General Assembly of the Church of Scotland in 1706, received its blessing and was recommended to Presbyteries as a project worthy of support. It was so favourably received throughout the Highlands and Islands and so many subscriptions on its behalf received that the government gave it official recognition through a Royal Proclamation issued by Queen Anne in 1709. Letters Patent were granted, giving powers to the Society to establish schools "for the further promoting of Christian Knowledge, and the increase of piety and virtue within Scotland, especially in the Highlands, and remote corners thereof, whose error, idolatry, superstition and ignorance do mostly abound, by reason of the largeness of the parishes and scarcity of schools, and for propagating the same in Popish and Infidel parts of the world."[3] The Society was empowered to "erect and maintain schools, to teach to read, especially the Holy Scriptures and other good and pious books; as also to teach writing, arithmetic, and such-like degrees of knowledge… and to use such means for instructing the people in the Christian Reformed religion as may be competent."

Presbyteries were commissioned to act as supervisory bodies in their respective parishes and given precise instructions as to the procedure to be adopted in managing schools.[4] A prospective teacher was to be examined by Presbytery to establish his Presbyterian credentials. He had to testify his allegiance to the Confession of Faith and the Presbyterian Government of the Church, and undertake to conform to the discipline of the church. After he had entered his post Presbytery was to visit his school to see if he had a suitable dwelling-house and schoolroom, was conducting his school according to Society rules, was teaching effectively and behaving in a proper manner. Particular care was to be taken that he did not teach Latin or "meddle in other business". Presbytery was enjoined to send in regular reports to the Society indicating that the school was being run according to these rules, and let them know what books were required.

Within two years sufficient capital had been raised to warrant the erection of the first school — at St Kilda, where "nothing had been taught for many a dark and dreary generation but the art of catching fish and solan geese, for the wretched support of mere animal life."[5]

Other remote areas were quick to present their educational needs to the Society, and in the same year, 1711, on 8th March, a petition[6] was received in Edinburgh from James Buchan, minister of Northmavine, in the name of the Presbytery of Zetland. Buchan was one of the most active protagonists for schools in eighteenth century Shetland, as was his son who was minister of Walls and Sandness from 1735 to 1778. His petition claimed that Shetland "lyes very discontiguous consists of several islands at a considerable distance from one another, and that it is impossible that one school can suffice one paroch… and that the country is so poor that they are not able to afford a maintenance for one legal school in all the paroches of Shetland." For these reasons he craved the Society to consider the erection of schools in Shetland.

Three months later the Society decided that Shetland's situation could best be met from the Society's limited funds by making the normal financial allocation for one school, i.e. £200 Scots, but dividing it among three itinerant teachers. Presbytery was to be responsible for finding suitable persons as teachers,[7] defined as "men of piety, prudence and gravity, who understand and can speak, read and write… and who can write a fair hand, and do understand the rules of arithmetic, and can cipher exactly and readily."

Whether through poor communications or an inactive Presbytery, this offer failed to produce a ready response from Shetland. Five committee meetings of the Society during 1712 commented on the lack of information from Shetland, three reminders were written, the final one in December stating that if no response were forthcoming the schools would be settled elsewhere.[8] The failure of Zetland Presbytery to react more promptly during those initial stages of their relationship with the Society was to have an adverse effect on education in Shetland for at least the next 20 years.

At last, on 1st January, 1713, George Duncan, minister of Walls and Sandness, appeared in Edinburgh to represent the views of Zetland Presbytery before the Society. He carried a recommendation that the Society school already designated for Shetland, should be settled in the united parishes of Walls and Sandness. Duncan undertook personally to provide a schoolhouse and lodging for the teacher, and agreed to accede to any decision by Presbytery to remove the school elsewhere. The Society then agreed that their first school in Shetland, which would be their ninth in Scotland, was to be established in Walls and Sandness, and undertook to engage a suitable teacher for the post.[9]

They wasted little time and within three weeks Adam Marjoribanks appeared before their committee for examination. His testimonials from Earlston Presbytery and his tests in writing and arithmetic being satisfactory he was given a commission to teach. Before leaving on his long journey to Shetland he was paid by the Society a half year's salary (£50 Scots) in advance, and given £2 sterling worth of books.[10] He presented his commission to Zetland Presbytery on 25th March, 1713 and commenced teaching soon thereafter.[11]

Marjoribanks was the Society's pioneer teacher in Shetland, and found a community eager for education. Within a fortnight 40 pupils had enrolled and the numbers were increasing daily.[12] But his work was destined to be short-lived for he died of a fever five months later.[13]

Some indication of the delays in communications between Shetland and Edinburgh can be gathered from the fact that it was not until June, 1714 that the Society was informed of Marjoribanks' death. In doing so, Zetland Presbytery claimed that as they were anxious to continue the good work initiated by Marjoribanks and provide some continuity of instruction for the 40 pupils who had been attending, they had elected as his successor Charles Ross, "a grave and pious young man" who had been teaching in a school in Northmavine. The Society agreed and Ross was appointed.

A Lethargic Presbytery

The establishing of this first real educational bridgehead in the islands would, one might think, be a challenge to the local ministers who had so frequently represented the clamant need for enlightenment among the people. But there is little evidence at the Presbyterial level of activity and enthusiasm; too often they appear to be neglecting their supervisory function the Society had allotted to them. When Mr Duncan, minister of Walls and Sandness, wrote to the Society in June, 1715 for Charles Ross's commission he was told they were unable to supply this until Presbytery had returned to them a certificate of Ross's suitability, which had already been requested.[14] Furthermore, although it was one of Presbytery's duties to inspect Society schools regularly, they had to be reminded in May, 1717 — FOUR years after the school had been established — that they had not sent in a Visitation Report.

Certainly, as has already been pointed out, the local clergy had many problems on their hands which tended to diminish the urgency of educational needs, and the appalling difficulties they laboured under must have made them wary of embarking on new enterprises. The derelict buildings they had to preach and live in were the result of the inability — or unwillingness — of heritors to fulfil their legal obligations to the church. The Delting heritors petitioned Presbytery in 1717 regarding "the grevious (sic) state of the Parish", with no church save a ruinous one, no manse and no school, and claimed that they were unable to bear the cost of building these premises, which they reckoned at £840 Scots — 40 per cent of the whole rents of the parish.[15]

There is no doubt the church made heavy demands on the heritors and the fact that many of them retained their Episcopal loyalties made them even more reluctant to support it. For them there was a genuine conflict between personal conviction and public responsibility.

Robert Sinclair, laird of Quendale, was an example of an Episcopalian heritor who was a thorn in the flesh of the local clergy. In 1718 he objected to the appointment of Walter Hugens as Minister of Dunrossness. After many unavailing protests to Presbytery claiming Hugens was an unsuitable person, Sinclair played his last card on the day Hugens was to be inducted at Sandwick Kirk. When the congregation arrived for the ceremony they found the laird had ordered his factor to lock the kirk door. The Moderator ordered the door to be broken down but "Alex. Fraser, servant to Quendaill, stood in arms before the door, and they desisted."[16] The Moderator bowed to the inevitable and the induction took place in the kirkyard.

In this friction between kirk and heritors the initiative did not always lie with the latter. In September, 1723 Presbytery heard charges against James Taylor, Chaplain to the Episcopal Laird of Lochend and tutor of his children. He was accused of beng opposed to the Government, of engaging in Episcopalian practices, and being critical of the Presbyterian church. It was also alleged that he had set up a school in Lochend's Lerwick house and was teaching children other than those from his patron's family. He was therefore summoned three times to meet the Presbytery to subscribe to the Confession of Faith, but ignored each summons. Local ministers were ordered to pray publicly for Taylor in his sinful state, and he would then be excommunicated. This sentence was eventually pronouced from the pulpit of Lerwick Kirk on 22nd October, 1727, and James Taylor, "the prelatical intruder", as he was labelled by Presbytery, decided to suspend his "intrusion" and leave the islands.

These two local cause celebres dominated Presbyterial affairs during the period 1718-1727 and give some indication of the tensions and disharmony which existed between church and heritors. During this decade these controversies filled page after page of Presbytery records absorbing virtually all the time set aside for their regular meetings, and it is not surprising that less clamorous issues such as education should have received a lower priority.

But, however pressing their preoccupations or problems, it was to the ministers that the community had to look for the intitiative in striving for schools. By virtue of their own training, the educational ideals of their church, and the fact that they were often the only educated persons in their respective districts, they were the obvious torchbearers of education. Unfortunately, too many of the 12 parish ministers in Shetland during the early years of the eighteenth century were, for various reasons, ill-equipped to play a positive role. Two of them — John Cattanach of Unst and Alexander Dunbar of Delting — were so advanced in bodily infirmity as to be incapable of carrying out their parochial duties. Robert Gray of Nesting, although a younger man, had not taken the trouble to administer the Sacrament from 1703 to 1722. John Duncan of Bressay while in Edinburgh as Presbytery Commissioner to the General Assembly of 1728, petitioned the SSPCK for more schools for Shetland but confessed, when questioned, that "he had no certain account of what parochial schools were erected in the country".[17] Moreover, he was in no hurry to report back to Presbytery and had to be reminded the following summer to make his report. Such ignorance of the local situation and obvious lack of interest are astonishing from a minister pleading his community's educational straits. It is possible to take the more charitable view that he was concealing that fact that there were no parochial schools lest the Society withdraw the existing school.

It will be recalled that the Society had to remind Zetland Presbytery in May, 1717 that a report on the progress of the Walls school was still awaited in Edinburgh. This report finally arrived in time for a Society meeting on 1st May, 1718.

The visiting committee were obviously well pleased with Ross's work. They found the children "grave and serious", capable of reading the Bible "very exactly and distinctly", while some of them had a reasonable competence in writing and "vulgar arithmetic". "They could all repeat part of the Assemblies Catechism, a good many from the beginning to the end very distinctly." There was subsequent evidence, however, that he was not devoting all his energies to the school. Indeed, his salary of £100 Scots (£8.33 sterling) was miserable enough and only half of what was being paid to most Society teachers elsewhere in Scotland, although it was subsequently claimed by John Scott of Melby[18] that his grandfather had paid "his (Ross's) salary for the most part." In 1718 the Society were petitioned by Shetland ministers attending the General Assembly that summer for an increase in salary for their teachers. The Society agreed that if Ross continued at his post "and will resolve to take no other business in hand that may divert him from attending his duty as Schoolmaster he shall be preferred to that Salary",[19] i.e. 200 merks or £133.6.8 Scots (£11.33 sterling).

Meanwhile Presbytery had decided that Walls must relinquish her school which was to itinerate annually, the next station being Tingwall, "a more populous parish with an area of population contiguous."[20] But Ross's enhanced salary was not sufficient to divert him from his "other business", whatever it was, to a school in Tingwall. He refused to move, although in 1724 we find him teaching a small school in Eshaness, Northmavine. We can only speculate what his other intesests may have been but it is most likely that he sought to augment his pittance from the Society by taking a place in a fishing boat. During the eighteenth and nineteenth centuries several Shetland teachers, mainly in adventure schools, went for a season's fishing. His refusal placed Presbytery in a predicament for they had no suitable qualified local candidate and were obliged to appeal to the Society for a teacher.

In November, 1718, Francis Beattie from Edinburgh received a commission from the Society to teach the school at Tingwall at a salary of 200 merks.[21] He arrived in Shetland on 16th January, 1719 and for the ensuing decade was the only officially recognised Society teacher in Shetland.

"Petty" Schools

During this period the sheer inadequacy of one itinerating school for the whole area was frequently pressed on the Society by Presbytery. In 1717 their Commissioner to the General Assembly had asked that a "considerable number of books be put in the hands of the Presbytery to issue to poor people" who might then teach one another, and that £300 Scots be allocated to Shetland to be used for salaries to persons who might undertake to teach the poor.[22] The Society granted the money along with 12 dozen Bibles and a supply of Catechisms, Confessions of Faith, Vincent's *Explication of the Catechisms*, and Guthrie's *Tryall of a Saving Interest in Christ*.

This request happened to be in line with the Society's current thinking. Faced with increasing demands for schools and inadequate funds to establish them on a proper footing, they had found themselves compelled to resort to the expedient of assisting small schools staffed by local "lads o' pairts", requiring a mere 50 merks (£2.83 sterling) annual salary. In 1719 they wrote to all schoolmasters that "where they find any boys of more than ordinary capacity for letters to take special notice of such, and be at more than ordinary pains about them, and when they are come that length as to be useful in the school to imploy them to assist in teaching the children under the master's inspection that they may be fitted to teach schools themselves."[23] This early experiment in the concept of pupil-teachers made Francis Beattie responsible for a number of future Shetland teachers.

Society schools in Orkney

The response in Orkney to these suggestions about 'pupil-teachers' and their eventual placing in small 50 merk schools was much greater than in Shetland. In 1721 the Society was sponsoring 12 schools in Orkney to Shetland's one, and Orkney Presbytery could write: "The Society's Schools in Orkney are blesed with great success and there is an emulation among the people who should have their children best taught, so that there is hope that in a lifetime the whole rising generation shall be taught to read, and be instructed in the principles of Religion, many in reading and arithmetick..."[24] At the same time the minister of Westray reported that the Society school in his parish had upwards of 112 scholars and more coming, "yea married persons... and servants have left their service for a time to come and learn, six of them 26 years, some 18 others 20 or so."

The disproportion between Orkney's 12 schools and Shetland's one was noted by Zetland Presbytery in a report to the Society in 1721,[25] to receive the tart response that whereas "eight schools are maintained [in Orkney] for about £236 Scots yearly... it is but very lately since £300 Scots was sent to said Presbytery of Zetland for maintaining small schools, and a great number of Books, and the Society wants to have a particular account of the small schools maintained upon the said money and the books sent there before they give any more to that Country... and one reason of giving so many schools to Orkney is the great success they have there as appears by the lists, and that the 50 merk schools will have upwards of 100 schollars, and the endeavours used in Zetland have not been so successful."[26]

The records are silent on the Presbytery's reaction to this rebuke and we are left to speculate as to the reasons for the marked difference between the educational response of the two neighbouring island groups.

Success in Orkney

Undoubtedly, part of the explanation lies in the realm of geography. In Orkney itself this must have been a major contributory factory to the existence of the three schools which were established in the island of South Ronaldsay in the 1660s at a time when the remainder of Orkney was virtually devoid of schools. The sea crossing from South Ronaldsay to Caithness is a matter of only eight miles and the fact that Canisbay, the nearst point on the mainland to South Ronaldsay, established the first Caithness parochial school in 1650, suggests that the remarkable achievement of three school in a small island at this time was not unconnected with its close proximity to Caithness. Orkney's parishes are, moreover, much more compactly situated than those in Shetland, and this allowed greater freedom of movement of pupils, frequently across parish boundaries. For example, the first Society school in Orkney, established in Harray in 1712, drew pupils from several surrounding parishes, so that two years later it had a roll of 119.[27] Tingwall, on the other hand, although the central parish in Shetland, had a roll of only 27 at its Society school in 1719.[28]

In fact, geography had accelerated the whole process of the Scotticisation of Orkney which, beginning even before the impignoration of 1468, was well advanced by the eighteenth century. Orkney was thus more receptive to Scottish institutions and ideas than Shetland where the old Norn language and indigenous customs were more firmly embedded in the local culture. By the middle of the eighteenth century a contemporary Orkney observer noted the results of the Society schools on local speech: "The customs of the inhabitants, like the rest, were all Norwegian; their language the Norse, or that dialect of the Gothic which is spoken in Norway, and disused only within this present age, by means of the English schools erected by the Society for Propagation of Christian Knowledge."[29] By 1773 an Orkney clergyman, George Low, could state: "The Language of these Islands... was called here Norn... but is now so much worn out that I believe there is scarce a single man in the country who can express himself on the most ordinary occasion in that language."[30] But Low's account of his visit to Shetland a year later suggests a cultural climate more strongly Scandinavian, and in Foula he found the Norn language still a living oral tradition although much debased and hybridised with Scots.[31] As late as 1809 a Shetland writer could claim that "The old Norse has long been wearing out... The island of Unst was its last abode and not more than thirty years ago several individuals there could speak it fluently."[32] Although these comments provide only superficial insights into the linguistic state of the islands they do suggest that by the early eighteenth century Orkney society was less oriented towards its Scandinavian past and more disposed to accept Scottish and English influences.

Orkney was not only culturally but economically less enclosed than Shetland, mainly through its communications with Caithness and the beginning of its links with the Hudson Bay Company, whose ships were calling regularly at Stromness by the 1720s to recruit Orcadians for service in Canada. Increasing opportunities must have been accompanied by a heightening of aspirations, and this in turn to an increased demand for education. The Shetlander had no similar avenue of escape from his narrow world of croft and fishing-boat. His attitude to learning could have received little stimulus beyond that provided in any area by the Presbyterian Church which equated illiteracy with sinfulness. Whether or not ministers were actively engaged in erecting schools their pastoral function in the community constantly highlighted the value of education. Their lengthy sermons, detailed scriptural expositions, and insistence on a literate Kirk Session, all emphasised the prime importance of literacy in the Godly Commonwealth. And it would naturally follow that the greater the personal influence of the minister the greater the desire for education among his parishioners.

While there is no doubt that conditions in Orkney in the early eighteenth century were more propitious for erection of schools, there is evidence that the Society was more cautious in committing its funds to Shetland. As has already been shown, the Society's early negotiations with Zetland Presbytery had obviously done little to inspire confidence in Presbytery's handling of Society funds, particularly in relation to small 50 merk schools. There was indeed justification for the Society's caution in committing themselves further in Shetland, but this general attitude tended to hamper developments in certain areas where energetic ministers had aroused local enthusiasm for education and had even collected small sums of money to help launch local schools. The General Assembly periodically issued instructions to Presbyteries to organise special church collections for Society funds and it must have been galling for both ministers and congregations who raised funds to be repeatedly told that no money was available for schools in their areas. The people of the island of Fetlar felt sufficiently strongly about it to inform their minister that they would not allow their collection to be spent otherwise than on a schoolmaster of their own choosing. The minister wrote to the Society that "some small thing" had been collected but explained why he was not sending it.[33] Several Shetland ministers had to report they were unable to raise money locally because of the "depauperate" state of their people.

REFERENCES

1 ZPM 19/6/1700 and 3/7/1700, SA
2 ZPM 13/8/1707, SA
3 Hunter, H., A Brief History of the Society in Scotland for Propagating Christian Knowledge in the Highlands and Islands, London 1795
4 SSPCK Comm., 13/6/1713, SRO
5 Ibid.
6 SSPCK, General Meeting, 8/3/1711, SRO
7 Ibid. Committee, 29/6/1711
8 Ibid. 10/12/1712
9 Ibid. General Meeting, 1/1/1713

10 Ibid. Committee, 24/1/1713
11 ZPM 25/3/1713, SA
12 SSPCK, Vol 56, 5/4/1714, SRO
13 Ibid. Committee, 5/4/1714
14 Ibid. Committee, 1/6/1715
15 ZPM 25/9/1717, SA
16 Ibid. 4/5/1720
17 Ibid. 5/6/1729
18 Ibid. 14/8/1764
19 SSPCK, General Meeting, 7/8/1718, SRO
20 ZPM 6/6/1717, SA
21 SSPCK, General Meeting, 2/7/1724, SRO
22 Ibid. 6/6/1717
23 SSPCK Comm., 29/10/1719, SRO
24 Ibid. 4/5/1721
25 Ibid. 3/8/1721
26 Ibid.
27 Ibid. Vol 11, p 365
28 SSPCK, General Meeting, 4/6/1719, SRO
29 Mackenzie, James, Grievances of the Isles of Orkney and Shetland, Edinburgh 1750
30 Low, Rev George, Tour through the Islands of Orkney and Shetland, 1774, Kirkwall 1879
31 Ibid.
32 Edmondston, Arthur, A View of the Ancient and Present State of the Zetland Islands, Edinburgh 1809
33 SSPCK Comm., 6/4/1727, SRO

Chapter 5

Society Schools Consolidate

Buchan of Northmavine

THE MOST successful fund-raiser and assiduous advocate for schools in his area was James Buchan, minister of Northmavine from 1700-1727. In 1720 the Society received a petition from Buchan[1] stating that his parish had had a small school for one year which, with about 50 pupils, was thriving but would collapse if the fund was withdrawn. Presumably the fund referred to was a share of the £300 Scots already mentioned which Presbytery had received in 1717 from the Society but had failed to report on its disbursement. The Society turned down Buchan's request on the grounds of shortage of funds, a decision which is difficult to reconcile with their comparative liberality in Orkney at the time.

Northmavine was a typical mainland Shetland parish, 16 miles long and 10 broad at its extremities, with five widely dispersed pockets of population. Buchan was one of the few local clergymen during this period who was prepared to devote time, energy and money to the cause of education. Undeterred by the loss of the Society's support he obtained within the next few months guarantees from three "corners" of his parish that they were willing to contribute £60 for maintaining schools. He then requested the Society to provide a salary for a schoolmaster for a fourth corner as the people there were so poor they could raise no money.[2] The Society commended Buchan's efforts but could go no further than send him 60 Bibles and other books. They further added that the establishing of a legal school in the parish "would much encourage the Society to assist with charity schools." This somewhat unhelpful attitude compares unfavourably with their policy in Orkney where several parishes without legal schools retained charity schools for lengthy periods.

But James Buchan was not a man to lose heart easily. He continued to raise money locally and the following year was able to report that he had four schools attended by 180 children, all were frequently inspected and the books previously sent had been disposed of.[3] His request that the Society grant £20 sterling annually for the maintenance of these schools was turned down, but he was promised more books and a quantity of writing paper.

The continued refusal of the Society to provide his local schools with a degree of permanence must have seemed hard to Buchan who had laboured not only to create these schools but to augment Society funds. In March, 1722, he had sent £27 sterling to the Society from local church collections, and at the same time was negotiating for a mortification of 500 merks (£28.30 sterling), which he had previously subscribed to Zetland Presbytery, to be transferred to the Society with the proviso that charity schools be fixed permanently in the parish of Northmavine. It was unlikely that the Society could commit itself to the establishment of schools in any area for an indefinite period, but at the same time it appears to have been slow to recognise and underwrite the great endeavours of this minister in his parish.

To raise sums of money adequate to maintain four schools and then to extract £27 sterling as a donation to the Society's general fund were remarkable achievements at a time when the majority of Shetland ministers were reporting they were unable to raise any funds for the Society. In terms of current values when a domestic servant's annual fee was £3 Scots, a crofter's house could be built for about £4 sterling and a church for £60, a sum of £27 represented considerable sacrifice from his community of about 1,200 people most of whom were, in his own words, "poor and indigent, and a great many... objects of charity."[4]

In June, 1724, Buchan sent yet another request for funds and books, together with lists of pupils from three small schools. The school at 'Occaness' (presumably Eshaness) taught by Charles Ross, back in Northmavine after his spell at Walls, had a roll of 33 boys and 30 girls; one at Hillswick, taught by John Clark, had 44 boys and 27 girls; while another at Gluss, Ollaberry — master not named — had 45 boys and 27 girls.[5] To have 206 scholars attending school out of a population of about 1,200 was evidence of the remarkable enthusiasm for learning which had been generated in this parish, and the Society were sufficiently impressed to grant £20 Scots to each of the schools for one year.

James Buchan had not achieved his ambition to have his schools given permanent status but he had at least convinced the Society of the reality of his educational enterprise. His personal contribution becomes even more apparent when we note the decline in the educational situation in Northmavine after his death in 1727. Two years later the Society complained there had been no report from Northmavine since 1726, and for almost 20 years thereafter the parish remains silent on the issue of schools. Indeed the next occasion when Northmavine features in the records is in 1744 when the minister, William Gifford, is ordered by Presbytery to find a teacher for the charity school which they proposed moving to his parish, or else the offer would be withdrawn.[6] Gifford was unable to find a teacher for the salary offered — £4.10/- sterling — and Northmavine lost the school. The fruits of Buchan's endeavours may have died with him but he passed on his interest and enthusiasm in education to his son James who, as minister in Walls and Sandness from 1735-1778, played a dominant role in the story of eighteenth century Shetland education and was largely responsible for the establishment of one of the first parochial schools in Shetland.

Buchan's experiences in Northmavine illustrate the Society's dilemma in endeavouring to deploy their limited resources in such a way as to ensure maximum educational benefits. Their assistance to "petty" schools was never regarded as anything other than an expedient, an attempt to keep alive locally sponsored schools until such time as a case could be made for a regularly established charity school or, ideally, the heritors erected a legal school.

"Petty" Schools

From 1713-1729, while maintaining one regularly based school in Shetland, the Society assisted small schools in Tingwall, Delting, Northmavine, Lerwick, Gulberwick, Nesting, Yell, and Unst, representing seven out of the 12 parishes. These schools operated on a precarious footing. The small Society grant of about £20-£25 Scots per year was obviously inadequate encouragement for a teacher, who was compelled to rely on additional support, financially and for subsistence, from the people of the district. This was not always forthcoming. John Anderson, appointed teacher of a small school at Gulberwick in Lerwick parish in November, 1724, was forced to quit in 1727 because, as Mr Waldie, the parish minister, wrote, he was not able "to live upon the salary given him, and the people there gave him no assistance. But now he had grounds to hope the people would be more kind and hoped the Society would allow him a school for another year and that £10 Scots for a half year due him would be paid."[7]

These "petty schools" were generally sponsored by the parish churches. Launched by the minister, who would find a suitable person to teach, they were nursed along by the Kirk Session, usually through funds from the Poor Box or Sacrament Collections, and by fees paid in cash or kind by parents. Tingwall Kirk Session allowed the schoolmaster 10/- Scots per session for teaching poor scholars.[8]

So little is known of these teachers that one can only conjecture as to their qualifications and personal circumstances. It would appear that they were sometimes proteges of the minister, who may have contributed to their own education with a view to their eventual employment as teachers, together with additional perquisites as session clerk and precentor. Such seems to have been the background of John Smith who as a lad was appointed schoolmaster at Dunrossness in 1726 and rapidly built up a school so that within a few months he had a roll of 102 scholars. He was maintained at the minister's house and his sole income from teaching was £5 sterling contributed by the people of the district. The heritors had refused to contribute.[9] To undertake to teach over 100 pupils at a salary of £5 Scots per month when a labourer building dykes received £7.14/- for a month's work, suggests either extreme dedication or an inability to undertake work more physically demanding. Certainly in the nineteenth century, when more details of individual teachers are available, there was a fairly high proportion of local teachers who suffered from some minor physical disability which, while preventing them from hard work on croft or fishing boat, provided the opportunity and stimulus for study. John Smith was two years later appointed Session Clerk but almost immediately left the distict and in the same year was appointed schoolmaster, session clerk and precentor at Tingwall, offices he still held in 1749 when he informed the Session of Whiteness in Tingwall parish that, because of bodily weakness he was unable, particularly in winter, to travel between his place of residence in Scalloway and session meetings at Whiteness — a distance of about nine miles. He suggested a local man might act as clerk and precentor. Some idea of the dearth of people able to write at the time can be gathered from Smith's suggestion that his successor be paid £6 yearly but that he (Smith) would continue to write the minutes in the Session Book if he were reimbursed with half the amount or its equivalent in kind, i.e. "three Lispunds of good and sufficient dry bear yearly at Candlemas."[10] If John Smith placed a considerable premium on the art of keeping minutes he did it with some justification for there is no finer hand in any of Shetland's Church records.

The survival of these small schools depended entirely on finding an adequate salary for the teacher. Each district which launched one invariably importuned the Society for assistance and invariably were told that Society funds were not available. It was left to the community to keep the master's head above water, and all too often it failed to do even this or, if at all, only at subsistence level. In 1731 Whiteness Kirk Session was informed that William Gaddie, late schoolmaster in Weisdale, had died and left a poor widow and several small children "having little to subsist upon". The session found "that in his life he had been very useful in his station",[11] and therefore provided for him a winding-sheet and coffin together with three pints Dutch waters for his funeral. The following month the session gave a crown to his widow "being in great necessity and his children."[12]

The Society's Ambulatory Schools

The Society's main commitment to Shetland during the period 1719-1729 was, of course, through Francis Beattie. From his arrival in Shetland on 16th January, 1719, until his death 20 years later he conducted schools in Tingwall, Unst, Yell, Fetlar, Delting and, finally, Dunrossness — from the most northerly to the most southerly parish in Shetland.

His first report from Tingwall, in the summer of 1719,[13] provides a list of 27 boys and six girls, 12 of whom were reading the Bible, six the New Testament, two Proverbs, and the remainder in the Catechism. A committee of Zetland Presbytery visited his school in the early part of 1721 and were satisfied with Beattie's diligence but as the numbers attending had dwindled from 55 to a mere 17 on the day of the inspection they recommended that the school be removed to Unst.[14] The Society approved this move and in 1723 Beattie writes that he is in this island where "the people were formerly very rude and ignorant" but that he expected numerous scholars to attend his school.[15] His anticipations were fulfilled for in the only report recorded during his two years in Unst he notes that 75 boys and 12 girls had been in attendance.[16]

He was then ordered to the adjacent island of Yell in 1725 where he spent almost three years, during which time he sent in one list showing a roll of 24 boys and 10 girls. His next station was Delting where he taught from 1728-1730, at one time having 50 scholars on his lists.

One would have thought that, with only one officially recognised Society school in their area, Zetland Presbytery would have taken care to carry out their responsibilities of regular visitation and reporting on the master's ability and pupils' progress. But after their visit to his school in Tingwall in 1721 there is no record of any presbyterial inspection of Beattie's schools until 1728 when he was in Delting.[17] By contrast, it will be remembered, Orkney Presbytery was regularly reporting on the great majority of the 13 schools in their area.

As already mentioned, the meetings of Zetland Presbytery during the 1720s were dominated by lengthy debates on Taylor "the prelatical intruder". During the same period there were frequent dissensions over repeated absences of ministers from meetings in Lerwick. These became so acrimonious that it was even suggested that the 12 parishes be divided into three presbyteries. These issues certainly ousted education from the presbytery agendas and oversight of schools suffered. At last, in 1729, we find that a deputation from Presbytery visited Dunrossness and as a result dispatched a petition to the Society representing "the clamant need" for a school in that parish, mentioning how well the people had responded to the school created by the minister.[18] This situation had arisen out of the departure of John Smith from his school of 102 pupils. The petition states that the minister is prepared to provide a schoolhouse and other accommodation for a master if the Society agree to transfer their school from Delting to Dunrossness. The Society agreed to this and Beattie taught at Windhouse, Dunrossness from 1730 until his death on 29th May, 1739. From 1735 he was catechist as well as schoolmaster.

During the 1730s Presbytery displayed much more initiative in educational matters and sent in reports, at least more frequently if not always as regularly as the Society deemed necessary.

In 1730 the Society established, in reponse to pressure from Presbytery, its second school in Shetland. Oddly enough, it was to go to Dunrossness which already had a Society school, but was to be situated in Sandwick, at the northerly end of the parish and 12 miles from Beattie's school. The teacher appointed was Andrew Balfour, at a salary of £20 Scots.

The Remote Islands

For some time Presbytery had been expressing concern to the Society about the religious and educational needs of Foula, Fair Isle, and Skerries. As early as 1716 a memorial[19] had been presented which included an appeal on behalf of these isles, which were said to be destitute of schools and could only receive gospel ordinances on 12 or 14 days in summer when the minister paid an annual visit. Foula, it was claimed, had 124 examinable persons, few or none of whom "ever saw the Sacrament and the Lord's Supper administered, tho' when your petitioner was there they seemed to be very much affected with the preaching of the Gospel and to have a very vehement thirst after knowedge, and attended punctually and without wearieing upon family visitation, Catechising and preaching for the space of twelve dayes, tho' it was the chief time of their fishing." Fair Isle, with a more numerous population, was also mentioned as in great need, while it was stated that Skerries had a population as numerous as Foula but were "far more rude and ignorant than any of the other two."

The Society received the plea sympathetically and agreed that as soon as funds allowed they would send a fit person to minister to the people of these remote isles. A further presbyterial petition was considered in 1720 by the Society who again acknowledged the plight of the isles and decided to give them first priority when funds became available. They were as good as their word and in 1722 James Williamson of Ormiston was appointed itinerant schoolmaster and minister for Foula, Fair Isle and Skerries. He appears to have landed on Fair Isle on his journey north on 20th September, 1722, for it is recorded that he was on that island from that date until 12th April, 1723. He then appeared for the first time in Lerwick on 29th May, 1723, when he produced a testimonial for Zetland Presbytery from the minister of Ormiston.

It would have taken considerable ingenuity to devise a more formidable itinerary for any man. Situated at remote fringes of the Shetland archipelago, these islands were each separated from the mainland by up to 20 miles of open sea. It is not surprising that Williamson was unequal to the task. In 1731 Presbytery received complaints that he was not dividing his time equally between Fair Isle and Foula but was remaining regularly for eight months in Fair Isle and two at most in Foula.[20] He appears to have abandoned his commitment to Skerries. Even in Fair Isle, which he seemed to regard as his headquarters, the people, while claiming to like Williamson, implied he was not undertaking any teaching.[21] He himself wrote to the Society asking that teachers be supplied for the three isles even if they could be paid no more than £1 sterling each.[22] The Society agreed to send the suggested £1 sterling to the isles recommending that school should commence by the following May.[23] But 1731 passed without Presbytery being able to find teachers and in May, 1732 the Society threatened to re-allocate these allowances to other areas if not used for their original purpose.[24] As it happened, William Strong commenced teaching a school in Fair Isle in January, 1732[25], and Thomas Henry opened a school in Foula on 1st August, 1733[26], but no suitable person was found for Skerries and its allocation of £10 Scots was used to augment the salary of a petty school at Nesting from £20 to £30.

Skerries was to continue a deprived area educationally for another century, but by a strange paradox the very remoteness of Fair Isle and Foula conferred on them a certain distinctive appeal which enabled the Society to keep schools alive on these remote isles for longer periods than in any other part of Shetland. With only a few short breaks both islands have had schools operating regularly from the 1730s onwards. The salary — a mere £1.5/- sterling in the 1730s, £1.10/- in the 1750s, increased to £12 a century later — was no inducement, but the teachers were generally local men with other means of income and subsistence. In Foula, the Henry family on their croft at Guttorm provided teachers — father, son and grandson — for 88 years. Thomas had the most rudimentary qualifications to teach others. He could not write and could only sign his name in printed capitals.[27] But he could teach reading and the establishing of this skill in a small community would have laid the foundation of a literacy which, however minimal, was something not enjoyed by many areas in Shetland during the eighteenth century.

Negligence and Incompetence

By the mid 1730s the Society was maintaining five schools in Shetland — two in Dunrossness, one in Fair Isle, one in Foula and one in Nesting. When a teacher could not be found for Skerries and the £10 earmarked for its school was added to the proposed salary for Nesting, a young man, John Campbell, came forward and was accepted for the post. By November, 1732 his school was in operation and a Presbyterial Visitation Committee found 32 scholars under instruction.[28] Campbell still regarded his salary of £30 Scots as inadequate and applied to the Society for further augmentation, but Presbytery's reports on his work did not help his case. He was charged with negligence, resulting in low standards and a drifting away of scholars, only 11 being present when the school was examined in January, 1735.[29] Campbell may well have been a rootless, unsettled person — in 1735 we find him in Edinburgh and in 1740 in London — but Nesting at this time must have been a particularly barren vineyard in which to labour. The parish kirk was "going very fast to ruin", the minister, Robert Gray, had no manse and, as reported by his elders, no reputation. They accused him of being greedy, inefficient, frequently "monstrously drunk", and that he had administered the Sacrament only once since his induction in 1703.[30] Not a man to provide inspiring leadership in the parish, nor to give his schoolmaster a very positive lead. But although Gray continued in his inauspicious ministry for a further 13 years, Campbell's career was cut short in 1735 when the Society dismissed him from their service.[31]

Although the Society had only five recognised schools in Shetland at this time, another of their teachers was to be dismissed for incompetence. Andrew Balfour had made an unimpressive start to his career when in 1729 Presbytery had examined him and found his qualifications unsatisfactory. Specific shortcomings are not mentioned but they recorded they were only "tolerably well satisfied." He was nevertheless appointed to a Society school in Sandwick in the parish of Dunrossness, but in 1733 the parish minister sent a report to the Society commenting on Balfour's negligence.[32] A more specific complaint was lodged in 1734 recommending his dismissal, their reasons being that he had given little or no attendance at his school since Whitsunday, 1732.[33] The Society dismissed Balfour and, on the recommendation of Presbytery, appointed Robert MacPherson to a school at Cunningsburgh in the same parish.[34] MacPherson was of more reliable material and taught in Cunningsburgh for over 40 years.

Society Curriculum

Society schools placed a heavy emphasis on religious education. Children began with rudimentary instruction in reading, commencing with the ABC, then on to the Catechism, Proverbs, and Old Testament. Various editions of the Catechism were used, beginners starting with a "Syllabing" version which broke down the bigger words into syllables. Much emphasis was placed on memorisation, particularly of the Catechism. Seven and eight year olds had to wrestle with and commit to memory its theological abstractions, progressing from the first question — "What is the chief end of man?" — through to number 107. They could have made little of the responses they had to give, such as "God is a spirit, infinite, eternal and unchangeable in his being, wisdom, power, holiness, justice, goodness and truth." They also had to memorise graces before and after meat as well as prayers for morning and evening. Reading was done on a mechanical basis with little or no attempt at encouraging understanding of what was being read.

Spelling was taught along with reading but it was only after the Old Testament had been read through and scholars were beginning it for the second time that writing commenced. The problem was that few parents were able to afford the cost of the paper although the Society did provide paper for children of poorer parents. That was their policy also regarding text-books. Parents who could afford it were invited to purchase Bibles and Catechisms while poorer parents were given free copies. Arithmetic had a relatively low priority and was only introduced after the Bible was completed. Even then the master was not obliged to teach it if his salary was less than 100 merks.

General Assembly of 1713 had recommended that Presbyteries consider, when appointing schoolmasters, that they were capable of teaching the common psalm tunes in order that there be a "more decent performance of the public praises of God."

Under James Buchan's regime in Walls and Sandness very detailed and regular reports were sent to the Society on the schools in Sandness, Papa Stour and Foula. The Report for 13th December, 1744 (Appendix C) is a typical example and gives a good idea of how these schools operated and the measure of support from parents. Scholars ranged in age from six to 19 and, out of the 60 on the roll, only 14 were regarded as "Frequent" or "Constant" attenders, the other 46 being classified as attending "Seldom" or "Very Seldom". Fifty-six were either learning the Catechism or had completed it, a number of the latter being eight or nine year olds. The variety of stages in reading must have required a degree of ingenuity in carrying it out, unless the more advanced scholars were left to read silently. All in all, James Cheyne, the teacher had a formidable task.

Salaries

The recommended salary for Society teachers was £200 Scots but it was decided that Shetland could most benefit from dividing a single salary among three itinerant teachers. In a further attempt to disperse schools as widely as possible throughout the community, "petty" schools were introduced. These were known also as "50 merks" schools but the £33.6.8 suggested by the title did not often materialise and teachers were generally paid no more than £20-£25, and in the remote isles a mere £10.

Teachers complained regularly, and with every justification, they were unable to live on what was a mere pittance even in those straitened times. Francis Beattie, the most experienced of the Society teachers, received unpaid help in school from his wife but when he appealed to the Society for "allowance to buy his wife a suit of Cloathes, she having this past nine years been labouring in the School which lays her aside from all other business"[35], he received no response. When Beattie died in harness in 1739, after teaching from one end of Shetland to the other over a period of 20 years, he had a mere £36 Scots salary. Even by the end of the century qualified teachers were receiving £48 Scots.

Society salaries were lean enough but an unusual occurrence in 1746 deprived local teachers of their annual amount. On 27th June, 1746 the sailing smack *Isabella* on which the minister of Lerwick was travelling north with the Society salaries was captured by a French privateer and all money and valuables taken. The salaries were subsequently reimbursed by the Society.[36]

In fairness to the Society it must be pointed out that their limited funds determined a policy designed mainly to assist areas which showed initiative and signs of self-help. One of the criteria used was the efforts being made locally for the establishment of legal schools and a consideration of what was happening in Shetland in this respect will help to throw some light on the Society's attitude as well as underline the difficulties encountered by those anxious to promote education in Shetland.

The Second Patent — An Experiment in Practical Education

When the SSPCK was launched in 1709 its main objective was a "Reformation of Manners" in the Highlands and Islands. Its schools would introduce the Highland clans to the Presbyterian religion and dispel the "ignorance and barbarism" which it was felt was a serious barrier to a united kingdom.[37] The Society envisaged schools as the engines of religious and social reformation in the area. In the unsettled period after the Fifteen Rebellion it became obvious that a diet of Bible reading and memorisation of the Catechism were making little impact on the social and economic life of the area. There was a need to provide instruction in "some of the necessary and useful arts of life." The Crown was approached for enlargement of the Society's powers and in 1738 the Second Letters Patent was granted.

The new Charter permitted schools to instruct children in skills necessary for their future lives — husbandry, trades, manufacture, and housewifery. The key occupations of agriculture, spinning, weaving, and knitting were identified.

This enterprising extension of the curriculum proved too radical for its time and achieved only limited success. Presbyteries were invited to suggest how the new Charter might be implemented but few ideas were received. Local intitiative was essential, ideally from the landlord and in the few areas where this was achieved, there was some measure of success, especially in agriculture and flax-weaving.

The Second Patent made little impact in Shetland apart from a brave attempt by Sir Andrew Mitchell of Westshore, Scalloway. In 1756 he presented a Petition to the Society[38] in which he stated that the Shetland terrain is "very Barren and unfruitfull seldom yielding as much as will afford Bread to the Inhabitants for eight months and sometimes not for six months in the year," that the soil is nonetheless capable of being cultivated into good arable and grass land by "people skilled in the knowledge of Agriculture, whereof the Inhabitants are entirely Ignorant." He proposed that the Society provide "some competent annual allowance… to one or two ploughmen, well skilled in Agriculture, and improving of Barren Ground, who could be prevailed upon to settle in Zetland under such Regulations as the Society shall think fitt to appoint, and if such person is fixed on any part of the petitioner's Estate in that Country, he will at his own Expence, for the Encouragement of such Person cause Erect a convenient House for him, and give him some acres of Ground contiguous thereto to Improve for the first three years Rent Free."

The Society were more than sympathetic. They not only undertook to send an expert ploughman to Shetland with an allowance of £5 sterling a year for seven years to "encourage the promotion and diffusion of knowledge of agriculture in Shetland", but offered a grant of £10 yearly for nine years to be paid to five young lads under 16 selected by Sir Andrew whom the Society would place for a maximum of three years with skilful Scottish farmers for instruction. Sir Andrew would then be expected to engage the young men on their return to Shetland, in agricultural pursuits.[39] There is no evidence that either of these was implemented but it may well have foundered on the traditional opposition to change typical of all peasant societies. A brutal example of this occurred not many years later. Sir Andrew's son John, who inherited the estate after his father's death in 1764, undertook to demonstrate the superiority of the heavier Scottish plough over the primitive Shetland single-stilted version. He brought in a Scottish plough with a heavier breed of oxen to draw it but "some of the people in the neighbourhood came in the night time, broke his plough to pieces and so mangled his oxen as to render them unfit for work."[40]

The Mitchell family were, for time and place, unusually enlightened landlords. After her husband's death, Lady Mitchell continued an interest in economic development. After the Forty-Five Rebellion renewed efforts were made to combat Jacobitism by bringing useful employment to the Highlands and Islands. The British Linen Company was formed and gave grants for flax spinning and linen manufacture. Linen Company money launched a number of manufactories in Orkney and, in 1766, Lady Mitchell obtained from the Society 220 spinning-wheels and reels, together with a grant to engage spinning mistresses. The Society imposed a condition that locally grown flax should be used and as flax was not grown in Shetland, Lady Mitchell obtained permission to purchase flax from the Scottish mainland and undertook to pay for the flax from the allowances made to each of the 220 girls to be taught and to supervise its allocation.[41]

It was possibly Lady Mitchell's interest in flax-spinning which led to her son, Sir John Mitchell, becoming involved in the establishment of the Company of Linen Manufacturers of Zetland. In 1770 he and four other principal heritors, with James Hay as manager and overseer, each contributed £750 towards the building of the factory, the importing of flax, and employment of workers. The Company, through the agency of Lady Mitchell, established at least one Spinning School in Lunnasting where each girl received a Wheel and half a Reel, together with some lint. The Spinning Mistress was paid 2/- for each girl taught.[42]

The enterprise failed to emulate the successful linen manufacture in Orkney and in 1776 collapsed. The main problems seemed to be the failure to grow flax locally in any quantity and, despite Lady Mitchell's efforts in establishing spinning schools, the lack of enthusiasm among Shetlanders for spinning.[43]

The SSPCK continued to make funds available under the Second Patent for the teaching of vocational skills but the only other example of this being taken advantage of in Shetland was in Sandness where, from 1802-1830, the wife of Laurence Moncrieff, Society teacher in Sandness, taught spinning of wool. She was being paid £3 in 1820, which by 1830 had increased to £4. She retired on the death of her husband and was superannuated by the Society.

REFERENCES

1. SSPCK General Meeting, 3/11/1720, SRO
2. Ibid. 10/3/1721, SRO
3. SSPCK Comm., 21/6/1722, SRO
4. SSPCK General Meeting, 22/3/1722, SRO
5. Ibid.
6. ZPM 7/11/1744, SA
7. SSPCK General Meeting, 30/8/1727, SRO
8. Tingwall KSM, 20/12/1724, SA
9. SSPCK Comm., 23/6/1726, SRO
10. Tingwall KSM, 6/8/1749, SA
11. Whiteness KSM, 3/10/1731, SA
12. Ibid. 28/11/1731, SA
13. SSPCK Gen. Meeting, 4/6/1719, SRO
14. SSPCK, Vol 1, 10/8/1721, SRO
15. SSPCK Comm., 31/10/1723, SRO
16. Ibid. 20/1/1726
17. Ibid. 13/12/1728
18. SSPCK Comm., 11/12/1729, SRO
19. SSPCK General Meeting, 7/6/1716, SRO
20. ZPM 3/6/1731, SA
21. Ibid. 24/6/1729, SA
22. SSPCK Comm., 4/8/1730, SRO
23. Ibid. 22/10/1731, SRO
24. Ibid. 23/3/1732, SRO
25. Ibid. 23/5/1732, SRO
26. SSPCK General Meeting, 6/6/1734, SRO
27. Walls KSM, Visitation of Charity School in Foula 28/5/1742, SA
28. ZPM 7/3/1733, SA
29. Ibid. 1/1/1735, SA
30. Ibid. 28/7/1735, SA
31. SSPCK Comm., 15/7/1735, SRO
32. Ibid. 24/5/1733, SRO
33. Ibid. 21/3/1734, SRO
34. Ibid.
35. SSPCK Comm., 4/4/1728, SRO
36. ZPM 6/8/1746, SA
37. Summary Account of the Rise and Progress of the Society in Scotland for Propagating Christian Knowledge, Edinburgh 1783
38. SSPCK Comm., 25/1/1756, SRO
39. SSPCK Comm., 3/3/1756, SRO
40. John Kemp, Observations on the Islands of Shetland and their Inhabitants, Edin. 1801.
41. SSPCK Comm., 13/8/1766, SRO
42. Bruce of Symbister Muniments, GD 144/90/78, SA
43. Low, George, A Tour through the Islands of Orkney and Schetland, 1774, Kirkwall 1879

Chapter 6

Legal Schools — Early Attempts to Establish

THE 1696 ACT reaffirmed the heritors' prime responsibility for establishing parochial schools in every parish, and also stated that if the heritors failed to build a school and lay on a stent, the presbyteries should apply to the Commissioners of Supply who, or any five of them, might establish a school, fix the master's salary and stent the heritors according to their valued rent. This placed very firmly on the kirk the onus of ensuring that the Act worked, and an unenviable responsibility it was. For in many areas, including Shetland, where the most influential heritors were also Commissioners of Supply, the legal provisions of the Act, however watertight in appearance, could be evaded — and were.

The General Assembly took the kirk's responsibility seriously and throughout the early years of the eighteenth century repeatedly issued injunctions to presbyteries to take action where heritors were neglecting to settle schools. In 1718 and again in 1719 presbyteries were specifically instructed to invoke the existing laws for establishing legal schools. In all areas where schools had not been settled, heritors and parishioners were to be instructed to meet on a certain day and at a certain place to stent themselves for salary and accommodation according to the Acts of 1633 and 1696.

The kirk's initiative met with some success but in general the parochial system of education evolved laboriously with reluctant heritors the main stumbling-block to progress. In early eighteenth century Aberdeenshire, for example, the heritors were being constantly pressed by the kirk to stent themselves for the provision of legal schools but failing to take action. On one occasion the Presbytery of Alford referred the situation to the Commissioners of Supply, from where it passed to the Lords of Session, who finally ordered the heritors to meet their statutory obligations.

Reluctant Heritors

Shetland landowners had more justification than most in seeking to avoid additional financial commitments. During the uneasy and confused transition from Norse to Scottish administration, land in

Shetland became burdened not only with the ancient Scandinavian taxes but with feudal dues and arbitrary impositions. In 1664 Shetland udal landowners were offered feudal charters of their lands by Douglas of Spynie, the crown chamberlain, a transaction which cost them £15,000 Scots.[1] Thomas Gifford of Busta, himself chamberlain for the Earl of Morton from 1706 to 1747, summed up the situation: "… for indeed the trifling land estates of Zetland, and the very inconsiderable value of the lands, together with the great few duties paid yearly out of them, renders the heritors of Zetland utterly incapable of being at the charge of these public securities and frequent confirmations required by law, as is practised in other places, where the subject is capable of bearing the charge, which Zetland is not, for the causes foresaid, and therefore has been laid aside since the granting of Spynie's charters."[2] Smarting under their disproportionate burden of taxation, the Shetland heritors had a readymade excuse to justify their statutory obligations being "laid aside". Furthermore, Shetland was the only part of the kingdom which had not had an official valuation of its lands, and it was on this valuation that public burdens such as parochial school-money was assessed. In the absence of an official assessment, a formula had been established by custom, by which Orkney paid two-thirds and Shetland one-third of all public impositions.[3]

And so, early in the eighteenth century, when Zetland Presbytery set about promoting parochial education, they could not have found the heritors' lack of enthusiasm altogether unexpected. Nor indeed could the kirk have anticipated much sympathy or co-operation from this quarter, considering that all but two of the principal heritors were Episcopalian.

In March, 1711, at a meeting of Zetland Presbytery, a letter from the General Assembly was read recommending that a legal school should be settled in every parish, with a schoolhouse and competent salary.[4] Presbytery expressed their regret that no legal schools had been established and undertook to remove the barriers preventing this. Subsequent records do not reveal the manner or extent of their endeavours but there is no evidence that Presbytery exercised its right to apply to the Commissioners of Supply to stent the heritors. The opportunity had certainly been created for them in 1707 when James Buchan, minister of Northmavine, and George Duncan, minister of Walls, represented to Presbytery "the want of schools in thair parochins and the abounding ignorance occasioned thereby" and that "having dealt with the Heritors to stent themselves, which being denied they address the Presbytery to make application to the Commissioners of Supply to the effect forsaid."[5] Presbytery undertook to do this but no evidence of action is recorded.

On July 29th, 1713, during a Presbyterial visitation of the parish of Delting, the assembled heritors and heads of families were exhorted to contribute to a fund for the salary to a schoolmaster. All agreed and Andrew Fisken, the minister, was appointed to carry out the arrangements. His commission cannot have met with much success for in August, 1717 he petitioned Presbytery that "Amongst many Crossing Difficulties he labours under, none the least is no school or public seminary of learning... which keeps the people in Profound ignorance and debars them from partaking of the Sacrament of the Lord's Supper and even straitens them from getting... a competent number of Elders."[6]

Thomas Gifford, Laird of Busta

Andrew Fisken was to find a more effective ally nearer at hand in countering his difficulties — his neighbour and brother-in-law Thomas Gifford, principal heritor in Delting and the most influential man in the islands at the time. In 1707, the crown granted the Earl of Morton a feu of the Earldom of Orkney and Lordship of Zetland, which not only entitled him to the crown rents of the islands, but invested him with powers as heritable stewart, justiciary, sheriff, and bailiff, together with judicial authority in virtually all civil and criminal cases. The Earl appointed Thomas Gifford as his Stewart-depute and as such, Gifford was virtually in supreme authority in Shetland. Apart from the power he exercised by virtue of his official posts, he was a man of great natural ability, shrewd and successful in business, an efficient and astute administrator, and a landlord who, in the best paternalistic tradition, conducted his estate with firmness but a measure of humanity.

When Mr Fisken was inducted to Delting in 1709 he found himself with a parish and congregation but no manse or glebe and the kirk ruinous. Thomas Gifford responded promptly. He provided alternative accommodation in a house on his estate and was active in promoting the erection of a new parish church. Undoubtedly Mr Fisken would have urged the laird to use his influence to obtain a school for the parish and in Gifford he would have found a man sympathetic to the idea of a local school, although at this particular time conditions were hardly favourable. As mentioned earlier, Gifford was encountering economic difficulties both in his private ventures and among the local population. James Grierson, minister of Tingwall, in a petition to Presbytery in 1716, claimed that "... the common people, especially since the Dutch had failed, are extremely poor."[7]

By the early 1720s, however, conditions were improving. In August, 1722, Fisken, in appealing to the SSPCK for support for a local school was able to state that his parishioners "not only contributed towards increasing the Society's funds but had bound themselves to pay £100 Scots yearly to a Schoolmaster."[8] Then, in 1725, at a Stewart Court presided over by Thomas Gifford, a petition was received from Kirk Sessions and heritors containing the statement that: "fulness of bread and plenty, which the Lord hath been pleased to continue for some time now, [is] sadly and sinfully abused by the generality of the ingrateful receivers thereof."[9] The "fulness of bread and plenty", looked upon so sourly by the Calvinistic establishment, would have been nothing more than a temporary boost to the subsistence economy from a series of good harvests from land and sea. At this time the lands of Shetland never provided enough oats and barley to serve the population for a complete year; and in bad years not so much as would serve them for four to six months. A smallpox epidemic in 1720 had drastically reduced the population and this, together with a few good harvests, would, however temporarily, have edged up the standard of living of the remainder.

Gifford's Initiative

Then, as so often happens, a fortuitous circumstance occurring at a propitious moment, triggered off a chain of events. In 1722, the eldest of Thomas Gifford's children was reaching the age of schooling and, in April of that year, Gifford engaged Alexander Mitchell, student of divinity, as tutor.[10] In engaging Mitchell, Gifford had obviously envisaged him as teacher, not only to his own family, but to local children, for when Mitchell appeared before Presbytery to present his testimonials and be examined in divinity he was designated as "Instructor of Youth and Schoolmaster to the Parish of Delting."[11] Gifford put into operation a system whereby his tenants contributed a proportion of Mitchell's salary, while he himself paid the remainder.[12] The tenants either paid their contributions to a local man appointed as collector or had the amount debited to their accounts with Gifford. Mitchell's account for 1722 reads:

> "Received from Gilbert Omand, colector of his Celarie from the people in the paroch —   £78 Scots
> By my own share of the Contribution —   £13 Scots"

The stent on the parish does not appear to have been levied consistently but was generally in the region of 1/6 per merk of land, the average total contribution being 9/-. Although on one occasion Gifford referred to the amount collected as "the parochiall scoolmoney", his own proportion of approx. one-seventh was nowhere near the one-half he was legally obliged to contribute. On the other hand, Mitchell's initial salary of £91 Scots was above the legal minimum of 100 merks (£66.13.4 Scots), although from 1728-1732 it fell below the minimum to £60

Scots. Mitchell's account in Gifford's Day Book is closed without comment on September 12th, 1732.

Meanwhile, in July, 1724, Presbytery had again discussed the great need for legal schools and had recommended that each minister endeavour in his own parish to further the requirements of the 1696 Act. There is no indication that Andrew Fisken informed his brethern of the Delting experiment but he would undoubtedly have discussed their decision with his principal heritor, and this, together with the fact that Delting had been operating a school on parochial lines for two years, would no doubt have encouraged Gifford to move beyond the local scene and use his powers as Stewart-depute to launch legal schools throughout the islands. The Stewart-depute was obliged to hold two Head Courts each year and at one of these, at Lerwick on 14th November, 1724, he presented his proposals for establishing a legal school in every parish. (Appendix B)

In the light of existing circumstances, Gifford showed remarkable initiative and public-spiritedness in presenting these proposals. The case is put forward with a ring of authority, a note of genuine concern and enlightened leadership, which make this document remarkable not only for Shetland at the time but for more prosperous parts of Scotland. The proposals were carefully worded to counter the usual arguments against legal schools. They stated that "if the parish is discontiguous so as one school cannot serve the whole parish, they are, upon a right representation thereof, intitled to a school from the Society for Propagating Christian Knowledge, whereas the parish where no legal school is settled has no title thereunto." And on the question of cost it was asserted confidently that there wasn't a parish in Shetland which could not raise 100 merks (the minimum salary). No doubt with his own present experiment in Delting in mind, Gifford said this could be done by the tenants initially advancing the whole amount, one half of which (the heritors' portion) would be subsequently rebated in their rents.

The heritors requested and were granted a final compromise — that they were to have complete control of the school money, the siting of the school, and nomination of schoolmaster. The 15 heritors present — all Episcopalian except for Gifford and one other — then accepted the proposals unanimously, although there is the strong possibility that for some at least it was no more than a token acquiescence. He later obtained the consent of the Earl of Morton, holder of all crown lands, whereupon the proposals passed officially through the Stewart Court and were engrossed among the Country Acts. It then became compulsory for parents to send their children to the local school.

Gifford's Plan Collapses

Despite its astute presentation this piece of local legislation, however enlightened in intention, proved a dead letter in practice. Gifford, writing nine years later, states that the Act[13] "now obtains in several parishes, and in others much neglected, just as the principal heritor of the parish stands inclined to promote such a public good work." In making this statement Gifford, perhaps from a sense of pride since the Earl of Morton was to receive a copy of the manuscript, was concealing the real extent of his failure. By 1733 the only parish to have operated a school on parochial lines was Delting — predominantly his own estate — and even there the experiment had lapsed. Even the Earl of Morton had failed to honour his pledge, for in 1731 an SSPCK delegation to the Earl informed him that all Society schools in Orkney and Shetland would be withdrawn unless legal schools were erected. The Earl responded by claiming he had given direction for a legal school to be settled in Birsay, Orkney, "but that he had reason why he would not concur in settling any more."[14] He forebore, however, to reveal the "reason" for avoiding his legal responsibility.

In May, 1725 Presbytery sent their thanks to Gifford for his efforts in procuring the Act.[15] But at the same meeting they recommend that "every Minister set about the settling of a school in each of thair parishes," which suggests that the ministers had already accepted that the initiative undertaken by Gifford had passed by default to the kirk. This situation tends to be confirmed in 1726 when we find the heritors actively opposing a school in Dunrossness although the local tenants had agreed to give the teacher, John Smith, an encouragement of £5 sterling for one year at least, and the minister had given him accommodation in the manse.[16]

Why then did the Act fail to produce more positive and lasting results? Had the signatories merely given their assent as a gesture to mollify the influential Stewart-depute? Or had Gifford genuinely convinced them that the scheme was feasible, based on his own experience in Delting, and they had failed to make it work? Or was it that in early eighteenth century Shetland the parochial system of education was only workable if launched and piloted round the many hazards by someone of the stature and with the commitment of Thomas Gifford?

The failure of the 1724 scheme underlines not only the degree of local inertia which had to be overcome but, more seriously, the great weaknesses of the 1696 Act when applied to remote rural areas with scattered populations.

REFERENCES

1. Gifford, Thomas, Historical Description of the Zetland Islands, 1733, Edin. 1879, p.38
2. Ibid.
3. Register of Proceedings of Heritors of Orkney, 22/11/1661, SRO
4. ZPM 8/3/1711, SA
5. ZPM 13/2/1707, SA
6. ZPM 1/8/1717, SA
7. SSPCK Gen. Meeting, 7/6/1716, SRO
8. SSPCK Comm., 22/8/1722, SRO
9. Gifford, op. cit. p.84
10. Gifford Day Book 1708-1732, MS, SA
11. ZPM 26/4/1722, SRO
12. Gifford Day Book Ibid., SA
13. Gifford, Thomas, Historical Description of the Zetland Islands, Appendix 3, 1733, Edin., 1879
14. SSPCK Gen. Meeting, 4/11/1731, SRO
15. ZPM 27/5/1725, SA
16. SSPCK Comm., 23/6/1726, SA

Chapter 7

Buchan and Walls

THOMAS GIFFORD had shown in Delting in the 1720s what leadership and initiative could do but Shetland had to wait a further 20 years before another man was to appear whose enterprise and energy were to transform the educational scene in his parish — James Buchan, minister of Walls and Sandness from 1735-1778. The story of his long ministry in this parish, particularly his commitment to schools, provides such a revealing picture of the many factors influencing education and provision of schools at that time, that it merits being told in some detail.

It will be recalled that the first Society school in Shetland was established in Walls in 1713. Despite difficulties it flourished, until Presbytery removed it to Tingwall in 1717.[1] Undoubtedly these four years laid the foundations of an interest in education in the district and threw up men and women who were prepared to conduct small adventure schools or instruct their own children in reading at home.

In the 1730s two small schools were operating in Walls and the session allocated Bibles to parents who undertook to instruct their children. In 1737 James Henry compeared "and represented to the Session that he had two fatherless children in his family, that they were now so far advanced in their Learning that he was about to enter them into the Bible, but he thought it sufficient for him to feed and clothe and... Teach the said children though he did not furnish them in books. In the meantime he had their education so much at heart that he thought proper to address the Session for a Bible to the said children."[2] The Session gave him a Bible, and well they might, for when one considers the general impoverishment of the time, his sense of responsibility towards his foster-children was indeed remarkable. If his interest in education was in any way typical of the district, then the situation in Walls was ripe for exploitation by someone with drive. And that person was to be James Buchan.

Buchan was no stranger to the problems of promoting schools in Shetland. He was the son of James Buchan, minister of Northmavine, whose efforts in establishing schools there have already been mentioned, and he himself had been schoolmaster in the island of Bressay for six years before being presented to the parish of Walls.

His predecessor, George Duncan, who had died in 1734, had

encouraged "petty" schools and been involved in setting up a so-called parochial school in Walls with his son John as teacher. John Duncan served for two years in Walls but refused to teach in either Sandness or Papa Stour as he "got not his maintenance free as in Walls".³ The Papa heritors therefore refused to pay their quotas of his salary and the principal heritor, James Mitchell of Girlsta, was obliged to advance most of the peoples' quotas. Not long before George Duncan's death, he had persuaded the SSPCK to send books to the parish, and one of James Buchan's first tasks as minister was to "pursue" a Lerwick merchant who had been authorised to bring the books from Edinburgh. Eventually, in September, 1738, the merchant was prevailed upon to produce the books — eight Bibles, 10 New Testaments, 12 Solomon's Proverbs, 12 Mother's Catechisms, and 24 Single Catechisms.⁴

It is interesting to note how these books were distributed. Of the eight Bibles, three were given to individuals, including the aforementioned James Henry, one retained by the minister, and four were sent to Sandness. The great majority of the remaining books went to Sandness which suggests that, although there was no identifiable school in the area, home instruction was being conducted in a number of families. Since reading of biblical texts was the principal, if not the sole, educational activity at this time, books were eagerly looked for and greatly cherished. Four years later, when the session checked on this particular batch, all were accounted for, although it was noted with disapproval that two copies were "sullied". These were set aside for the use of the very poor.

A Sympathetic Heritor

In Walls and Sandness there was obviously a groundswell for learning, and in this James Buchan was fortunate. He was doubly so in that his arrival in the parish coincided with that of a young and forceful heritor who had just inherited an estate comprising approximately half the lands in the parish, and who had a genuine interest in education. John Scott came to the 465 merks estate of Melby in 1736. Unlike many of the principal heritors in Shetland his landed interest was confined solely within the bounds of the one parish, and this enabled him to concentrate his considerable energies in tackling his responsibilities as principal heritor.

He found the parish, and Sandness in particular, in sore straits: "… whereas in all or most of the unprovided [with schools] Parioches in the Country besides Sandness, there are some Gentlemen, Merchants, or substantial Tenants residing there in, that can imploy teachers upon their own charges which may Instruct both their own children and those of the poorer sort in their neighbourhood, matters are quite otherwise here; there being no Gentlemen, no Merchants, no Tenants of any tolerable stock or Substance residing in that Parioch, nay few, very few that are capable to pay half of their just debts, but the far greater part are (to my experience) so plung'd in Debt, that I question if there be any Paroch in the countrey so deeply and universally depauperate."[5]

Scott's assessment of his parish was unlikely to be exaggerated as it was part of a Petition he presented for the scrutiny of Zetland Presbytery whose members would have been fully aware of local conditions and sensitive to special pleading from any particular area. But, however "depauperate" the people of Walls and Sandness were at this time, their condition was only relatively worse than that of any Shetland parish.

Famine and Pestilence

Famine and pestilence darkened the lives of Shetland people throughout the eighteenth century. As mentioned previously, the land never produced enough grain to serve the population for a complete year, and in bad years, which frequently occurred, barely enough to suffice for four to six months. Survival depended on fish, particularly the "piltock" (one-year-old coalfish) caught in the voes from boats or from suitable stances along the rocky coasts. In 1701 Brand commented: "... for bread failing many of the people in the summer time, that often for four or five months they will not taste thereof, these fishes [piltocks] are almost their only meat, and especially the livers."

While dearth of grain and poor fishings occurred with malignant regularity, certain periods of scarcity were so disastrous as to be remembered vividly and documented in some detail. Such was the early 1740s. The harvest of 1739 had been poor, followed by a hard, snowy winter. By the spring of 1740 there was great "extremity among many householders" because of "skersity and dearth of Victual",[6] and to make matters worse the harvest in that year was ruined by a prolonged fall of snow under which the corn rotted. At Hillswick a merciful shoal of beached whales gave the starving some relief. The spring of 1743 was again disastrous "wherein the weather has been and is like to continue so stormy and tempestuous that it threatens universal death to the beasts of the field and to render it impracticable for the husbandman to Labour or Sow the ground."[7]

The famines of the early eighteenth century did not come alone. At that time smallpox epidemics were recurring in 20 year cycles. In 1700 Lerwick and the South Mainland were most seriously affected, Lerwick losing approximately one-eighth of its population. The 1720 outbreak appears to have been most virulent in parishes to the West. It is claimed that on this occasion only six men in Foula were left alive to bury the dead.[8] The epidemic of 1740 was more widespread, with victims occurring all over Shetland and from all classes. Five of Thomas Gifford of Busta's children died during this epidemic.[9]

It is against this background of grinding poverty, with destitution and sudden death a commonplace of daily living, that we have to place the efforts being made to promote education and the response of the people to them.

Certainly James Buchan could not have begun his campaign for the erection of schools at a more difficult time than in the early 1740s, nor in a more difficult area. Yet such was the measure of local support for schools that, in February, 1740, in famine conditions, church collections in Walls in aid of the SSPCK came to £41.11.6 from approximately 150 families.[10]

Armed with this money and instructions from his Kirk Session that it was to be donated only if the Society appointed a teacher to Papa Stour — a small island to the west of the parish — Buchan set off for Edinburgh and, on 2nd April, 1741, promptly petitioned the Society for three schools — in Walls, Sandness and Papa Stour. It was an audacious request, considering the Society had only three schools in the whole of Shetland at that time, including one in his own parish, in Foula.

The Society had already, in preparing its scheme for Shetland for 1740-41, decided to augment the salary of 200 merks which had been paid to the deceased Francis Beattie by an amount to take it up to £12 sterling, and divide this among three schools to be designated by Zetland Presbytery. But they must have been so impressed by Buchan's case that they pre-empted the authority they had given to Presbytery and promised an allocation of £36 Scots to Buchan for a school in Papa Stour. Buchan's response was characteristic of his single-minded loyalty to his own parish, not to mention his toughness as a negotiator. Having got more than he might have expected under the circumstances, he said nothing about the money which had been collected for the Society but, as he reported to the Kirk Session upon his return, the Society "had not as yet sent any Books for the poor schollars to be taught here. Therefor, as he forsaw that the want of said books would much Impede the Design of the School, he thought fit to lay out the money forsaid for purchasing books for said School and other poor Scholars within his Ministry."[11]

His next task was to persuade Presbytery of the merits of his case, particularly as he had short-circuited normal proceedings in going straight to the Society with his petition. Here again is impressive evidence of his persuasiveness, for not only was his petition successful in convincing Presbytery of the needs of Papa Stour but he managed to procure one of the three new schools for Sandness.

It is reasonable to assume that an important factor in Presbytery's eyes would have been, not Buchan's initiative, unusual though it was, but the fact that in his petition he had indicated that his principal heritor had promised that, if a charity school were to be allocated to Sandness, he (Scott) would contribute his legal proportion towards a parochial school, and he would also use his influence to persuade other heritors to do likewise. Under regular pressure as they were from the General Assembly and SSPCK, Presbytery would have no doubt been prepared to allow any minister his head, provided he looked like getting closer to that oft talked of, but elusive institution — a legal school. And in the Shetland of the mid-eighteenth century James Buchan was more likely than most to achieve that goal.

Local Men as Teachers

Buchan found two capable local men who, after due examination by Presbytery in reading, writing, arithmetic and church music, were certified as qualified Society teachers: for Papa Stour, John Greig, already catechist there, and for Sandness, James Cheyne, session clerk and a descendant of the Cheynes of Esslemont, landed proprietors in the district during the 17th century and earlier.[12]

Within a few months the two schools were in full swing and by the summer of 1742 Buchan had prodded Presbytery into making official visitations, which were conducted according to Society guidelines and fully documented in the Session Register. These records reveal the wholehearted response which came from these small, impoverished communities. Sandness, with its 45 families, had 68 scholars on the roll, 37 of whom were recorded as either "constant" or "frequent" attenders. Their ages varied from five to 22 the majority being in the six to 14 group. Papa Stour, with 40 families, also had 68 scholars on the roll, 31 recorded as "constant" or "frequent" attenders. In both schools there were as many girls as boys on the roll. An indication of the cruel conditions of the day is that in Sandness approximately 20 per cent, and in Papa Stour almost 30 per cent of the children were orphans or fatherless.

Problems of Ambulatory Schools

When Presbytery were informed in 1741 that they were to receive an allocation of £12 sterling to be divided among three schools, they decided they would launch these on an ambulatory basis, each school

1. Anderson Educational Institute with teachers and pupils c.1880.
Photo: George Washington Wilson, courtesy of Islesburgh Community Centre Summer Exhibition Committee.

2. Staff and pupils of the Anderson Educational Institute, c. 1880. The headmaster, Mr Allardyce, is the bearded man in the back row. The poet J. J. Haldane Burgess, then a pupil teacher, is in the front row, fourth from the right.
Courtesy of Mrs Hilary Harmer and the Shetland Archives (papers of the late Dr T. M. Y. Manson).

NEW SCHOOLHOUSE AND SCHOOL.

SANDNESS, SHETLAND, 10*th January* 1871.

SIR,

The above woodcut gives a view of the Schoolhouse and School which, through the liberality of Clergymen, Schoolmasters, and other friends of education in the South, I have succeeded in erecting in this locality.

It is a plain, neat, and substantial building, well lighted and ventilated, erected on a piece of ground granted by the landlord to the School for ever, and will, I hope, prove a blessing to the poor people of the district for generations to come.

The district benefited by the School is situated on the north-west of the Mainland of Shetland, contains a population of 606, is distant 10 miles from the Parochial School, and the School attendance has of late years increased from 30 to 70 Scholars.

The old School buildings, which were built in 1790, and were at best of an inferior description, had fallen into such a ruinous condition as to become uninhabitable, and they either had to be rebuilt or the salary would be withdrawn.

The general poverty of the people was such that they could do nothing, and I could not think of their losing their School without my doing everything in my power to help them. It has been a hard struggle, has occupied every spare moment of my time for upwards of two years; and had the appeals on behalf of the sick and wounded soldiers not seriously interfered with my scheme, I believe I would have succeeded in raising funds to complete my buildings in a satisfactory manner; but I am sorry to say that I am still £35 short of the sum necessary to finish the Schoolroom.

The School is open to all, and is attended by the children of every denomination in the district; and as I have no sympathy with the advocates of a secular system of education, I have done my utmost to secure that the Bible shall always be taught in the School.

I am sorry to trouble you, but I am anxious to finish my Schoolroom so as to enable my Scholars to pursue their studies in comfort; and if you will be kind enough to favour me with a small subscription, or bring my case under the notice of any lady or gentleman whom you think might sympathise with me, you will exceedingly oblige,

SIR,

Your obedient Servant,

ROBERT JAMIESON.

Address.—ROBERT JAMIESON,
SCHOOLMASTER, SANDNESS, SHETLAND.

THE MANSE, WALLS, SHETLAND, 1*st October* 1870.

I CERTIFY that MR ROBERT JAMIESON, Schoolmaster at Sandness in this Parish, who is making laudable efforts to complete the erection of a suitable Schoolhouse and School in that district, has my entire sympathy in the object he has in view. The property on which the School stands is much burdened, and the proprietor therefore able to do little more than grant a site, with a small patch of ground. The people are almost entirely fishermen and small crofters, and can give no effectual aid. They are very desirous, however, to give their children a good education—have great respect for, and like their teacher well, who, in a numerous and well-conducted School, is doing a great deal of good in the district.

ARCHIBALD NICHOL,
Minister of the Parish of Walls and Sandness.

Courtesy of Shetland Archives.

4. Andrew D. Mathewson, Headmaster of East Yell Parochial and Public School 1823-1878.
Courtesy of Old Haa Trust, Burravoe, Yell.

5. Robert Jamieson, Headmaster of Sandness School 1858-1899.
Photo C. Spence, Lerwick.

6. East Yell Parochial School, built 1822, on left. East Yell Public School, built 1879, on right. *Courtesy of Anna Thomson and Old Haa Trust, Burravoe, Yell.*

7. General Assembly School, Laxfirth, Tingwall.
Photo Jack Peterson, courtesy of Shetland Museum

8. John Ross, Headmaster at General Assembly School, Laxfirth, Tingwall 1839-1843 and at Bressay Parochial School 1843-1878. Photo taken outside East School, Bressay.

9. Charles C. Beatton, Headmaster at Gott Public School 1873-1887. Previously at General Assembly School, Laxfirth, Tingwall 1843-1873.

continuing for two years at a chosen station then moving to another as determined by Presbytery. The first three stations were to be Sandness, Sandsting, and Tingwall, followed two years later by Nesting, Northmavine, and Yell. Both Presbytery and Yell appear to have accepted the idea of "ambulatory" schools as a device for spreading meagre resources over a wide area, without really thinking seriously of the implications. Certainly they were soon to be confronted with practical difficulties. The people of Sandness in particular were loth to lose their school after only two years and petitions on their behalf were sent to Presbytery and Society by Kirk Session and principal heritor. Scott argued[13] that Buchan had considerable difficulty in getting the people to build a schoolhouse for a teacher who would remain with them only two years, and had finally persuaded them after "repeated exhortations and arguments" by an assurance that Presbytery might consider their case if further representations were made. The people had then erected a schoolhouse "upon a piece of centrical ground, gifted for that end by your Petitioner, of about Thirty feet long, and furnished it with a sufficient door, Tables and forms on their own charge and pains, which you may believe would cost such a poor people a hard enough pull. Now if this house be rendered so suddenly desolate and waste and fall to ruin with its furniture, the Presbytery will easily foresee the hurtfull consequence of such an unhappy Incident, and how much it must weaken the hands of the Minister of that place, as it will make the People deaf to all future motives to do or expend anything for the Education of their Children. Wherefor your Petitioner cannot but hope that the Presbytery will indulge the poor people the benefit of their labour and charges about their Schoolhouse by addressing the Society to appoint them a fixed standing school."

Appeals of this nature found both Presbytery and Society with a rather irresolute grasp of their prescribed intentions regarding ambulatory schools, and both vacillated from meeting to meeting. In October, 1741 the Society instructed Presbytery that James Cheyne be removed from Sandness to Dunrossness. Presbytery, having received John Scott's Petition and been converted to its views, reacted by describing the Society's policy, to which they had already agreed, as being "attended with no small inconvenience, it being hard for parishes to build schoolhouses....and Immediately thereafter to have the School removed." Then, in December, 1742 the Society revealed a similar inability to abide by their declared policy when, after receiving a Petition from Walls requesting that James Cheyne remain there, they concurred, adding lamely that another teacher be found for Nesting, "where James Cheyne was to have gone." (They had apparently forgotten their instruction 14 months previously that Cheyne go to Dunrossness.) Meanwhile, amid this flux of uncertainty, a further meeting of Presbytery in September, 1743 swung back into line behind the original ambulatory policy by expressing disapproval of the Society's decision that James Cheyne remain at Sandness, regarding "this decision as a loss to the Country" and approving of an additional Society school being fixed at Sandness, but not one of the three "ambulatories". In accordance with that decision they recommended that John Greig be removed from Papa Stour to Yell.

The ambulatory principle was proving difficult to maintain. Apart from the local communities of Sandness and Papa Stour being reluctant to lose schools which were flourishing, the teachers were local men with local affinities and not anxious to pull up roots and move.

A Blast from Buchan's Trumpet

At the next meeting of Presbytery, in November, 1743, Buchan presented a "Remonstrance and Supplication of the Church and Session of Walls, Sandness, Papa Stour, and Foula, with a Scheme Subjoined for providing all the Ministerial Charges in the Country with Proper Means of Education."[14] This was, in reality, a blast from Buchan's trumpet against the attempt to remove John Greig from Papa Stour, as well as the general ambulatory principle. But the four other members present voted against the paper to a man and also rejected his plan for parochial schools. This was based on a scheme for raising the necessary funds by firstly, the "sinking" of Catechists, wherever appointed, and diverting their salaries to an educational scheme, and secondly, by a scheme of land assessment. Buchan was certainly single-minded but rather short on diplomacy. He could hardly have expected his Presbyterial brethren to support his unilateral scheme for his own parish. Nor could it be imagined that they would take kindly to his implied criticism of themselves. For, in his condemnation of the ambulatory system, he asked rhetorically if Nesting and Yell had made any preparations to accommodate Cheyne and Greig — knowing well they had not. So it was not surprising that a group of ministers presented a report to Presbytery in March, 1744 for transmission to the Society in which Buchan is singled out for unfavourable comment.[15] They criticised his tactics in approaching the Society directly and using unfair influence so that "the ministry of Walls alone for some time past has had three of six Charity Schools appointed for this country" and "has enjoyed as many means of instruction as all the other eleven put together."

But Buchan was not the man to be deterred by opposition. If anything it acted as a stimulus and he came armed to the same meeting with a massive reply to Presbytery's rejection of his remonstrance. However much he antagonised his Presbytery colleagues he would not have endeared himself to the Presbytery clerk who took 15 pages to engross his statement in the Minute Book. The burden of Buchan's complaint was that the decision of the previous meeting was unrepresentative, only one-third of the members being present; that the Society's ambulatory scheme had foundered on the "precarious... and random management" of Presbytery as operated by local ministers who had not ensured that their respective areas were provided with schoolhouses to receive the teachers, nor supplied with peats and kailyards; and that a period of only two years in a district gives incentives to neither teacher nor parents.

These points were certainly all arguable but Buchan allowed his enthusiasm for his case to so carry himself away as to claim that Walls had a legal school and therefore was entitled to extraordinary support from the Society. He was referring here to a small school built by John Scott in 1742, maintained partly by subscriptions from the people, but mainly by Scott himself. As Presbytery pointed out, "although there is a schoolmaster who teaches the Youth... and obtains some salary, yet there is no legal settlement according to the Acts of Parliament, no Decreet for a salary to the Master, nor any proper steps nor application (that the Presbytery can hear of) made to the Judge competent for pronouncing Decreet on that matter, on which account the said school in Walls must necessarily be precarious and uncertain." And Buchan must have known this all too well. The extent to which he had taxed Presbytery's patience is revealed in the sentiment which concludes this minute: "... they have spent much time (having sat about three days) in this cause, and they have been so fatigued with long narratives, trifling protests and repetitions that they were now sick of this affair."

Their disfavour was further emphasised by reiterating the instruction that Greig move from Papa Stour to Nesting this time, and Cheyne from Sandness to Northmavine. Buchan predictably protested in vain, although he would have derived some satisfaction from the rebuke delivered by the Society three months later indicating dissatisfaction with Presbytery's decision to move the Papa Stour and Sandness schools when the Society had already ordered them to be fixed.[16]

The three-cornered tug-of-war between Buchan, Presbytery, and Society continued inconclusively, with Presbytery enacting the annual ritual of ordering Cheyne to move to another area, and Cheyne standing fast. Finally, in 1754, Cheyne, now an old and failing man, and having once more been instructed to move — this time to Delting — informed Presbytery that he wished to demit office in favour of his son George.[17]

This was agreed and George, having been examined and certificated in reading, writing, arithmetic, and church music, undertook the long-postponed move to Delting. But his stay was brief for, two years later, Presbytery were informed that Cheyne had "again and again intimated his wish to demit office." Whether he found teaching in Delting an unrewarding exercise or simply wished to return to his native parish, we do not know, but he is later recorded as teaching in Sandness.[18]

Buchan's Grand Design

Buchan's grand design was to create a pattern of schools throughout his parish, drawing on all possible forms — charity, petty, and legal — which would bring education within the reach of every family in the parish. It was an ambitious scheme for such a widespread area, involving schools in Down-Walls, Mid Walls, Sandness, Papa Stour, and Foula. But, by the late 1740s, the plan was virtually a reality although, like all educational schemes in similar areas, "precarious and uncertain".

As mentioned earlier, two small schools — at Braebister and Curkigarth — were functioning in Walls in the 1730s. In Down-Walls — the south-east part of the district — the school at Curkigarth had been taught by James Moncrieff, at least since the early 1730s. The Kirk Session had guaranteed him a salary for teaching children of poor parents, which for the two years 1735-1737 amounted to £9. He would also have received fees in money and kind from parents and a contribution from John Scott. The Kirk Session continued to pay Moncrieff until 1737 when he is reported deceased.[19]

At this stage, Buchan and his session reviewed the pattern of schools in Walls and decided that as the school at Braebister in the Mid Walls area drew on two-thirds of the entire Walls population, thus leaving the school in Down-Walls inadequately supported, the families of the townships of Riskaness, Howll and Burraland should attend at Down-Walls. And to site the school more centrally within the revised boundaries it was decided it be moved from Curkigarth to Stove. This was accepted at a meeting of the session with 38 heads of families in the area, who agreed to contribute yearly £29.6/- Scots as salary to the teacher. The session offered to supply the materials for the building of the schoolhouse but expected the people to be responsible for its erection and maintenance. Duncan Moncrieff, son of the previous teacher, was invited to be schoolmaster. He accepted but for only one year. His lack of enthusiasm was understandable in that the salary offered was less than one-third of the minimum legal salary for parochial schoolmasters at that time.

Meanwhile, Mid Walls had also had problems of continuity. On 19th

October, 1746 Buchan announced from the pulpit that a meeting of the inhabitants of Mid Walls — from Elvista to Turdaill — would take place the following day to endeavour "to set up a school for teaching English at this place."[20] The only opposition at the meeting came from the people of Dale who claimed that the Burn of Setter, which lay between them and the school, was too dangerous for their children to cross in winter. The session was sympathetic to their situation and agreed to provide material for erecting a foot-bridge across the burn if the people of Dale would assist in its erection and maintenance. A local man, Thomas Henry of Hivdigarth, was elected as teacher and he agreed to commence duties at the beginning of December, by which time the schoolhouse at Bendrie would be made habitable.

The school continued for two years at Bendrie then Henry, not having received the promised salary, left and Mid Walls was again without a school. The session had not provided the promised bridge across the Setter burn and the parents of Dale withdrew their children and withheld payments to the teacher.[21] Moreover, the parents as a whole found the agreed contributions a burden and suggested that the session endeavour to lighten it by finding an unmarried teacher who could receive lodging and maintenance from house to house.

This episode was a further bitter illustration to Buchan and his session that, for all the general desire for education, obligations entered into voluntarily did not, in the face of economic reality, always hold. An element of authority was lacking and it is an interesting commentary on the hierarchy of power in the local community at the time that it was to the principal heritor that they turned to give the necessary imprint of authority to their plans. They wrote to John Scott asking that he strengthen their hands "in their pious design" by requesting the people to pay the sums they had voluntarily undertaken towards the master's salary. A postscript to their letter reveals how Buchan saw this petty school in his overall strategy for education in the parish: "We are of the mind that the keeping or dropping the School in Walls will have much influence on the Society's resolutions with respect to the removal or continuance of the Charity School in Sandness."[22]

This move could, however, be interpreted not just as a request that Scott interpose his authority but a device to involve him in the scheme and thus, inevitably, underwrite the people's financial undertaking. Fourteen years later, by which time it appears that the once congenial relationship between Buchan and Scott had become somewhat soured, Scott stated that the people, having undertaken to contribute towards teachers' salaries and subsequently finding themselves unable to do so, expect the heritors to advance money towards payment of these salaries, whereby the people enter into debt leaving "the Heritors [to]… carry the whole burden of paying a school-master's salary, and never get payment again from the most part of the people neither of that advance nor their own Land-meals and other Debts due them."[23] This "protestation" from Scott stemmed from almost 30 years of frustrating efforts to establish a system of education for his area and all too often finding that the erection of schools only helped to swell the credit side of his ledger. It also, no doubt, expressed the disillusion of an old and ailing man. He died within the year.

There is no evidence as to how Scott responded to the request from Buchan and the Kirk Session in 1750 but a year later, at a further meeting of heads of families of Mid Walls, Buchan "did Judicially Interrogat them anent their inclination" in reviving the school at Braebister (i.e. Bendrie), and it was agreed that James Jacobson in Netherdaill be appointed schoolmaster with a salary of £22.16/- Scots as specified at a meeting in November, 1749.

"That Laudable End"

In 1757 the SSPCK reiterated its now familiar threat that they would withdraw all allowances to schools in Shetland unless Presbytery "use proper endeavours" to have legal schools established in every parish. Presbytery again went through the now routine motions and instructed all its members to make every effort to implement the law.

Buchan duly summoned a meeting of heritors and heads of families where the predictable objections were ventilated. John Scott stated he was "heartily willing to contribute to that laudable end"[24] but pointed out that it was unreasonable to expect the people of Sandness, Papa Stour and Foula to contribute to a parochial school in Walls unless they could expect some benefit from it. Since Papa Stour and Foula already had charity schools virtually fixed, Sandness remained the problem area, not having had a regular school since James Cheyne demitted office in 1754 and his son George went off to Delting.

Scott proposed that the Society be informed that, if they settled a charity school in Sandness, he would contribute his quota towards a legal school in Walls and that, in the meantime, he would be "willing to encourage and Assist his Tennants and others he had influence among in this Parish in maintaining and keeping up little schools", as he had hitherto been doing in Down-Walls and Mid Walls.

During the late fifties and early sixties Presbytery kept the issue of legal schools to the forefront of their business and held meetings on this topic in various parishes. In August, 1764 they were at Walls to meet heritors, elders, and heads of families. John Scott, in what was to be his swan-song, laid before them a rambling and contentious "protestation" containing an account of his family's long association with educational endeavour in the district, and voicing strong opposition to the notion of a legal school so long as specific areas were left unprovided. He also hit out at Buchan, accusing him among other things, of "his litigious humour".[25] Buchan advocated that steps be taken to establish a legal school and was supported in this by two small heritors and three elders. But the remainder of the elders together with all heads of families and one small heritor joined with Scott in opposition. Faced with this division of opinion Presbytery felt unable to proceed further but requested Buchan to petition the Commissioners of Supply to stent heritors in accordance with the law, with half of the total amount being borne by tenants.

There is no record of Buchan having pursued this request but it is possible that the events of 1764-5 in Walls, particularly as they affected the Melby family, inhibited Buchan from putting pressure on that source. This was a gloomy period for the Scotts. In 1764 John Scott's son and heir was killed by a fall from the cliffs on the isle of Vaila.[26] He himself died in August of the following year, leaving a five-year-old grandson as heir in line. While not always seeing eye to eye with Buchan, John Scott had, for almost 30 years, been a positive force in promoting education in his district, and his passing meant that the initiative now lay more than ever with Buchan.

"A Lasting Foundation"

In 1768 Buchan told his session "that he had for a long time been meditating a plan for the erecting of a School in Walls upon a lasting foundation with an encouragement sufficient to procure a well qualify'd Schoolmaster for the time to come…".[27] He was now well into his sixties and had been minister of the parish for 33 years. He was a man of means and property. He wanted very much to make a lasting contribution to the educational provision of the parish. What was needed was a combination of circumstances which would concentrate his aspirations.

After the bleak years of the 1740s people's lives had improved, however marginally in the 1750s and for part of the 60s. There had been a series of good harvests and fishings, and whaling ships bound for Greenland had been calling regularly at Lerwick to enlist crews.

In 1768 the SSPCK ordered George Greig, Society teacher in Papa Stour, to be transported to Walls if a house could be provided for him. Buchan must have seen this as the opportunity to exploit. Greig was a man of considerable ability who, as session clerk, had been Buchan's ablest lieutenant. His minutes of the period amply testify to his painstaking zeal, his general level of learning, and his overall sense of proportion. He had also, in his time, been merchant, factor, baillie, and ruling elder in Papa Stour.[28] Buchan knew his worth and must have seen that, now he was in Walls, this was the sort of man around whom a strong and lasting school could be built.

At a session meeting in 1758, Buchan demonstrated to his elders the extent of his commitment to a school.[29] Firstly, he would mortify to the schoolmaster of the proposed school, for all time coming, four acres of land at Voe. Secondly, he undertook during his lifetime, to pay the schoolmaster £20 Scots annually. Thirdly, that whoever succeeded him in his own house, gardens and nine merks land in Voe, should be burdened — he and his heirs — with £30 Scots annually to the schoolmaster at Walls. And fourthly, that he himself would contribute £30 towards the erection of a schoolhouse on the site he had gifted. This was indeed a substantial basis for a permanent settlement and the session unanimously agreed to augment it by granting £6 sterling from the Poor's Box towards wood for the schoolhouse and workmen's wages. The house was to be 32 feet long, 14 feet broad, and 10½ feet high. It was further agreed that, at the next service in Walls, Buchan should summon the congregation to assemble and find out what they were prepared to contribute, either in money, labour, or maintenance of workmen.

Buchan had certainly given a positive and generous lead to the community but he must have been heartened by their magnificent response. On a stormy March day 65 heads of families — out of about 108 — turned up and all agreed to be responsible for maintenance and service, for one day each, to the workmen — six masons, two wrights, two barrow-men, and one man for clay — during the 25 days it was estimated they would take to complete the job. Mrs Scott of Vaila, unable to be present because of the severe weather, had authorised Buchan to promise £30 on her behalf. Archibald Henry, a local merchant, offered £30 and there was an anonymous donation of a guinea. Further, 11 young men who were present, offered jointly to supply half an anker[30] of waters as drams to the workmen, and one of the elders offered a further ½ anker for the same purpose. This encouraged the session to look for further similar support and they drew up a list of 42 other young men from the district who might contribute drams and tobacco to the workmen.

Happyhansel

Even with the drams and tobacco the schoolhouse took longer to complete than the anticipated 25 days but Buchan was able to report to the session in November, 1768 that the work "as far as it can be accomplished this year is well-nigh finished." In fact, it would appear that the elders, ranselmen, and workmen whom Buchan interrogated as to the length of time required and who estimated 11 men working 25 days, were not fully aware of the scale and type of building Buchan was envisaging. Certainly, he specified that it was to be 32'x 14' x 10½' high, which was bigger than the normal schoolhouse of the period. Tingwall Parish School, for example, which was erected about the same time, was 30' x 14' but only 7' high.

There is no evidence that Buchan revealed fully to the session his intention that the building would not only contain the schoolhouse and the master's accommodation but also have provision for a dormitory. It was also to be roofed with slates instead of the customary thatch. These things considered, it is not surprising that the work took much longer than estimated and cost almost twice as much as the school at Tingwall. The latter was erected for £265.11.4 Scots[31] whereas the Walls school cost £479.6/- Scots (labour — £157.7/-, materials — £321.19/-) and that was exclusive of the voluntary contributions towards workmen's maintenance and creature comforts.

We do not know precisely how long the building took to complete but, as indicated above, the major part of the work had been completed during the summer/autumn period of 1768. Apart from the contributions to the building fund outlined above, Buchan also contrived to draw donations from as far afield as an ex-Collector of Customs in Lerwick and Sir John Mitchell in Scalloway, an important heritor but without a stake in Walls.

Indeed the whole enterprise had behind it such a wealth of goodwill that the school was named "Happyhansel", a name which continues to be associated with the school in Walls down to this day.

In the Shetland context the post of teacher at Happyhansel was an attractive one. Greig's salary from the Society was £5 sterling; Buchan's Mortification was valued at a further £5; salary as session clerk together with perquisites arising from this office amounted to £2. This gave him a guaranteed minimum annual income of £12 sterling which could be augmented by fees. Furthermore, the four and a half acres of ground and the privilege of grazing one cow was far in excess of the statutory kailyard provided for parochial schoolmasters. At a time when a teacher's income was generally on a par or little more than that of a labourer, George Greig was in a position which enabled him to earn more than a tradesman. About 1790, a skilled mason could, at best, earn 1/- per day and sometimes only 6d (the rate they were paid for their work at Happyhansel). This meant an annual income of from about £8-£15, whereas Greig could earn at least £15.

In 1769 the school was recognised officially by the SSPCK and Greig awaited recognition by Presbytery. All seemed well but Buchan felt that a school launched was only half the battle. From bitter experience he knew that schemes which got off to promising starts invariably collapsed through lack of continuity of funds, principally for the maintenance of the fabric of the building. He therefore presented a scheme to the session[32] "to prevent the schoolhouse and its appurtenances going to ruin in time coming". A maintenance fund was to be established from the following sources:

> 1) the old practice of penalising ante-nuptial fornicators — £6 Scots from the man and £3 from the woman — which had lapsed, was to be revived, with 40 pence of the fine to be paid into the fund. Sin was to subsidise learning.
>
> 2) another practice which had lapsed — the payment of a "spousing kjob" by couples whom the minister married — was to be revived. The minister was now to demand from couples to be married sums not exceeding half-a-crown from the richer nor below a shilling from the poorer.
>
> 3) a voluntary collection was to be taken up from the marriage company — "before the blessing be pronounced, after celebrating the marriage."
>
> 4) collections to be taken up at Sabbath worship conducted by a Reader.

The scheme, although designed with Happyhansel very much in mind, was recommended to be applied to the other areas within the united parish for the building and upkeep of schoolhouses. After three years the balance in the school fund stood at £13.11.3 Scots. The average "spousing kjob" appears to have been 12/- Scots and the marriage collection about 5/-.

A School for all Seasons

Buchan now had a substantial schoolhouse, a sound teacher, and a scheme for regular maintenance. It was a scheme which would have filled most educationists at this time with a great deal of satisfaction. But Buchan saw yet wider possibilities.

As has already been mentioned, the schoolhouse was built to generous proportions designed to accommodate, not only the teacher and family, but a number of boarders coming from all over Shetland. Buchan's design was to encourage the growth of Happyhansel, almost by fait accompli, into a legal school serving not only the parish of Walls but the whole of Shetland; a school where pupils could be sent for advanced studies including Latin, book-keeping and navigation, which could prepare them, if necessary, for college.[33] (Appendix D). To that end he was prepared to assist Greig by not only giving him lessons in Latin but, at the same time, assisting in the instruction of pupils in Latin and navigation.

This picture of Buchan, then approaching 70, cramming into the already arduous duties of his widespread parish, the additional duty of teaching the young and coaching the schoolmaster, also in his sixties, provides an illuminating glimpse of the degree of commitment this man had for education in his parish and further afield.

Progress towards the establishment of Happyhansel as a legal school depended on the normal statutory procedure involving agreement by heritors. Since his scheme envisaged Happyhansel operating as a school for pupils from all over Shetland he sought support from the most powerful heritor, Sir Laurence Dundas, who controlled the Lordship Estate in Shetland. He despatched a detailed account of his plans for making Happyhansel a legal school, to Balfour of Trenaby in Orkney who, at the time, was chamberlain of the Lordship Estate. (Appendix D) What response came from Balfour or Dundas is not known but the document itself is unique in that it gives the clearest picture we have from this period of current educational thinking and attitudes.

Buchan called it "Plan for turning the School of Happyhansel into a Legal School to be as extensively useful as Possible both to the Parish and the Country."

This document is interesting in a variety of ways. If it is regarded as a feasibility study for the setting up of Shetland's first legal school, undertaken by a man who, more than most, knew the problems and pitfalls of setting up schools in Shetland, we are provided with a valuable compendium of information pertaining to this time and place. Buchan outlines the form the school was to take, the subjects to be taught, the master's qualifications, his salary and how it would be raised, his other perquisites and, since Happyhansel would be Shetland's first school to provide instruction not available elsewhere, provision for accommodating boarders.

Perhaps the most revealing part is that which deals with "Principal objections." The Shetland minister, in seeking the landlord's approval and support, would have been anxious to allay any fears the project may have prompted. And who was in a better situation to interpret those fears than Buchan with his long experience of the Shetland scene and his close associations with local lairds? If he has in this document put his finger on their fears then it provides strong evidence to suggest that the lairds' reluctance in establishing legal schools sprang from social as well as financial reasons.

The local system of fishing tenures depended for its full development on as large a labour force as possible. The Shetland lairds regarded fishing as the basis of the local economy, with fishing tenures an integral and essential part of it. It followed therefore that the more men who fished the greater the success of the economy and by definition the better the well-being of the community. Anything which directed men away from their rightful places in the sixerns, be it Greenland whaling-ships, Press gang, emigration — or education — was a bad thing.

Although it could be argued that Buchan in this document is playing the casuist in order to enlist the support of Balfour, and ultimately Dundas, it is not difficult to read his own attitude between the lines. And like any person at any time, his attitude would have been a complex of several things. As an eighteenth century Scottish Presbyterian minister his views would have reflected the traditional religious doctrines of his age including the central conviction that schools were essential in bringing the Bible to the people; his economic and social outlook would have been largely determined by the prevailing view of the time that prosperity depended on a growing population, a view which would have been reinforced by the current economic practices of the Shetland lairds; and, synthesising all, would have been his own particular character and temperament.

For example, in his letter to Balfour, he never deviates from the Presbyterian commitment to a school in every parish, yet he regards it as "unjust and unnatural" for young men to leave their homes to seek opportunities outside Shetland and declares that he preaches against this practice. He also appears to give, at least, tacit acceptance to the doctrine that the children of the commons should receive only a basic education in reading, spelling and religion, and that it is fortunate their parents lack the means to obtain a more ambitious education for them.

He was typical of his age and station in his rigidly authoritarian view of a Society held together by "Magistrates, Ministers, Parents and Schoolmasters… in their Respective Spheres." It could indeed be argued that his enthusiasm was nothing more than an expression of his belief that schools were agencies for maintaining the natural order of Society. In which case all his struggles with Presbytery, lairds, the Society, all his time-consuming journeys, supplications, protestations, his personal contributions in land and money, could be interpreted as little more than the means of keeping the ordinary people in their predestined place in Society. But when we compare James Buchan with his fellow-ministers and realise the extent to which he stood head and shoulders above them in his efforts to bring education to his parish, it must be accepted that in many ways he transcended the prevailing mood of his times and displayed a concern for his parishioners that sprang from very personal and intimate sources.

A Legal Foundation at Last

Like many men and women possessed by a dream, Buchan was inclined to close his eyes to certain formalities which might inhibit his progress. In launching Happyhansel officially as a charity school but with legal school pretensions he transgressed the Society regulations that Latin was not to be taught in their schools. Presbytery picked him up on this point and on two occasions in 1771[34] refused to attest George Greig as a Society schoolmaster. At the third attempt[35] Buchan produced the argument that Greig did not "at present teach Latin during school hours nor to any charity children", but conducted his Latin lessons to private pupils and in the schoolhouse.

This argument must have been accepted by, at least, the Society, for Greig is included among the five charity schoolmasters in the Scheme for 1773-1774.[36] Happyhansel had now received official recognition by the Society.

Buchan then proceeded with his plans for establishing it on a proper legal footing. Within a few months of the Society's acceptance of Greig, Buchan petitioned Presbytery to visit Walls "to take proper steps to establish a legal school."[37]

Within a month Presbytery met the heritors in the Kirk of Walls, and once again the latter displayed their concern for an educational provision which covered all quarters of the parish. They agreed unanimously to a legal school in Walls but made their consent contingent upon the Society maintaining schools in Sandness and Papa Stour. If this could be achieved the heritors agreed to stent themselves to the exent of £100 Scots: if not, they would consent to no more than 100 merks.[38] In the meantime George Greig was chosen as teacher and presented in March, 1774 for trials to Presbytery, who ordered him to enter on his office on 1st May. All seemed poised for the consummation, when the almost inevitable rupture appeared between Buchan and Presbytery.

Anxious that the parish should not lose the charity school with Greig's new appointment, Buchan promptly petitioned Presbytery to certify Greig in order that his salary be secured for the ensuing year. But Presbytery reiterated the old objection that he could not be certified as "he teaches Latin in his school which is contrary to Society rules." To raise this technical objection at the eleventh hour, particularly when Greig had only three more days to serve as a Society teacher, was surely carrying legalism, if not the vendetta, to the extreme. But it was only a token resistance, for the Society, prompted by Buchan, agreed that Greig's salary be transferred to George Cheyne, a previous Society teacher, who was to conduct an ambulatory school between Sandness and Papa Stour. With his customary initiative, or high-handedness, Buchan had already installed Cheyne on 10th March. And so Happyhansel officially became a legal school on 1st November, 1774, when the legal salary commenced.

In 1777 the Society intimated their scheme for Walls parish. It was to consist of £10 per annum, comprising £5 to Sandness and Papa Stour, £3 to Foula and "£2 additional salary allowed to these schools in the parish of Walls to be divided among the schoolmasters as the Rev. Mr Buchan shall think fit." Buchan's immediate thought was to allocate the additional salary to Papa Stour, thereby fixing a school in each of the focal points of his united parish. He suggested that William Henry, Reader in Papa Stour, should be the teacher and that he should receive £5, the extra pound being obtained by deducting it from the Foula salary.

And so, after 40 years of unremitting and contentious effort, Buchan's dream was as near to reality as was possible in that place at that time. Education was accessible to the great majority of people in his widespread parish. The schools — one legal and three charity — were placed on a firm financial footing, each with a schoolmaster reared in the parish with all that meant in terms of stability.

There is a certain symmetry about James Buchan's contribution to the educational provision in Walls, for in 1778, the year after this final settlement, he died. George Greig, his able lieutenant, died in the following year, to be succeeded by his son Archibald.

Under Archibald Greig, Happyhansel school developed along the lines envisaged by Buchan in that it became an educational centre not only for Walls but the whole of Shetland. It acquired a notable reputation and the sons of lairds and merchants from elsewhere in Shetland came to board at Happyhansel. In 1797, for example, William Bruce, laird of Symbister, Whalsay, paid an account of £22.3.8 to Greig for board and school fees for his nephew for the four years 1793-1796.

Buchan's struggles in the educational field are classic illustrations of the problems facing anyone attempting to provide schools in scattered rural parishes in the eighteenth century. Thomas Mouat of Gardie, a prominent heritor, sums it up rather neatly in a pamphlet written in 1802: "We all wish to encourage the proper Education of the lower classes, but find that we can only obey the Spirit by deviating from the Letter of the Law. A wise legislature and a moderate clergy will be satisfied therewith… the people have alwise found it more for their advantage to employ some times men and some times women teachers as they could be procured in the various districts of the Parish whom their children could reach with conveniency and whose demands were so moderate as to lay them under no hardship; and that these are the only schools which can be of material benefit in a Country like Shetland."[39] Although Mouat's view embraces a very narrow and limited view of public education, it contains in essence the case against the 1696 Act as applied to rural areas. It also underlines the important role of small adventure schools in achieving a degree of literacy, however minimal, among the people. The notion of a network of small schools supported by the people had an obvious appeal to the heritors, thereby relieved of the statutory responsibilities for half the cost of salaries.

The ideal was a combination of legal schools supported by Society and adventure schools. This was achieved by James Buchan but only after unremitting effort, considerable negotiation and ultimately a degree of personal and financial commitment. For these to coincide was a rare occurrence in eighteenth century Shetland.

REFERENCES

1. SSPCK Gen. Meeting, 5/6/1718, SRO
2. Walls KSM 4/7/1737, SA
3. ZPM 14/8/1764, SA
4. Hjaltland Miscellany, Vol. 2, p.xxiv, ed. Reid Tait, Lerwick 1937
5. ZPM 30/6/1742, SA
6. Walls KSM 1/3/1740, SA
7. Hjaltland Miscellany, Vol.3, ed. Reid Tait, Lerwick 1939
8. Cowie, Robert, Shetland: Descriptive and Historical, Aberdeen 1871
9. Grant, Sir Francis, The County Families of the Zetland Islands, Lerwick 1893
10. Walls KSM 10/3/1740, SA
11. Walls KSM 14/9/1741, SA
12. Hjaltland Miscellany, Vol.2
13. ZPM 30/6/1742, SA
14. ZPM 16/11/1743, SA
15. ZPM 7/3/1744, SA
16. ZPM 13/3/1754, SA
17. ZPM 8/5/1754, SA
18. Walls KSM 2/12/1774, SA
19. Walls KSM 4/7/1737, SA
20. Walls KSM 20/10/1746, SA
21. Walls KSM 20/8/1749, SA
22. Walls KSM 4/3/1750, SA
23. ZPM 14/8/1764, SA
24. Walls KSM 11/9/1762, SA
25. ZPM 14/8/1764, SA
26. Grant, Sir Francis, The County Families of the Zetland Islands, Lerwick 1893
27. Walls KSM 6/3/1768, SA
28. Hjaltland Miscellany, Vol. 2, ed. Reid Tait, Lerwick 1937
29. Walls KSM 6/3/1768, SA
30. An anker was 8⅓ gallons
31. ZPM 5/12/1769, SA
32. Walls KSM 25/12/1769, SA
33. MS Letter (c.1770) Buchan to Balfour of Trenaby, SA, Appendix D
34. ZPM 20/3/1771 and 27/3/1771, SA
35. ZPM 19/6/1771, SA
36. ZPM 10/3/1773, SA
37. ZPM 16/6/1773, SA
38. ZPM 14/7/1773, SA
39. Mouat, Thomas, A Letter by the Landholders of Shetland, Feb.1802

Chapter 8

Legal Schools — the Long Struggle

THE WEAKNESS of the 1696 Act, as summed up by Thomas Mouat and regularly illustrated throughout the remoter areas of Scotland, was one of the early examples of the inadequacies of blanket legislation in a country with widely varying physical conditions. What was considered appropriate at the centre all too often proved impracticable at the periphery.

Yet no modification of the obviously flawed legislation was attempted during the eighteenth century and, in the meantime, the agencies involved had to go through the statutory routine although time after time it ground to a halt at the critical stage of financial commitment by heritors and tenants.

The heritors viewed warily their obligations regarding schools. They recognised that the landlord/tenant relationship of the period, whereby the great majority of the tenants were in perpetual debt to the landlords, inevitably meant that not only would they be responsible for their statutory half of the costs of the schoolmaster's salary, but they would also have to underwrite a considerable proportion of the tenants' half. The tenants' outlook was well put by John Scott of Melby: "Inhabitants of Walls and Sandness — all of them — are generally against a Legal School as well as the Heritors for this reason that they can have their children educate cheaper and get the schoolmaster's salary payed in an easier way as the advance of ready money which they cannot have nor afford to pay the Superior and Land Tax or the Minister's tithes."[1] The tenants, thirled as they were to the credit system, were incapable of envisaging a system of cash payments to the teacher, and would rather provide labour — or maintenance.

Nonetheless, General Assembly and SSPCK kept up pressure on Presbyteries to establish legal schools, with the Society threatening from time to time to withdraw their schools if no action were taken. Just as regularly, Presbyteries instructed ministers to convene meetings of heritors in their parishes to take the necessary steps.

These processes were little more than ritual acknowledgments of the existing statutory obligations of the various authorities, and little was achieved. But at least they kept the issue alive in the minds of those responsible for taking the appropriate legal steps.

11. Ruins of original Happyhansel School, c. 1960.

10. Thomas Gifford of Busta.

12. SSPCK School, Tangwick, Eshaness.

13. Gilbert Williamson, teacher at Twatt Parochial and Public Schools 1856-86.

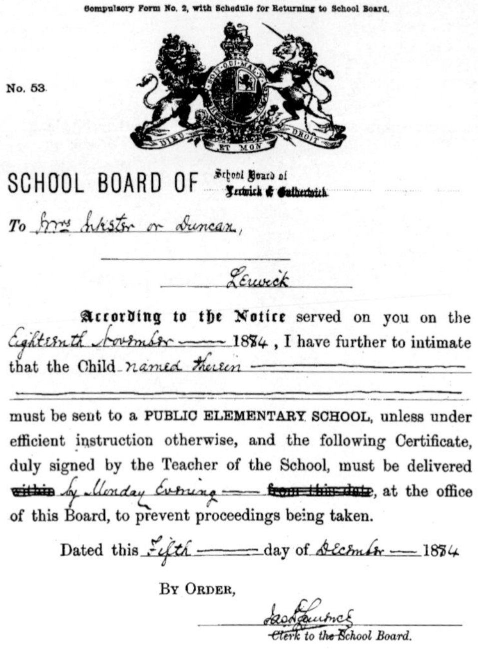

14. School Board letter re enrolment. *Courtesy Shetland Archives.*

15. Malcolm Gaudy, Headteacher of Free Church School, Cunningsburgh c.1850-c.1874.

16. Arthur Anderson (1792-1868). Founder of Anderson Educational Institute.

17. Quarff bairns c.1903. *Photo R. H. Ramsay.*

18. John Allardice, Rector of Anderson Educational Institute 1874-1883

19. Robert Young, Rector of Anderson Educational Institute 1894-1899.
Courtesy of Anderson High School

20. Lerwick Parochial School c.1872. Pupils with headteacher Mr James Hunter, far left back row.

21. Weisdale Public School c.1895. Pupils with Miss Low, teacher. Back row: John Wilson, Jas. Barclay, ? Burnett, Wm. Isbister, ? Johnson, Robbie Arthur, Jas. Isbister, John Jas. Johnson, Davy Arthur, Tammy Wilson, Bob Leask, Isa Morrison, Helen Morrison, Ross Jamieson, ?, John G. Robertson, Gifford Arthur, John Smith, Peter Robertson, Wm. Smith. Middle row: Bina Smith, Babsy Morrison, Leebie Burnett, Ruby Morrison, Kitty More, Madge Murray, ? Mary Irvine, Janet Morrison (Sound), Janet Morrison (Tubie), ?, Mary Allan, Teenie Burnett, Kirsty Leask, Jeannie Anderson. Front row: John L. Morrison, Jas. W. Morrison, Adam Leask, Wm. P. Leask, Jas. White, David Smith, Magnus Robertson, James Wilson, Jas. W. Anderson, Wm. More.

The Society's Ultimatum

The Society's ultimatum of 1757, already mentioned in the chapter on Walls, appears to have sparked off more positive action than previous threats. This may have been partly due to the marginally improved economic climate in Shetland during the 1750s when heritors were prepared to contemplate expenditure on education. Within 18 months of the ultimatum six of the 12 parishes had had meetings of heritors on the question of schools.

The Tingwall heritors tried to dodge their responsibilities by claiming[2] they already had a legal school. This presumably was the Scalloway Grammar School, which was not funded in the recognised statutory manner and did not have the complete support of the parish.

In his response to the Society's questionnaire of 1755, the minister had stated[3] that the grammar school was funded by a tax of two pence per merk of land together with subscriptions to the value of £20 sterling per annum. This tax raised about £13 sterling, the whole of which was paid initially by the tenants then the heritors' half was deducted from their annual rents. The minister indicated that the tenants paid grudgingly since few of their children could benefit from the school, placed as it was at the southmost end of the parish. Apart from the Grammar School there were three schools in the parish — a Society one in Weisdale and two others which taught reading and were paid for by the parents of children who attended.

Dissatisfied with the heritors' response, Presbytery convened a meeting in Tingwall of heritors and heads of families.[4] The turnout was disappointing. Only four of the 19 heritors appeared — although two more sent letters — and a mere 22 heads of families out of a possible of over a hundred. All but two present agreed to the establishment of a parochial school but Presbytery felt unable to proceed in view of the inadequate representation from the parish.

The minister of Lerwick reported[5] that his principal heritors had indicated their support in principle of the idea but proposed that the question "should be laid before the whole heritors at their first meeting about the town's affairs." He subsequently reported to Presbytery[6] that the heritors had met and, while agreeing that there should be a school, felt that its establishment was not possible until they had got rid of the burden of public debt upon the town.

The minister's report to the SSPCK in 1755 had stated that Lerwick had a grammar school which was maintained by a combination of subscriptions, 50 shillings annual interest on a mortification of £50 sterling by the Earl of Morton, and the master's dues as precentor and session clerk.[7]

The Rev. John Mill of Dunrossness reported[8] that he had written all the non-residing heritors except one, and that he had spoken to the residing heritors. The initial response had been encouraging but it took another two and a half years for Mill and the Presbytery to take a more positive initiative. In 1760 Presbytery convened a meeting[9] at Dunrossness which produced a good turnout — 21 of the 51 heritors and approximately half of the four hundred or so heads of families. This was indeed remarkable considering that the year had seen an end to the period of good crops and fishings and the people were suffering from a great scarcity.

Dunrossness was the largest parish in Shetland — 14 miles long, from two to six miles broad, and with a population of 2,600. (The 1872 Education Act criteria required seven schools to serve the area). All those assembled agreed in principle to have a parochial school and to be stented 2/- Scots per merk, but they wanted the salary to be divided among three teachers who were to be ambulatory among six areas. Although such an arrangement was contrary to the provisions of the 1696 Act, it is interesting to note that the 1803 Act did provide for a division of salary to enable two teachers to operate in large areas. In the event, Presbytery felt unable to sanction this unorthodox, if quite sensible, demand and no further steps were taken. So far as Dunrossness was concerned the matter appears to have rested there, for nothing further is heard from that area until 20 years later when the Society threatened to withdraw their school at Quendale unless heritors undertook to erect a legal school.[10] The well-rehearsed threat appears to have been ignored without any further action by the Society, for there is a continuous record of Society schools in Dunrossness from the 1780s until 1854.

In his response to the SSPCK's questionnaire of 1755, Mill had reported that Dunrossness had no parochial school but Society schools in Fair Isle and Cunningsburgh.[11]

John Mill, minister of Dunrossness from 1742-1805, was a man possessed of strong Calvinistic principles and committed, after his own bleak fashion, to the spiritual welfare of his parish. But, in all his long ministry, little emerges from local church records or his own diary[12] of any continuing concern for educational provision. The little that is recorded mentions payments in 1755 and 1756 from church collections of small amounts, varying from 12 pence to 4/6d, to a woman Katherine Grott for "schoolage" of poor children.[13] Compared with his contemporary, James Buchan of Walls, he obviously saw education as a relatively low priority.

In 1760, the year of the important Presbyterial visitation regarding schools in Dunrossness, his diary contains no references to this occasion but has an entry inveighing against his sinful flock: "It grieved me much to find so little stir among the dry bones, the generality here and elsewhere being so immersed in the body and world that the most rousing sermons and awful alarming providences make no impression on their blind heads and obstinate hearts, though a pestilential fever that began in 1758 raged for several years, which, together with the smallpox in 1761, carried off upwards of 200 young and old; yet alas made but little impression. In February and March said year by a long tract of snow and severe weather numbers also were cut off, horses sheep and cattle. Great scarcity of victual ensued, while the sea yielded no fish; and by reason of a great drought, the cows yielded little milk, whereby the inhabitants were generally brought to great straits, as a just judgment for abuse of plentiful seasons by gluttony and drunkenness, which oft broke out in scandalous uncleanness of all sorts. Nor was any suitable improvement made of such awful dispensations in any serious and hearty concern for salvation and preparation for the Day of Judgment and Eternity — every one looking about them how breaches might be made up in the loss of husband, wife or child, etc."

This censorious note, unrelieved by any feeling of compassion, runs through his entire diary, and one is left with the strong impression that his preoccupations with the Day of Judgment and Eternity blinded him to such earthly requirements as schools.

Unlike Buchan of Walls, Mill was not over-zealous in seeking for his large parish a fair share of Society schools. In 1779 the Society school had been moved from Cunningsburgh in the north part of the parish to Quendale in the south. In 1797 the elders and heads of families in Sandwick and Cunningsburgh petitioned Presbytery asking for their fair share of the school at least three years out of nine.[14] They claimed that 12 years after the school had gone to Quendale they had petitioned Mill to have it moved but he had said that was only possible if they built a schoolhouse. This they had done, whereupon Mill then said they had to have some heritors' security for implementing the Society's regulations regarding cows' grass, kailyard and peats for the teacher. This guarantee was given by several small local landowners but still Mill took no action. "Baffled in every attempt", the petitioners employed a young lad as schoolmaster and paid him a salary although few could afford to maintain him. They ultimately had to abandon the project. The petition requested Presbytery either to settle a parish school in Sandwick or require that the Society school move there. Presbytery decided to ask Mill to set about establishing a parish school but that aim was not achieved until 1801.

Sandsting and Aithsting made what appeared to be a promising start.[15] Fourteen of the 15 heritors met and agreed to provide a salary of

100 merks with a surplus of £1.6.8 Scots to be paid to the appointed collector of the various proportions. The agreement placed the onus on the tenants to be the first advancers of the salary, the landlords' half being provided by reductions in the land-rents. This device, however legal it might have been, bore too heavily on the tenants for them to give it their full support, and the scheme was stillborn.

The minister had not responded to the Society's questionnaire of 1755.

John Barclay, minister of Delting, met his heritors who agreed in principle but with the fatal proviso — unattainable in virtually every Shetland parish — that the school had to be beneficial to the whole parish.

Barclay's reply to the Society's questionnaire of 1755 had indicated that Delting had no parochial school because of extreme poverty of the people and the scattered nature of the district but that there were two to three schools at various times in different corners to teach children to read English.[16]

In Walls, as indicated in a previous chapter, James Buchan called a meeting of heritors who agreed to establish a legal school but only if other parts of the parish could be provided with Society schools.

Buchan's reply to the Society's questionnaire of 1755 stated that Walls had no parochial schools but that there were several little schools supported by voluntary contributions and that the people were too poor to support a qualified teacher.[17]

William Archibald, minister of Unst, intimated that his local heritors had agreed unanimously and that he was to consult those non-resident.[18] This spasm of activity in Unst was followed, incredibly, by almost 20 years of inaction, and then equally incredibly, it was a heritor, Captain George Ross, RN, who in 1803 appeared before Presbytery craving them to take steps to establish legal schools in Unst.[19] This unusual initiative appears to have galvanised Presbytery into what can only be interpreted as embarrassed action whereby they instructed the Unst minister to call a meeting of heritors and "if they fail to decide on a school the Presbytery will as there are no Commissioners of Supply in the Country be under the disagreeable necessity of bringing the matter immediately before the Court of Session."

There was no reply from Unst to the Society's questionnaire of 1755.

Commissioners of Supply

This is the first occasion we hear of Presbytery contemplating the final sanction given to them by the Act of 1696, i.e. the power to place their case in the hands of the Commissioners who, in turn, could establish a school, fix the master's salary, and stent the heritors according to their valued rent.

Commissioners of Supply were first created by Act of Parliament in 1667, their function being to act as authorities for the administration of Scottish counties. Their appointment was made on the basis of a property qualification, initially of lands of the annual value of £100 Scots. This qualification was altered by subsequent legislation but remained based on possession of landed property. The Commissioners were thus the principal heritors and the landed interest still remained central to the establishment of legal schools. The Act stated that a minimum of five Commissioners was required to implement this provision, a condition which, theoretically, should not have caused any problem in Shetland which had 20 Commissioners in the 1760s.[20] But it appeared to be otherwise in practice. The earliest extant records of Commissioners of Supply in Shetland commence on 11th October, 1763, an occasion when only five members were present.

Poor attendance of Commissioners must have been a feature of the time for on 5th March, 1760,[21] following the inconclusive responses from heritors' meetings, Presbytery decided to request their representatives to the next General Assembly to find out whether three or four Commissioners would be legally sufficient to stent a parish if the stipulated five could not be obtained. And further, if the Commissioners of Supply were to refuse to undertake their legal responsibilities, and no Notary Public were available, whether the Presbytery Clerk and two witnesses could register an official protest. Such a request would also have sprung from an awareness that, in their role as Commissioners, the heritors were unlikely to be any more committed to schools than they had already demonstrated. As it happened, the Procurator of the Church of Scotland ruled that he could not suggest any alternative course of action if the Commissioners refused to stent the parish, the law, as he claimed, being defective on that point. In short, the efficacy of the Act depended centrally on the heritors.

In 1763, however, Presbytery made an attempt to enlist the support of the Commissioners. The ministers of Bressay, Lerwick, and Tingwall made representations at a meeting of the Commissioners,[22] asking them "to interpose their authority" to enable schools to be established in their respective parishes. The Commissioners adopted a cautious line. They declared that, not being in possession of rentals of these parishes, it would "be precipitate to proceed immediately" and instructed the ministers to call a further meeting of heritors to seek agreement on a legal assessment.

The ministers duly embarked once more on the procedural treadmill. James Mitchell of Tingwall was successful in obtaining the consent of a number of his heritors at a meeting in March, 1764.[23] His appearance before the Commissioners may not have been in vain for one of the leading members was his principal heritor, Sir Andrew Mitchell. Sir Andrew had been influential in maintaining the grammar school at Scalloway and, as was revealed at the heritors' meeting, had paid out of his own pocket arrears of salary, amounting to £32.15.2 Scots, to the recently deceased schoolmaster, William Brown.

Under Sir Andrew's chairmanship, the meeting of heritors agreed to establish a legal school in the united parishes of Tingwall, Whiteness and Weisdale, and to that end to stent the 1595½ merks of land in the parish, half to be paid by the heritors and half by the tenants. A sum of 100 merks Scots was to be set aside for the master's salary with any surplus going towards the cost of erecting one or two schoolhouses.

The payments from heritors and tenants were to commence at Martinmas of that year, 1764, but as it was unlikely that a schoolmaster could be obtained by then they ordained that the assessment should be laid aside for the erecting of a schoolhouse to be located centrally in the parish. The suggested site was somewhere in the proximity of Tingwall Kirk but as they could not agree precisely where, it was decided to appoint a small committee to investigate. The schoolhouse was to be 30 feet long, 11 feet wide, and seven feet high, to have windows and to be divided into two apartments — one for the schoolroom and one for the accommodation of the master.

William Mitchell appeared before the next meeting of the Commissioners of Supply[24] to report the resolution reached by the heritors and to request that the Commissioners make an assessment of the levy to be laid on the lands of the parish. This was fixed at 1/- Scots per merk, the sum obtained thereby being considered adequate for a salary of 100 merks and the erection of a schoolhouse.

Legally, the road ahead for the Tingwall school seemed clear but the wheels of eighteenth century public administration ground slowly and the impetus from the heritors would have been seriously affected by the death in June, 1764 of Sir Andrew Mitchell. Almost two and a half years after the heritors' agreement, in September, 1767, Mr Mitchell reported to Presbytery[25] that, despite the decreet of the Commissioners of Supply, no schoolmaster had been appointed. Nor had a schoolhouse been built. Presbytery, inured to such impediments, once more instructed the heritors to meet — upon the first day of October — and to elect and present a schoolmaster, failing which Presbytery would elect one themselves. In November Mitchell again appeared at Presbytery to report that the heritors had failed to meet on the day appointed. Presbytery then proceeded as they had warned and elected Thomas Stout, precentor and session clerk at Tingwall, as parochial schoolmaster. It would appear that Stout had been waiting in the wings for the appointment for it is recorded that he demitted office as Society teacher in Fair Isle on 1st November, 1766.[26]

Presbytery then turned to the building of the schoolhouse, the other responsibility evaded by the heritors. They interviewed a mason and a wright who estimated that the building would cost £150.12/- Scots. Mr Mitchell was instructed to call a meeting of heritors in order that they might stent themselves for the proposed schoolhouse. Once again the heritors failed to meet as requested, whereupon Presbytery appointed Mr Mitchell to collect the necessary amounts from the heritors.[27]

The sum of £150.12/- estimated by the tradesmen was an extremely modest assessment in the light of the school at Happyhansel which had cost in the region of £500 Scots. As it turned out, the job when completed in late 1769 cost precisely double — £300.9.4 — and the burden on the heritors escalated from the original 1/- Scots per mark to 4/9d.[28]

There is no reference in church records to the date of opening of Tingwall Parochial School but, with Thomas Stout qualified and available, it can be assumed that it took place in early 1770. Certainly, in November 1771, Presbytery reported to the Society that a parochial school was operating in the parish of Tingwall.[29]

As indicated on previous page the Bressay and Lerwick ministers had, along with Mr Mitchell of Tingwall, attended the November 1763 meeting of the Commissioners of Supply. Mr Mair of Bressay responded to the Commissioners' request for a rental of his parish by compiling a list of lands amounting to 671 merks which he presented to the Commissioners in April, 1765.[30] Events moved swiftly thereafter and in September of that year Presbytery gave their approval to the appointment of John Smith as parochial schoolmaster of the united parishes of Bressay, Burra and Quarff.[31] The school opened in 1766 when John Smith is referred to as "legally established as Parochial Schoolmaster."[32] This gave Bressay, Burra and Quarff the honour of having the first properly constituted parochial school in Shetland and prompts the question as to why it was established there with such relative ease.

It was an unlikely candidate for success given that it was the least compact of any of the parishes, its three parts being separated not only by sea but by the Mainland of Shetland, with Bressay off the east coast and Burra off the west. A single school could serve only one of those three areas and while all Shetland parishes had scattered populations, to be separated by stretches of sea made regular communication difficult and frequently impossible. Because of the smallness of the rental the stent of 2/- was relatively heavy compared with Tingwall's 1/-, and that at a time of great economic depression, and with the principal estate in Bressay heavily in debt.

The fact that Burra and Quarff received no benefit from the school was bound to be a bone of contention and so it emerged — almost 20 years later over the erection of a new schoolhouse for another teacher. James Scott of Scalloway, principal heritor in Burra, appealed to the Court of Session[33] to suspend Letters of Horning requesting him to pay £20.13.3½, his contribution as heritor to the building of a schoolhouse at Bressay. He argued that he had not been informed of Presbytery's Decreet, that the schoolhouse in Bressay was of no benefit to him, and that the schoolmaster had been appointed by a junto (sic). This final point may have also applied to the appointment in 1766. Bressay's principal heritor, Andrew James Henderson, owned virtually all the land, was a dominating figure and would have tended to hold sway at heritors' meetings. Scott's appeal was turned down and he then petitioned Presbytery regarding the unfairness over the past years whereby the Burra heritors had contributed almost half the salary of the Bressay schoolmaster without any benefit to Burra.[34] He asked that an SSPCK school should be settled in Burra. Children in his area, he claimed, were growing up in ignorance for lack of a school and this point was incidentally reinforced in that two of the three kirk elders who witnessed the petition could not sign their names.

Despite the relative ease with which the Bressay school was established its continuance was precarious. In 1772 Mr Mair reported to Presbytery[35] that the pupils were not attending. A Presbyterial visitation on 13th October that year revealed that this was due to the school not being situated centrally and, perhaps more pertinently, that it was in "a ruinous state". John Smith, the teacher, described it more vividly as having "walls quite open as a 'skeo'".[36] Smith indicated how far short the heritors had fallen in providing a schoolhouse, teacher's accommodation, garden ground and peat-moor, by pointing out that he had no personal accommodation and had to rent a house from the proprietor at £13.10/- per annum. He claimed that the people naturally objected to having their children educated in such a derelict building and were sending them to private schools conducted by women of the district. He indicated that the minister had frequently from the pulpit and in private enjoined them to put their children to the parochial school but to no avail.

It should have been possible to find an accessible site in an island four miles by two and this was what Andrew James Henderson, principal heritor, undertook to do and to bear the cost himself. But, as we read earlier, James Scott appealed to the Court of Session in 1787 over the building of this proposed new schoolhouse in Bressay and this would suggest that either Henderson's promise was unfulfilled or that late eighteenth century schoolhouses were not built to last.

By the end of the century only four parochial schools had been established — in Bressay, Tingwall, Walls, and Northmavine — and, of these, only Walls had a record of continuity. Like many other remote Scottish parishes with scattered populations, Shetland was ill served by the Act of 1696 and there was no groundswell in Parliament to correct the inadequacies. The minority of Scottish members in the London Parliament, even if they had been united in their views on educational improvement, had scant opportunity to introduce reforms affecting remote Scottish areas. The 1803 Act was the first attempt at reform for over a hundred years but it failed to address the central question of providing enough schools for the population and dealt mainly with teachers' salaries and their accommodation.

The Kemp Controversy

In Shetland, the main sticking-point had been the reluctance of heritors to commit money to legal schools. At the beginning of the new century their benighted attitude was to be pilloried by a distinguished visitor to Shetland — Dr John Kemp, secretary of the SSPCK who had made a tour of inspection of almost three weeks in 1799 and returned to Edinburgh infuriated at the miserable provision of legal schools in the isles, the root cause in his opinion being that "proprietors are adverse to the establishment of schools, for this reason, that the more ignorant their tenants are, the less are they capable of emancipating themselves from the bondage in which they are held."[37]

Kemp presented his highly critical report to the Society on 5th September, 1799. He said he had found only two parochial schools in Shetland to set alongside the Society's eight. Orkney was little better with only three parochial schools as against 11 provided by the Society. He had attended a meeting of Shetland Presbytery where he had reiterated the Society's old threat of withdrawing all Society schools if the required number of legal schools was not established.

The Society's reaction was to send a memorial[38] to the most influential landowner in the northern isles, Lord Thomas Dundas, reminding him of the Society's fundamental principle that they would not grant funds for any school in a parish which did not have a legal school and that they had resolved to suppress every Society school in Orkney and Shetland in parishes where no legal school was established within one and a half years in Shetland and one in Orkney. At the same time, they indicated that they had no wish to withdraw any Society funds from the northern isles and were aware that even with a full complement of legal schools many additional schools would be required. They earnestly asked Lord Dundas to take a lead.

Dundas, who was not in the category of repressive landowners, but always on the lookout for any cause which might burnish his reputation in political circles, responded promptly and positively. Within a matter of a few weeks he replied that he gave his "entire consent to the... erection of parochial schools in all the parishes of Orkney and Shetland in which my property lies; and hereby direct my factors, in all meetings of heritors or of commissioners of supply... to agree, in my name, to grant such salaries, and such accommodations to the several schoolmasters as the particular circumstances... may render necessary and proper."[39]

Dr Kemp's strong feelings about the situation he had found in Shetland were not fully relieved by submitting his formal report to the Society and he published in 1801 a pamphlet[40] which tackled the heritors head-on, accusing them of oppression and exploitation of their tenantry. This stung the heritors into action and Thomas Mouat of Gardie assumed the role of spokesman for his fellow landowners. He published anonymously "A Letter by the Landholders of Shetland to the Hon. the Highland Society of Scotland" in February, 1802 in which he trotted out the old argument: "That in various instances in the widely detached Parishes of Shetland, not one fourth and in some instances perhaps not one tenth part of the inhabitants can possibly derive any benefit from such schools."[41]

Later the same year a counterblast in pamphlet form came from "Vindicator" — pseudonym of the Rev. David Savile, minister of Canongate Kirk, Edinburgh, and a friend of Dr Kemp. He challenged the heritors' main argument against the founding of parochial schools: "[Unst] is but 8 miles long, and from 2 to 3½ miles in breadth. Now, is this an extent too great to receive the benefit of a parish school? And might not one charity school added accommodate all the inhabitants? Yet the heritors choose rather to have old women, and half-educated men teaching private schools. Why: because they cost heritors nothing."[42]

"Vindicator" was making a very valid point. While the principle of one legal school per parish was far from ideal, such schools, if centrally situated, were capable of making a substantial contribution to the education of local children. For example, the parish school of Tingwall had, in 1785, 99 children between six and 14 years old within a three mile radius.[43] In the relatively compact island of Unst, had Thomas Mouat taken a lead, he could well have been instrumental in providing a legal school for a considerable number of children.

The controversy rumbled on, and in 1804 "A Friend to Zetland" (again Thomas Mouat) produced a pamphlet reply to "Vindicator".

In the same year the first of a series of articles by Patrick Neill, secretary of the Natural History Society in Edinburgh, appeared in the Scots Magazine. They were based on a tour through Orkney and Shetland and, while mainly connected with the study of Natural History, commented vigorously on the poor condition of the people: "... it was almost impossible", Neill declared, "not to take some notice of the state of the Inhabitants... ". The articles were published in book form in 1806[44] and in his introduction he stated that "The freedom of my remarks... on the unfortunate condition of the common people in Shetland, has brought upon me the censure of certain of the landholders; which they have, very unnecessarily, vented in unmeaning scurrility, through the medium both of newspapers and of Grub-street pamphlets."

Dr Kemp had certainly triggered off some explosive feelings. Undoubtedly the heavy charges laid at the door of the heritors, together with Kemp's threat that Society schools would be withdrawn, had had their effect. And this was to be seen in more practical ways. In January, 1801, Mr John Menzies, minister of Lerwick, informed the Society that no less than seven out of the 12 parishes had agreed to establish parochial schools forthwith.[45] In fact, only two materialised within the Society's time limit — Delting and Dunrossness in 1800 — and Aithsting and Sandsting, just outside, in 1802. Unst followed in 1805, Lerwick in 1816, Mid and South Yell in 1822, and North Yell and Fetlar in 1827.

The long struggle was, to a certain extent, over. Twelve parochial schools had been established and schoolmasters appointed but, in many if not most cases, the system remained precarious. Schoolhouses fell into serious disrepair, long vacancies prevailed from time to time, teachers' salaries often remained at the minimum, and attendance was erratic.

Another visitation by a representative of the SSPCK — Patrick Butter — was made in 1824. Although virtually every parish now had a legal school, Butter echoed Kemp's views of the landowners: "Shetland landowners are suspicious SSPCK would take over their land. They are indifferent if not adverse to the instruction of their poor tenants. The remains of a most rude system of slavery and despotism are quite visible."[46]

REFERENCES

1 ZPM 14/8/1764, SA
2 ZPM 2/2/1758, SA
3 SSPCK, Returns by Parish Ministers, 1755, SRO

4 ZPM 5/3/1760, SA
5 ZPM 2/2/1758, SA
6 ZPM 20/6/1759, SA
7 Ibid.
8 ZPM 2/2/1758, SA
9 ZPM 2/9/1760, SA
10 SSPCK Committee Mins., 26/6/1786, SRO
11 Ibid.
12 The Diary of the Rev. John Mill, ed. G. Goudie, Edinburgh 1889
13 Dunrossness KSM, 9/3/1755; 14/9/1755; 29/2/1756, SA
14 ZPM 28/6/1797, SA
15 ZPM 30/5/1758, SA
16 Ibid.
17 Ibid.
18 ZPM 20/6/1759, SA
19 ZPM 17/3/1803, SA
20 Mins. of Comms. of Supply for Shetland, vol 1, 1769, SA
21 ZPM 5/3/1760, SA
22 Mins. of Comms. of Supply for Shetland, vol 1, 4/11/1763, SA
23 Tingwall KSM 28/3/1764, SA
24 Mins. of Comms. of Supply for Shetland, vol 1, 27/4/1765, SA
25 ZPM 9/9/1767, SA
26 ZPM 18/3/1767, SA
27 ZPM 15/6/1768, SA
28 ZPM 5/12/1769, SA
29 ZPM 27/11/1771, SA
30 Mins. of Comms. of Supply for Shetland, Vol 1, 27/4/1765, SA
31 ZPM 12/9/1765, SA
32 Bressay KSM 31/3/1766, SA
33 SRO, CS21/Box 1249
34 ZPM 13/3/1790, SA
35 ZPM 24/6/1772, SA
36 A building for wind-drying fish, so constructed as to allow wind to pass freely through stones of wall.
37 Kemp, John, Observations on the Islands of Shetland and their Inhabitants by Dr John Kemp, Edin. 1801
38 SSPCK Comm. Minutes, 27/1/1800
39 Vindicator, Edinburgh 1802
40 Kemp, John, Observations on the Islands of Shetland and their Inhabitants by Rev. Dr John Kemp, Edin. 1801
41 A Letter by the Landholders of Shetland to the Hon. the Highland Soc. of Scotland, Feb 1802
42 Vindicator, Edinburgh 1802
43 List of Inhabitants of Tingwall, 1785, SA
44 Neill, Patrick, A Tour through some of the Islands of Orkney and Shetland by Patrick Neill, Edin. 1806
45 SSPCK Comm. Minutes, 1/1/1801, SRO
46 Journal kept by Mr Patrick Butter during his visits to SSPCK Schools in Shetland, 8th May to 11 Nov, 1824, SRO GD95/9/3

Chapter 9
Mathewson and Yell

JUST AS an examination of the campaign of the Rev James Buchan to establish schools in Walls enables us to get closer to the parochial fabric of a Shetland community in the eighteenth century, so does a scrutiny of the life of Andrew D. Mathewson, parochial teacher in Mid and South Yell from 1822-1877 take us inside the local educational scene during a period which spanned the greater part of the nineteenth century. It reveals in personal terms the inadequacies of schooling in Shetland in the early years of the century, the hunger among the people for a basic education, the diffusion of oral tradition, the role of the heritors and the church, the struggle of a family man to survive on the pittance he received as a parochial teacher, as well as many more glimpses of the nineteenth century educational world as seen from the man at the centre.

Andrew Dishington Mathewson was born in Houll, North-a-voe, Mid Yell, on 2nd April, 1799, at a time when conditions in Shetland were as poor as they had ever been; a time of poverty, harassment from the Press Gang, and with the thralldom of the fishing tenures at its height. The Mathewson family on their croft at Houll lived, like all their neighbours, in the shadows of these dark days. But they had one inherited advantage. On the mother's side there was a strong tradition of literacy unusual in those days of limited education. Andrew wrote that it was his aunt, Dorothy Fordyce, "who was the first that told me of Sir Isaac Newton and the wonders of Astronomy;"[1] and it was she who taught him to read so that, by the age of five, he had read the whole of Proverbs and the New Testament, could write and do some basic arithmetic.

In any situation at any time this would have been a remarkable achievement but in Yell in 1804, with no organised education and at the same time a widespread longing for literacy, it must have seemed little short of miraculous. Other parents in the district, hearing of this prodigy, brought their children, and when he was only six years old, young Mathewson was instructing pupils to read from the Bible.

He had been grounded in the three R's at the knee of his mother and aunt, but testified later to the wider education which circulated in the community, transmitted mainly by old men: "Books and apparatus being wanting much instruction was given orally by those well tried and often well informed men… The long winter nights were the most favourite seasons. All possible plans for collecting an audience were adopted — weddings, Feasts, Holydays, Funerals, Baptisms, etc. — and their Religion and Morality became impressed and diffused, every old man and woman was honoured and revered and expected in his turn to teach his children and grandchildren. Never shall I forget the lessons of these men."[2]

It is interesting to hear Mathewson, a confirmed believer in formal pedagogy, extolling the virtues of oral tradition. He saw the ongoing diffusion of community learning as an important process. The arts of survival involving weather lore, knowledge of tides, boatmanship, fishing and crofting techniques, preparation of food, folk medicine, would, as he records, have been passed on through the contacts of daily living. Social customs and traditions, music and dance and, above all, the dialect, were all part of the local culture and as such were absorbed by each growing generation to be passed on in turn to the next.

Mathewson had a strong conviction as to the importance of the heirarchical diffusion of moral and religious education. Late in life he wrote of the close-knit community influences he experienced as a boy: "… the Minister nursing the Parents with the Bread of Life — the Parents the Children… Friend stimulating Friend — and all the relationships of neighbours, Parish, Island, District, Country and Nation employed to unite in raising a Barrier for the Preservation of Religion and Morality and as books were few and Libraries far distant the Oral Instructions of the Aged were never wanting in the house and in the field, when we lay down and when we rose up — when we went to the fishing the oldest in the Boat began at Seafield and continued till we reached the fishing grounds south of Hascosay… For the oldest to keep the rest in peace order and instruction was the rule both by land and sea."[3]

His attachment to the local heritage, however profoundly felt, was to come into conflict with the standards of English culture and book-learning to which he was so committed throughout his long professional life. And this conflict certainly must have contributed to the complex and often contradictory aspects of his character.

Removal to Fetlar

In 1809 his father, who was not a fisherman, was evicted from Houll to make room for a tenant who was prepared to fish for the laird. The Mathewsons crossed with their possessions, including 300 sheep, to the island of Fetlar — four miles away and more fertile than Yell. Although a disruption to the family it was a fortunate move for Andrew. Whereas Yell had no organised school at the time, an SSPCK school, taught by Magnus Hoseason, was operating in Fetlar. Andrew attended the school and befriended young Horatio Hoseason, an illegitimate son of Mr Hoseason's brother in Liverpool. Horatio had been to school in Liverpool before his father dispatched him to Fetlar and was evidently an athletic, rather extrovert character. Young Andrew, emulous as always of superior attainments, enthused that Horatio could do "almost all that hands and feet could accomplish and taught me the same such as Running, Jumping, Standing on our hands and going from end to end of the table when Mr Hoseason was out, and how to attack and defend, jumping over dykes without touching them, swimming, diving, etc. etc. By practice we acquired proficiency till he and I could face 20 or 30 Fetlar boys."[4]

The school was examined annually in February by the parish minister, James Ingram, who also conducted young communicants' examinations in the late summer. In August, 1813, Mr Ingram passed young Mathewson as a communicant, his only objection being that he was too young at 14.

Fetlar was a small place and anyone showing unusual ability at school would have been talked about. Apart from his skills in reading and arithmetic, which would have placed him well ahead of his contemporaries, he was a gifted calligraphist and some of his coloured books with examples of penmanship had been sent to the manse, together with hand-printed Collects he had made from a prayer-book sent home by his brother Arthur who had enlisted in the Army. His unusual talents did not pass Mr Ingram who, after confirming them for himself at the communicants' examination, sent for young Andrew and his father in October, 1813. Father and son went with some trepidation, for a summons to the Manse generally meant a rebuke for some breach of church law. But on this occasion it was to inform Andrew that he had been chosen as teacher to young people at the north end of the isle, too far away to benefit from the Society school at the south end.

The local tacksman had offered two rooms in his fishing-booth at Urie — one as a schoolroom, the other for the youthful teacher's bedroom. Some of the prospective pupils would be young men in their early twenties who had made trips to the haaf or to the Greenland whaling, but Mr Ingram assured the diffident 14-year-old that these bigger lads would help in maintaining law and order. Mr Smith, the tacksman, was to be responsible for collecting fees and parents were to provide peats for heating. Andrew accepted the post and taught at the Booth of Urie for three winters.[5]

Ingram took a very positive interest in the budding schoolmaster and arranged for him to attend the school in Unst to receive instruction in vulgar and decimal fractions as Hoseason was apparently weak in this area.

Teacher in the Making

Andrew Mathewson was now almost acting out a predestined role as teacher. Chosen originally by the community on the basis of his precocious talents, he now began deliberately preparing for what was to be a life-time career. As he said: "My parents would have made me a fisherman, friends would have made me a Merchant, brothers a sailor, but I was influenced all along in favour of teaching by something in my own mind."[6]

During the winter of 1814-15 Mr Smith, tacksman, obtained Alexander Marshall of Edinburgh as tutor to his own children. Andrew sought and obtained the opportunity to study under Marshall, and in the evenings from 7pm-9pm he was instructed in English grammar, rudiments of Latin, Euclid's elements of geometry, and church music using the flute. When Marshall returned to Edinburgh in 1816 Andrew took over as tutor to the Smith children.

His reputation as infant prodigy, enhanced by his teaching experience in Fetlar, would obviously have followed him, and in 1818 he was invited to open a small school in Aywick, East Yell. He remained there for a year and in 1819 undertook a similar job in the adjoining district of Gossabrough where he spent a further year. John Finlayson, minister of Mid and South Yell, then persuaded him to teach the small school he was running in his manse at Mid Yell, where he spent a further year.

For several years pressure had been mounting for a parochial school in Mid and South Yell and, particularly from his base in the manse, Andrew would have had his ear close to the ground regarding progress. Experienced in teaching though he was for one so young, he would have realised the inadequacies of his own formal education and the need to obtain more advanced instruction before he could contemplate tackling the post of parochial teacher. Fortunately, he found an interested patron in Gilbert Duncan, writer in Lerwick, and Trustee of the Gossabrough Estate in East Yell. Duncan had been one of the founder members of Lerwick Subscription School in 1817 and offered to sponsor Andrew for a year there. Andrew attended from May 1821 to May 1822, and was taught by John McMorine, a young Divinity student.

The young and ambitious Mathewson became the self-confessed disciple of McMorine. It was not only his teacher's superior and apparently effortless command of learning which impressed Mathewson but, as frequently revealed in the series of letters he wrote to him, he was greatly influenced by McMorine's maturity and sophistication. In virtually all his letters he craves advice on life and learning as well as in the more routine techniques of grammar and punctuation.[7]

During his year at Lerwick Subscription School Mathewson's natural abilities again became evident. He was invited to assist McMorine in the Sabbath School which was associated with the Subscription School and, when the school was examined by the Lerwick minister, Andrew was passed as a Higher Class teacher.[8] Since McMorine had to go to Edinburgh at this time for a part session of training for the church, his able pupil was recommended to take his place temporarily.

Candidate for Parochial School

As has been shown in an earlier chapter, parochial schools came slowly to Shetland. Yell lagged behind all the others and it was not until the 1820s that a final commitment came from the heritors. The need was great. In 1821 less than 20 children were receiving education in the small schools in South Yell.[9] Early in 1822 the heritors of Mid and South Yell agreed to set up a legal school, to be situated in East Yell. Mathewson's local reputation and his further progress in Lerwick made him a strong candidate for the job. But he was soon made aware of opposition. James Robertson, parochial teacher in Delting, approached him with the suggestion that he allow Robertson to obtain South Yell and that thereafter he, Mathewson, could apply for Delting. Robertson was a minister-in-waiting and, knowing there was an impending vacancy in Mid and South Yell Church, was anxious to be established in the district. Mathewson would not hear of it. He claimed he was a Yell man and had an ambition to establish education in his native isle. Furthermore the appointment was not in their power but in the hands of the heritors. Putting that point into practice he wrote in February to the 30 local heritors soliciting their support. At this stage, Mathewson was not to realise that, in baulking Robertson's plans, he was making an enemy for the future. Robertson became minister of the Yell parish in 1828 and for sixteen years was a thorn in Mathewson's side.

The heritors met at Mid Yell on 19th June, 1822 and Mathewson was elected by nine votes with a salary of £17.16.3 sterling plus fees. Two weeks later he was called to Olnafirth, Delting to be examined by Presbytery. Mathewson's personal description of his examination,[10] apart from the detailed account of the procedures, reveals something of the lack of co-ordination and the degree of tension between heritors and Presbytery in appointments of parochial schoolmasters.

At the beginning of his examination Mathewson produced the Extract of Heritors' Minute containing his appointment but the Moderator protested that the heritors should not have presumed to settle the candidate, that being Presbytery's prerogative. One of the ministers present had copies of all the acts relating to schools and confirmed that Presbytery had authority to confirm teachers' rights to emoluments, etc. The Moderator then asked Mathewson if he had taken the oath of allegiance and when Mathewson said he had not, the ministers felt that they could not proceed. This possible impasse was avoided by Arthur Gifford of Busta intervening to say that, as a J.P., he could administer the oath. Mathewson then had to produce a testimonial from his local minister which Presbytery found acceptable. His Confession of Faith could not, however, be heard as, unaccountably, no copy of the text was available, although he declared his willingness to sign it. Two of the ministers supervised the scholastic part of the examination, comprising a reading test of a half-page from Willison's "Sanctification of the Sabbath"; a spelling test; parsing; writing; arithmetic (675 cwts. 3 qrs. 27 lbs. @ 22/4½ per cwt.); and several questions on religion including repetition of the Lord's Prayer.

Presbytery then considered Mathewson a suitable person to be a schoolmaster, and now that he had satisfied both his spiritual and secular masters he was duly elected and instructed to open the school, which had just been built at East Yell, on Martinmas — 12th November. Mathewson makes the interesting observation that, although appointing him to his new school, Presbytery gave him no instructions as to his duties and obligations.

Presbytery may have found Mathewson's abilities satisfactory but his old mentor, Gilbert Duncan, was not so easily satisfied. A week after his examination by Presbytery, Mathewson received a letter from Duncan designed to puncture any complacency the newly-appointed schoolmaster may have felt. Duncan complained: "Your letter you say was written in a hurry and I suppose I must therefore excuse you for a good deal of bad spelling but in future when you write to any person on any subject be sure you consult your Dictionary till you are certain you can do without it."[11]

At this critical stage in his career Mathewson was all too conscious of his shortcomings. He wrote to Marshall and MacMorine for advice and was fortunate in having mentors with sound ideas, many of which, 170 years on, still make good sense. "As your scholars" Marshall wrote, "will be first all strangers to you, take care to begin with a proper tone of authority. Then, your authority will not be questioned or opposed, if at all reasonable, but if by too great familiarity, or permitting improper liberties, you lose it, your usefulness is at an end. Begin then as you would wish to proceed; nothing but firmness is necessary to preserve authority, but when lost, nothing can restore it... Beware of any sudden changes of rules, or of practice; for when the scholars see <u>you</u> changeable they will be apt to introduce innovations which <u>you</u> do not wish. In conducting the classes, the best rule is never to let the lessons be too difficult and never to pass it till it is well said."[12]

MacMorine advised "you should beat them [pupils] as seldom as possible; never but when the good of your other pupils require it, or when the omission of it would expose you to be accused of partiality. For nothing is more exasperating both to parents and pupils than any seeming partiality… The stubborn kind are often spurred on by a reasonable dose of praise by encouraging emulation and by reasoning gently with them and shewing them the usefulness of what they are learning."[13]

Marshall's advice to "Aim at speaking with care and as much correctness as possible and never use vulgar expressions" dealt a blow to the dialect and, for the aspirant teacher, signalled that English was the only mode of speech to be used.

"A Sufficient Schoolhouse"

The Parochial Schools (Scotland) Act, 1803, specified that the heritors had to provide a proper schoolhouse, a room-and-kitchen dwelling house, and a garden for the master. These very general guidelines left much for local interpretation and the East Yell schoolhouse could well have fallen within the category of "proper" for the local situation. The school building consisted of two storeys 28' x 15' x 12' high, with the classroom downstairs which had an earthen floor, and attic accommodation upstairs for the teacher, comprising one large living-room/kitchen, 6' x 12', two small bedrooms, 6' x 9', and a small closet. There was common entry to the classroom and teacher's quarters by a single door. An area of 1¼ acres ground was allocated for the master's use — one acre before the house and one-quarter behind for a yard.[14]

No furniture had been provided for either schoolroom or dwelling area. As summer and autumn passed, Mathewson found that the bare schoolhouse was symptomatic of the heritors' grudging support for the new school. No indication had been given by heritors or Presbytery as to hours or fees, so he wrote for information to his colleagues in Fetlar and Unst.

Meanwhile interest was growing locally, with parents seeking assurances as to when the school would open. Martinmas came and went and still no furniture appeared. Parents even offered to bring boards as temporary tables and forms.[15] Mathewson still held off but, at last, on 25th November, he felt obliged to open the school "as Greenland men would be thrown out of their quarter."[16] These were young men anxious to put in a quarter's schooling before joining the Greenland whaling fleet in the spring. One such young man was James Hoseason who lived in a remote part of the island and wrote to Mathewson asking for accommodation or "room to sling a hammock" while he revised his navigation.[17] Mathewson replied that if he brought his own provisions from home he would undertake to give him a bed for 1d and cooking and attendance for ½d per day which, together with instruction, would amount to 10/6 per quarter. He also suggested that, as no schoolroom furniture had arrived, Hoseason might take a table with him "what severals design to do."[18]

The School Opens

On 25th November, 1822 the parochial School for Mid and South Yell opened to enrol nine girls and 18 boys and young men. In the absence of any specific instruction Mathewson fixed the school hours for winter at 10-12 and 1-2 or 3, and for summer at 9-11, 12-2, 3-5. He also announced that the quarterly fees would be: reading 1/-, writing 2/-, and arithmetic 2/6 — all to be paid in advance — a stipulation designed to provide him with some income until he received his salary in six months time. But he very soon discovered that he had fixed the fee for writing too high and had expected too much in asking for advance payment for fees.[19]

The fact that the school was in operation did not appear to stir Gilbert Duncan or the heritors he represented into very positive action concerning school furniture, for another six months were to pass before tables and forms arrived from Lerwick, and even then they were only adequate for seating 24 pupils whereas at that time 42 were in attendance with a further five or six expected shortly. Mathewson thought to touch the heritors' sense of decorum by suggesting to Duncan that the deficiencies be made up by placing boards on stones or "feals" (turves), although he made clear that he personally felt this would be "unseemly", and finally offered to make the extra furniture himself if only the wood could be provided.

The local Kirk Session should have been a useful support at this time but there is no evidence that either minister or session made any efforts to persuade heritors to supply the necessary furniture. The Rev. John Finlayson was a weak vessel and unlikely to take a strong lead. He was in 1813 dismissed by Presbytery for antenuptial fornication, not visiting parish in seven years, misappropriation of church funds, blaspheming and unseemly conduct. The General Assembly reversed the sentence because of lack of firm evidence, but found him to have been guilty of great impropriety.[20]

Inside the Classroom

However careful Presbytery had been in establishing that Mathewson was of good moral character, a loyal Presbyterian, and competent in reading, writing and calculation, they took no steps whatever to lay down any regulations regarding the administration of the school or what he should teach. Almost nine months after the school was opened Mathewson had to write to Presbytery for guidance on school hours, vacations and fees. He was told that the school should be open for five hours daily in winter, seven in summer, the actual times to be decided by the Kirk Session; that seven weeks vacation was allowed; and that school fees were to be fixed by the heritors. As elsewhere in Scotland, the operation of the school was determined by local control rather then national decree.

What does not appear to concern Mathewson, Presbytery, or heritors is what he should teach, and implicit in the whole appointment procedure is the assumption that there was a recognised basic curriculum which every teacher should follow. Schools were expected to advance the word of God and therefore, as in Society schools, the Bible was the principal reader. This was supplemented by the Catechism in a variety of versions — Shorter, Mother's, Brown's, Communicants, Proof. In his opening year, Mathewson also used spelling books, English grammars, and a selection of abridged literary readings.

Although the greatest demand by far for education at East Yell was for reading and writing, Mathewson's real interest lay mainly in his more advanced pupils. Indeed his educational aims tended to be lofty and somewhat divorced from reality. He was a strange mixture of pioneer and poseur. He had good ideas but too often would present them in an inflated manner. His decision to set down a scheme of work for his school was very commendable but can have amounted to little more than pious aspiration. The scheme, as presented below, looks impressive on paper but in effect the normal school day would have consisted almost entirely of instruction in religion and the three R's with an occasional pupil receiving additional instruction in mathematics, navigation, book-keeping — subjects in which Mathewson was very competent.

Private Regulations
Parochial School of Mid and South Yell
entrusted to the care & government of
Andrew D. Mathewson, Nov 11th, 1822

As the hours of attendance are from half-past Nine to 12 & from half-past 12 to 4 that is 2½ hours A.M. and 3½ h. P.M. : 6 hours per day —

and as the Classes are or may be numerous I begin to feel the necessity of acting in some fixed plan so that I may find peace in my mind by knowing I have done my duty and also that I may accustom the children to a regular steady perseverance.

The Classes are or may be

1 Morning Lessons
2 Bible
3 Testament or Collections
4 Proverbs
5 Catechisms (or Spelling Books)
6 Elocution the best B(ible) readers
7 Spelling
8 Writing
9 Arithmetic
10 Book-keeping
11 English Grammar
12 Latin
13 French
14 Geography
15 Elements of Geometry & of Plane & Spherical Trig.
16 Navigation
17 Lunar Observations
18 Astronomy, Zoography, or Mechanics
19 Drawing and Designing
20 Church Music

Now $2\frac{1}{2}$ h. A.M. divided by 150m/20 = $7\frac{1}{2}$ Minutes to each class;[21] but this is by far too little for the greater part of them and likely some of these classes may rarely or never exist. $\frac{1}{4}$hr. is a very good time for a class & 150/15 = 10 lessons say their A.M. 10 lessons x 15m. = 150 = $2\frac{1}{2}$ h.
 thus -

	Lesson	H. M.
<u>Morning Lessons</u>	1 x 15	9.30
I shall take assistants[22] if these be numerous and shall hear the assistants first		
<u>Bible Class</u>	1 x 15	9.45
Send 2 from the Testament Class to hear the Proverbs and Catechisms		
The remainder of T(estament) Class prepare for reading by taking their lesson verse about; 2 & 2 together		

A very little attendance may now be given to
Arithmetic,
Book-keeping, Navig. Astr. etc. if necessary

<u>New Testament Class</u>   *1 x 15*   *10.00*
Send 2 from the Bible Class to hear the Prov. & Catechisms
Bible Class write their copies
Attendance as above if called for

<u>Proverbs Class</u>   *1 x 15*   *10.15*
Test. Class write their copies
Bible Class Arithmetic and Grammar
Catechism Class — Writing

<u>Catechisms</u>   *1 x 15*   *10.30*
Bible Class as above — Ar. & Grammer
Testament Class — Arith, Wr. etc.
Proverbs Class — Writing
Very little assistance to any other class

<u>Elocution</u>   *1 x 15*   *10.45*
B(ible) — Ar. & Grammar
T(estament) — Ar. & Grammar
P(roverbs) — Writing, etc.
Cat(echism) — Writing

<u>French & Latin</u>   *1 x 15*   *11.00*
B. Prepare their Lesson
T. Ar. & Grammar (If no Fr. & Latin)
P. Prepare for reading (attend to Ar. &)
C. Writing

<u>English Grammar</u>   *1 x 15*   *11.15*
B. Prepare for reading
T. Prepare their lessons
P. Send one from B. to hear them
C. Prepare for reading

<u>Bible Class</u>   *1 x 15*   *11.30*
T. Prepare for reading
P. Read 2 and 2
Cat. Send one from T. to hear them

<u>Testament Class</u>   *1 x 15*   *11.45*
B. Prepare for reading
P. Send one from B. Class to hear them
Cat. Read 2 and 2
School shut ½hr.   *1 x 30*   *12.00*
School opens   *12.30*

Bible Class	1 x 15	
T. Prepare for reading		
P. Prepare their Lessons		
Cat. send one to hear them		
Testament Class	1 x 15	12.45
B. Write their copies		
P. Prepare for reading		
Cat. Read 2 and 2 or Writing		
Proverbs	1 x 15	1.00
B. Ar. & Writing		
T. Write their Copies		
C. Prepare for reading		
Catechisms Class	1 x 15	1.15
Elocution	1 x 15	1.30
English Grammar	1 x 15	1.45
Geography	1 x 15	2.00
Arithmetic & *Book-keeping inspected*	1 x 15	2.15
Navigation and Lunar Observations	1 x 15	2.30
Astronomy etc. & *Algebra*	1 x 15	2.45
Elements of Geometry, Plane or Spherical Trigonom.	1 x 15	3.00
Bible Class	1 x 15	3.15
Testament Class	1 x 15	3.30
Vocal Music, etc.	1 x 15	3.45
School Shuts		4.00
Dinner	15	
A walk or work for recreation	60	4.15

Mathewson's scheme of work, meticulous in its detail, provides a close insight into the school day in Mid and South Yell Parochial School. Religious education was the core of the curriculum and the time-table was organised around its four components — Bible (which meant the Old Testament), New Testament, Proverbs, and Catechisms. These, along with writing and arithmetic, occupied most of the morning session, leaving the afternoon to be mainly devoted to the more advanced subjects. He does not indicate what the pupils studying the basic subjects were doing in the afternoon when he was dealing with geography, book-keeping, astronomy, etc., but exercises such as writing, reading, and preparation which had occupied their unsupervised periods in the forenoon would no doubt have kept them engaged. He obviously used senior pupils to supervise younger groups and listen to their reading while he dealt with more senior pupils.

This question of one person teaching a variety of subjects to differing groups of pupils has always been a problem of small schools. Mathewson complained "I have to teach Alphabet to one class and Great Circle Sailing, the Longitude and Sea-Charts to the other."[23] He preferred teaching advanced work to older pupils than to be "chained", as he put it, "to plod on with helpless infants in the alphabet."

Parents were not unaware of this preference as Hugh Robertson of Gossabrough hinted in a note he sent along with his young son, stating that he could not afford to keep him in school very long: "We have to toil hard for very little return — it may be we cannot give him the time he would require — You could subtract 2 years from L. Williamsons time and add that to little Tom."[24] Laurence Williamson, an exceptionally gifted boy and Mathewson's star pupil, would then have been 15 years old and eager to sample his teacher's more esoteric offerings in the realms of Euclid's elements, conic sections, astronomy, etc.

Mathewson's reputation as a teacher of navigation attracted pupils from all over Shetland. Young men with some sea experience and ambitions to become captains came to East Yell during spells of leave from sea. They would frequently lodge at the Schoolhouse or request "room to sling a hammock". His navigation instruction comprised two courses — Great Circle Sailing and Lunars and Chronometers — costing 15/- each. Mindful of his early, difficult days, Mathewson placed knowledge before remuneration. He fixed his charge "but to any who have not the payment I would rather they got Navigation perfect and pay when they become Mate or Master than go without it to be only servants all their days."[25]

At times, particularly when conscious of ingratitude, he half-regretted such generosity: "I have often laboured here without School Dues from many for years — not widows and poor men's children but often of those received best in Parish… Books, Slates, Ink and Paper sold on Credit, given on Loan and often given gratis entirely to get them forward has been conceded to the utmost of my ability…".[26]

Unlike some areas, Mid and South Yell had no scheme for Kirk Session or heritors paying school fees of poor children, but Mathewson claimed he operated a school which was "open and ready to all who could reach it with money or without it."[27]

In the 1840s he wrote to his Member of Parliament presenting a petition from Shetland schoolmasters containing, among other things, a suggestion "that school fees be abolished for initiatory branches" and that schoolmasters be compensated by a very moderate sum in their salaries. Such an idea was stillborn in that the heritors were unlikely to dip further into their purses and the state was only beginning to contemplate the possibility of education being a central government responsibility.

Discipline

Mindful no doubt of the advice he received from his role models, McMorine and Marshall, he seldom used corporal punishment — although threatening it. He preferred solitary confinement after 4pm or additional tasks.[28] His colleagues in Shetland suggest[29] that, while the tawse was always an option for serious delinquency, other forms of punishment such as extra work, detention, or losing place in class, were favoured.

Laurence Williamson, already mentioned as Mathewson's prize pupil, has left a few brilliant snapshots of ADM at work in the classroom:[30]

"If you please Sir, can you sell me some pens"

"No I have no pens to sell — but I can give you a pen — there, there is one to keep and one to lose."

"If you please Sir, can you lend me a pencil."

"No, I object to all borrowing and lending. Let every one have his own. I remember lending an aitch (adze) to a man and I forgot who it was. Some years later there was a man in and I asked if he could lend me an aitch. Oh, he said, I have an aitch of yours. I never said I had forgot about it, but said send it up as soon as you can. So let every one have his own pencil. Here's a small bit for yourself."

"James, what are you making a noise for… and with your cap on too. I'll rap your heads together. If you'll demean yourselves like gentlemen, I'll treat you like gentlemen, but if you'll be treated like horses I'm prepared for you. I managed six horses when I rode the peats of Mongersdale [in Fetlar]. I'll thrash you like sheaves, I'll thrash you within an inch of your lives. If I take you in hand you'll remember it as long as you live."

The following scene is interesting in that it shows, apart from the master's opposition to the cult of the ball, pupils using the dialect, uncorrected by the master. According to one of his descendants in Yell he never used "du" in addressing people

"They tell me you had a ball here yesterday."

"Hit wizna wis, Sir."

"Who was it?"

"I never ken Sir."

"You do not know. Do you not know you are telling a lie. There's not a boy in the school that does not know. It's a temptation you cannot stand. The one bringing it is the cause of all. Your mind is laid upon it. You disregard all else. Evil needs only a beginning. It is for that reason, not for the exercise. Exercise is excellent. It is the taking of your time, your attention. You can't see you have no necessity for play. Just as I told you about the two Mid Yell boys who quarrelled about the seat in the window. They went home and something kept them away next day and other things and circumstances kept them away the day after and behold they never came back. Now never let me have to call your attention to the ball again. You have not a moment to spare, nor any of you, if you only just knew it."

Text-book

Parochial schools had no uniform set of text-books apart from the Bible and Catechism. Several Shetland teachers, Mathewson included, used books published by the Scottish School Book Association.[31] The Association's English set of 10 books was used in East Yell. A number of schools used books published by a Committee of Established Schoolmasters. Parents were responsible for buying the books although some could afford little more than those for English and arithmetic.

Sabbath Schools

Mathewson did not see his role as educator confined within the four walls of the East Yell Schoolhouse. He was very much in the central tradition of Scottish education which saw schools as the gateway to Biblical literacy and thence to a Christian community.

The East Yell School opened at a time when the spiritual welfare of the parish was at a low ebb. The minister, John Finlayson, was notorious for his loose living and poor pastoral care and Mathewson, who had been tutor at the Manse from 1820-1821, knew only too well the extent of his intemperance and his indulgence on those occasions in profanity which, in a letter to Finlayson, Mathewson delicately referred to as "the language of infirmity."[32] Mathewson could never be accused of such forms of intemperance but his enthusiasm, together with a vein of self-righteousness, led him all too often in his career to adopt a prickly and rather tactless approach designed to encourage opposition rather than co-operation.

Convinced that he had a role to play in raising the spiritual tone of the parish, he decided that Sabbath schools, which he already had had experience of in Lerwick, could make a real contribution. He had met a William Stephen from Edinburgh who was a teacher to the tacksman's children in Fetlar. Stephen had pointed out the benefits of joining the Sabbath Schools Union which enabled members to buy books at reduced prices and helped with the provision of local libraries. Mathewson went ahead and opened a Sabbath school despite opposition from Finlayson who said he should be attending the church at Mid Yell on the Sabbath rather than spending his time teaching. By April, 1823 he had a maximum of 17 pupils, mainly girls.

About this time he had been conducting a survey on behalf of the Inverness Society for Education of Poor in Highlands and discovered to his mortification, as he put it, that 14 families in the parish had no Scriptures whatever in their homes. Without consulting Minister or Kirk Session he decided to wield the cudgel himself.

In November, 1823, in preparation for the opening of the East Yell school for its second year, he pinned a note on the church door intimating that he had for sale at very cheap rates a few Bibles and Testaments, then added the tactless exhortation: "I am very sorry to say... that some Families are without the word of God altogether and those should take this opportunity of acquiring Scriptures. Their names have already been taken up and may be made public in the Parish to their own disgrace if they continue much longer insensible to their eternal welfare."[33]

At the same time Mathewson was anxious to show the Presbyterian flag in the face of "more active undertakings" such as the Wesleyan movement which, in the summer of 1823, had sent two missionaries — Brothers Dunn and Raby — to Yell. Dunn preached to large gatherings where he received a warm response. He had heard John Finlayson preach but was not impressed: "the greatest burlesque of Preaching I have ever heard, at the conclusion he warned his hearers against hearing us."[34]

Mathewson as the self-appointed spiritual watchdog of the parish, saw a network of Sabbath schools as the answer to the situation, and solemnly addressed Minister and elders:

> As not only you but also every enquiring person has discovered the nowise agreeable truth — how that very little is doing for the Rising Generation in the greater part of the Parish — how that the Sabbath is spent to very little purpose by many — how that few families...are careful of Family Worship....

He therefore proposed the following:

> 1) That several Sabbath Schools be established through the Parish under the Superintendence of the Parochial Teacher, and denomination of the Mid and South Yell Sabbath School; in connexion with the Sabbath School Union for Scotland.
>
> 2) That the Elders and other persons eligible be requested to take charge of the school which may be in their neighbourhood during the Teacher's absence, as he can come round only once in 4 or more weeks — according to the number of schools — and as the exertions of any one individual are inadequate for such a task, considering the Children would certainly require a weekly attendance.

3) That one or more of those Elders who may not be at Church be also requested to assist the person who may more immediately have the charge in the way either of preserving order, or of communicating instructions.

4) That as many people on account of the great distance, badness of weather, etc. can rarely hear half a dozen sermons in the year — the Minister be requested for allowance to read a sermon in these cases in the forenoon and for the sake of preserving a connexion he will grant some little sum for so doing and a few Sermon Books for the purpose.

I beg leave only to state further that the design of these propositions… is to leave little room for people to break off from our establishment in quest of more active undertakings.

Mathewson obviously envisaged himself as the superintendent of these schools with support from elders and others either as teachers or assistants. He was also suggesting that a reader or readers be appointed within the parish and no doubt saw himself in that role.

There is no evidence that his Sabbath school plans were put into operation or that he realised his ambition to stand in a pulpit and deliver a sermon, albeit from a book, but there is no doubt that his drive for education and enlightenment of the parish continued. In the early days of his school in East Yell he endeavoured to raise money from heritors and heads of families for a parochial library; he set up a juvenile library containing religious and moral material along with juvenile miscellanies; he planned a singing school in church music. And there was the constant drive for self-improvement. He appears to have had an arrangement with John Ross of Westsandwick, a minor heritor, to exchange books and magazines. In 1825 he sent Ross three copies of *The Philosophical Journal* and three copies of *The Methodist Magazine*, receiving in return from Ross Captain Parry's *Discoveries in Quest of a New Passage.*

Conflict With Parish Ministers

Mathewson's interest in *The Methodist Magazine* may well stem from his growing disillusion with the Established Church as he had experienced it through Finlayson. In a letter to Arthur Anderson, later to become MP for Orkney and Shetland, Mathewson writes:

… clergy and gentry unite in prolonging the reign of ignorance (among Shetlanders), the common people kept down in order to be the more passive… But while the Heritors & Tacksmen thus held his B… (word indistinct) the Minister was not remiss in attending to his part of the play… Every mummery was kept up & of course the common people taught to know the difference between them and their superiors. It was not to be supposed that such instructors were to go from house to house as Ministers of Christ. No, no, they had quite a different duty to perform. They liked better to blow and bellow away from the Pulpit for 20 minutes to an audience of gazing ignorants either about errors of which they never before heard or about arguments they could not understand

and that generally in language above their comprehension. The Christian doctrine of humility was taught because it rendered people more manageable and allowed these autocrats to crow over them with less restraint — the best illustration of their motives was that offered by their own conduct — avarice, lying, hypocrisy.[35]

The continuing feud between Mathewson and local ministers would, almost certainly, have contributed to such scathing criticism. After Finlayson's dismissal by Presbytery in 1812 and subsequent re-instatement by the General Assembly but with a warning to be more circumspect in future, he was a "lame duck" parish minister. He kept his distance from Mathewson to such an extent that in January, 1823 Mathewson wrote to Charles Cowan, minister of Fetlar, asking if he would examine Mid and South Yell School, claiming that Finlayson "does nothing", neither visiting nor examining. He eventually resigned in 1824 to be succeeded by John MacGowan who remained only two years, to be succeeded in turn by the James Robertson who had been parochial schoolmaster at Delting and had clashed with Mathewson in 1822 when the Mid and South Yell post was looming. The rather tart correspondence that passed between them at the time did not augur well for their future. The inevitable clash was not long in coming.

Absences from School

Robertson was ordained on 8th May, 1828 and within a matter of days had visited and inspected the school. His inspection concluded with an exhortation to the scholars and then he went upstairs with Mathewson where he stated that he had heard reports from a local heritor that the school was being neglected because of Mathewson's absences on private surveying work. Mathewson explained that he undertook surveying assignments purely because of financial necessity. In 1821-1822 he had spent what little savings he had at the school in Lerwick and after starting teaching in November, 1822 he had received no salary until the following Martinmas (November). During this year he had incurred debt to survive which had increased with each succeeding year although he was not extravagant. He had undertaken surveying during the school vacations but had, on occasion, continued the work if no pupils attended the school.

At a meeting of Presbytery early in 1829 Robertson, while not making a formal complaint, conveyed the impression that Mathewson was not paying sufficient attention to the school. Presbytery duly reminded Mathewson of his responsibilities and on 15th August of that year he felt constrained to give them an assurance: "In accordance with the advice I have this day received from you… it is my determination to attend to the duties of the Parochial School at Mid and South Yell... and that I am truly sorry that any misunderstanding has occurred between the Rev. James Robertson and me."

There was never any question about Mathewson's commitment to the school but, like all parochial schoolmasters of the time, he had to struggle to exist on the minimum salary, paid half-yearly, of £16.13.4 plus school fees. From 1829 to 1861 it was £25.13.3½ and after 1861 — £35.6.4. He married in 1827 and rapidly acquired a large family of six sons and six daughters. Caught in the dilemma of trying to fulfil his obligations to both his school and his family he became obsessed with justifying his absences and resorted to all sorts of devious reasoning. He argued that since few, if any, pupils came to school at voar and hairst he might as well be engaged in remunerative work. Much given to committing his thoughts to paper, he prepared an elaborate balance sheet of days owing to him, setting vacation periods against days spent surveying. From January, 1823 until May, 1829 he showed how he had spent over 33 weeks surveying but still had five weeks and two days vacation time in hand. He also claimed that, to compensate for openings lost, he had occasionally extended the school day from 8 to 8 and had opened on Saturdays. He could make these claims without any apparent thought for his pupils. There were times when the uncertainty of his presence at school resulted in a mere handful of pupils attending.

By his own account[36] Mathewson reveals just how he allowed his surveying to stray beyond vacations: "Next vacation began on October 8th [1828]. I finished Funzie [Fetlar] October 17th. Two rooms in Lunnasting October 28th... Now I ought to have begun school on the 29th but as my chief design was to divide lands in Sandsting at first I was sorry to find that unless I took another week I could not do so. The papers not being ready I was detained in Lerwick on the 31st continued Sunday November 2 with Mr Brydon [Sandsting and Aithsting minister] commenced Surveying and Valuing on the 3rd and finished the 3 rooms on the 15th taking two weeks to complete them as I had Maps to draw and calculations to perform." In order to complete the job he worked throughout three nights and re-opened the school on 17th November — almost three weeks late.

The dispute with Robertson over attendance at school developed into a feud which seemed to consume Mathewson. He set down on a sheet of paper[37] a list of Robertson's accusations and his own counter-accusations. Robertson claimed:

1. Neglect of duty by absenting himself 21 or 15 weeks annually in Vacations
2. Injuring the Scholars by attending to other business in the School, such as drawing Maps
3. Injuring the Scholars by not coming into the School before 12 (noon)

4. Injuring the Scholars in not closing the School by Prayer
5. Professing to teach the Latin Rudiments
6. Jesuitism
7. Misleading people by empty professions
8. Writing Mr R. that the cause of his writing so much regarding the Chain was that of hatred, etc.
9. Going about the bush in argument and begging the question

Mathewson accused Robertson of:
1. Jesuitism
2. A going about the bush in argument and a begging of the question
3. Endeavouring to mislead the ignorant. Misleading people by empty professions
4. Empty protestations of friendship
5. Neglect of duty in refusing to grant advice on critical points
6. Degrading the Clerical character by propagating and disseminating lies — or stories injurious to the character of ADM
7. Unfairness in argument by not allowing ADM to prove and reply
8. Violence and Passion when professing to have come to settle differences with ADM
9. Discouraging genius and learning
10. Unfairness in argument by using means calculated to put ADM off his guard.
11. Using endeavours to make ADM ashamed for the purpose of silencing him unconvicted and uncondemned
12. Coming for the purpose of carrying away a report of (unfinished)

This uncompleted charge sheet is a sad document revealing Mathewson's need to justify himself at least to himself. There were obviously faults on both sides. Robertson, the university graduate, appeared to denigrate Mathewson's self-taught skills and academic pretensions; and Mathewson refused to face up to the fact that he was not devoting all his attention to his school.

Of the nine parochial school teachers in Shetland who responded to a Government questionnaire in 1841,[38] Mathewson was the only one to state he had "any other employment or occupation", which he recorded as "during vacations, sometimes prosecutes land or marine surveying, etc., being jack of all trades."

Despite Mathewson's promises to Presbytery he continued to allow his surveying to encroach on school terms which, in turn, brought him into conflict with the minister. Robertson moved on in 1844 to be succeeded by James Barclay who had been parochial schoolmaster at Lerwick for 11 years. The conflict continued and indeed intensified as Mathewson, in seeking to justify his actions, developed a good-going persecution complex. But it wasn't just the minister who criticised his actions. The parents were also becoming disillusioned. On 23/11/1855 his wife wrote to him in Lerwick imploring him to come home "as all people of Gossabrough [district in East Yell] is going to send children to

Mr Bain of Burravoe as you have been away so long and People are saying you were surely been long enough away before now and that you might a kept school for one winter quarter." This appears to suggest that, early on in the Martinmas term, he had failed to open the school and that this was a not uncommon practice.

The conflict with Barclay continued during the remainder of Mathewson's teaching career to be intensified with the minister's appointment in 1873 to Mid and South Yell's first school board. Mathewson, now well into his seventies, was reluctant to conform to the new regime and continued to run the school in his old ways. In February, 1874 he received a terse letter from John Walker, Chairman of the Board:[39] "The Clerk to the School Board has informed me that you continue to use the Bible as a class book and otherwise refuse to carry out the School Board's instructions to you... the Treasurer also informs me that you admit Pupils without his Receipts... after consultation with the Edinburgh Board I have to warn you that unless you at once comply with and conform to the orders of your School Board I shall... take necessary steps for your dismissal in terms of Section 6 (2) of the Educaton Act."

This was followed later in the year[40] by a most unfavourable Inspector's Report which found a record of poor attendance, registers poorly kept, the Bible as the sole reading book, unintelligent reading by pupils, and "the absolute absence of organisation" in the classroom. The report went on to say that "The teacher is 75 years of age — an age from which no great improvement, or adoption of better methods, can be expected." The general conclusion was that Mathewson could not be regarded as capable of receiving the teacher's certificate and that the school could not be recommended for receipt of Government Grant.

This devastating report, followed in 1875 and 1877 by further unsatisfactory reports, drove the board to request Mathewson's resignation which he tendered in 1878. He was aware of the Inspectors' criticisms but the old paranoia prevailed and, writing to his son Laurence, said the board had been actuated by "the policy adopted against me in 1844", (the year of Barclay's induction to Mid & South Yell).

It was a sad end to an extraordinary teaching career of 56 years. He had been a lynch-pin of the community as session clerk, precentor, Sabbath School teacher, registrar, postmaster, apothecary, surveyor, and freqently organised protests and petitions for better local conditions. He was a highly talented teacher and original thinker far ahead of his day.

One of the more understanding members of the school board[41] touched on the core of the situation: "I am well aware that the proper working of the School under the new arrangement must be a matter of some difficulty at first: and that, after your long virtual independence, such control as the School Board must exercise, cannot fail to be irksome...". Like so many of his parochial school colleagues, the relaxed supervision of heritors and Presbytery had left him "virtual independence". The Act of 1696 had given Scottish teachers almost absolute security of tenure. They held office under the law on the basis of *ad vitam aut culpam* and could only be dismissed after a lengthy process involving the church authorities. This degree of independence together with the absence of visits from educational specialists to re-focus their thinking and practice, left them with a reluctance to accept any change whatsoever.

REFERENCES

1 Mathewson, A.D., Letter intended for Lady Nicolson, Fetlar but not sent, 22/6/1865, SA
2 Ibid. Letter to James Jameson, 4/4/1882, SA
3 Ibid. Letter, 1/9/1873, SA
4 Ibid. Letter to James Jameson, 4/4/1882, SA
5 Ibid. Letter op cit.
6 Ibid. Letter to John McMorine, 8/5/1823, SA
7 Ibid. Letters to John McMorine, 1822-23, SA
8 Ibid. Letter to Alex. Marshall, 13/12/1821, SA
9 Ibid.
10 Ibid. Letter to Gilbert Duncan, 16/7/1822, SA
11 Ibid. Letter from Gilbert Duncan, 10/7/1822, SA
12 Ibid. Letter from Alex Marshall, 12/8/1822, SA
13 Ibid. Letter from John MacMorine, 1/12/1822, SA
14 Ibid. Letter to Gilbert Duncan, 2/12/1822, SA
15 Ibid. 28/11/1822, SA
16 Ibid.
17 Ibid. Letter from James Hoseason, 6/11/1822, SA
18 Ibid. Letter to James Hoseason, 10/11/1822, SA
19 Ibid. Letter to Gilbert Duncan, 28/11/1823, SA
20 Scott, Hew, Fasti Ecclesiae Scoticanae, Edinburgh 1928
21 Mathewson's calculations are unrealistic in that he is basing his working day on the maximum number of 20 subjects whereas he would normally have had to teach about half that number.
22 He is referring here to "pupil teachers"
23 A. D. Mathewson, Letter to J. Dickson, Secretary to Scottish School-Book Assoc., 4/8/1864, SA
24 Ibid. Letter from Hugh Robertson, 19/9/1870, SA
25 Ibid. Letter to John Jamieson, 29/3/1869, SA
26 Ibid. Unfinished letter, 15/7/1864, SA
27 Ibid. Letter to Wm. Sievwright, 10/5/1856, SA

28 PP, 1841, xix, 64
29 Ibid.
30 Laurence Williamson Papers, SA
31 PP, 1841, xix, 64
32 A. D. Mathewson, Letter to John Finlayson, 12/3/1824, SA
33 Ibid. Notice on Church Door 8/11/1823, SA
34 Samuel Dunn's Shetland & Orkney Journal 1822-1825, ed. by Harold R. Bowes, 1976
35 A. D. Mathewson, Letter to Arthur Anderson, 14/6/1838, SA
36 Ibid. Undated letter, SA
37 Ibid. Undated document, SA
38 PP, 1841, xiv, 64
39 Letter from John Walker, 13/2/1874, SA
40 HMI Report, 31st July, 1874
41 Letter J. Rainier McQueen to ADM, 10/11/1873, SA

Chapter 10
A Patchwork System

A Changing Society

FROM 1790-1840 Scottish society was undergoing radical changes. The American and French Revolutions had unleashed a spirit of scepticism and secularism which coincided with a rapid expansion of commerce and industry. The vast numbers of people flocking into the growing urban centres placed great stresses on the old accepted values. There was an increase of crime and indiscipline, often affecting the young. The feeling grew that education had a key role to play in countering these forces and the question arose as to whether the old established parochial system was equal to the challenge.

The parochial system of education had become ossified during the eighteenth century. Politicians seemed blind to its shortcomings and the church, from its central position in the system, did little to appraise them of the need for change. The Statistical Account of the 1790s had pointed out the depressed state of schoolmasters, barely existing on salaries which had remained fixed for over a century while the cost of living had soared. At last, in 1802, the General Assembly of the Church petitioned Parliament claiming that schoolmasters were:

> entitled to public encouragement, yet from the decrease in the value of money their emoluments had descended below the gains of a day labourer; that it had consequently been found impossible to procure qualified persons to fill parochial schools; that the whole order was sinking to a state of depression hurtful to their usefulness; and that it was desirable that some means should be devised to hold forth inducements to men of good principles and talents to undertake the office of parochial schoolmasters.

Parliament responded to this appeal and the Act of 1803 raised the teachers' minimum salary from 100 to 300 merks (£5.10.10 to £16.12.6 sterling) and provided for a review of salary to take place every 25 years based on the current price of oatmeal. The Act also reaffirmed the ultimate authority of the church in the appointment of teachers and continuation of Presbyterial examination of schools.

One would have thought that when an Education Bill appeared before the House politicians would have attempted to address the major problems of the parochial system, if indeed they were aware of them: the inadequacies in meeting the educational needs of the population; the lack of any co-ordinating organisation at the centre; the failure to devise a method of supervising teachers, and of training them. But no such fundamental appraisal was undertaken.

If the Act of 1803 took only very limited account of the inadequacies of the old system it paid no attention whatever to the new forces at work in society. It was only after the conclusion of peace in 1815 that Parliament began to investigate and consider how the parochial system might be improved and how it might be used as an instrument of social improvement.

In Shetland, the old, enclosed society of the eighteenth century was also beginning to crumble by the 1790s. A new, outward-looking mood was appearing, at its core the development of business enterprises by a new class of people — the merchants. These men had made money in trade with Dutch fishermen, naval vessels, whaling ships, as well as the lucrative business of smuggling. On a wider front, the return of almost 3,000 men from the Royal Navy at the conclusion of the Napoleonic Wars, opened up wider perspectives to local communities. These ex-seamen brought with them, apart from some capital in the form of bounty money, an aura of adventure and the lure of new horizons to captivate the young. Whaling ships began to call regularly at Lerwick to complete their crews and by the 1820s there were something like 1,000 Shetlanders sailing regularly to Greenland and the Davis Straits.

Lerwick, as the principal mercantile base, grew rapidly. Between 1791 and 1821 its population doubled from 1,259 to 2,578. People from country districts moved into the town in search of work. Many remained in impoverished conditions but there were a number whose initiative and ability enabled them to clamber up the mercantile tree. One such was Lowrie Tait, a young man from a very poor family in Fetlar who came to Lerwick in the 1790s hoping for a berth on a Greenland whaler. He wasn't successful but on the whalers' return he noticed that when they had been paid they frequently threw away their oily clothes. With an eye on future business, Lowrie gathered the old clothes, washed them and had them ready for sale the following spring when the whalers were re-fitting for another voyage. As he could sell his outfits more cheaply than the recognised shipping agents he rapidly acquired a reputation as a good man to deal with. He had a sharp mind and a flair for business and within a few years established himself as a flourishing shipping agent.[1] Lowrie's story entered the lore of Fetlar and would no doubt have been used as an example to the young of the importance of education in the process of getting on in the world. Other examples of young men who used their basic education in a local school to make progress in the world were the growing number of Shetland shipmasters in the merchant navy.

A. D. Mathewson never tired of listing those of his former pupils who had risen to become sea-captains. People were now beginning to see that, apart from its value in advancing the Christian life, education offered means of material advancement.

In a letter to the editor of a local paper in 1878 an elderly Shetlander recalls the value of education. He writes of the 1820s when he was a lad in a country district:

> We had two neighbours, one on each side of us;.... and ....each of them had only one child, a boy, who were named Tammy and Jamie. Both were sent to the school. Tammy attended two summers and four winters, and his father paid in all six shillings of school fees for him. The last winter he attended he wrought at Arithmetic, the fee for which was two shillings. When the father came to pay and heard the charge he flew into a passion, declared it was extravagant, told the schoolmaster that he was keeping the coat on his back — and it looked like it, as the coat was old and carefully mended — and that his son should never return to school more.
>
> Tammy grew up a raw, easy-going sort of man, with his mouth constantly open, as if he were momentarily expecting some of heaven's gifts to drop into it. He went a summer or two to the haaf, then to Greenland, married young, and became the father of a large family. He and his parents lived together, but as years rolled on their substance became gradually less, and eventually they became dependent on their son, whose assistance was so very feeble that they died recipients of the parish charity.
>
> Jamie attended school regularly until he was 15 years, and became a good scholar. His father paid thirty shilling of fees for him, and paid cheerfully. He served some time in a grocer's shop, and then commenced business for himself, but not succeeding as he expected he removed to the colonies, became a prosperous and leading merchant in one of our colonial cities, and settled £25 a year on his parents, which they lived to enjoy for the period of thirty years. Thus, for the sum of thirty shillings spread over a period of eight years, this man received £750, and perhaps the money was nothing to the satisfaction he felt in having done his duty, and the pleasure he derived from the affectionate solicitude and prosperity of his son. Had he been like Tammy's father he would have lived poor and died unmourned.[2]

This tale, for all its Samuel Smiles overtones, was not untypical of the attitude towards education of a fair number of local people at the time. The ability to read was regarded highly and the degree of literacy among the population, however minimal, was unusually high.

Educational Surveys

Parliament's growing concern at the apparent failure of schools to measure up to the social problems of the time led to a succession of enquiries into the state of education. Between 1818 and 1838 there were no less than four surveys and for the first time we can obtain some idea of just how many children were attending schools in the various areas. In

1818 Lord Brougham was instrumental in launching a Commission of Inquiry.[3] This was followed in 1826 by Returns from Sheriffs of the Scottish Counties showing the state of parochial schools in 905 parishes[4]. Then, in 1834, an enquiry was conducted pursuant to an Address in the House of Commons[5]; and in 1838 Answers by schoolmasters[6] were investigated. These four major investigations give us, for the first time, a reasonably comprehensive view of the state of education in the islands. Not every parish responded to the requests for information but by combining details from all four surveys a good general picture can be obtained.

By 1827 each of Shetland's 12 parishes had a parochial school with some 393 scholars in attendance altogether. This is an average figure for attendance which varied considerably depending on the season. From April through to September, parents kept children at home to help with the croft work which involved almost entirely manual labour — digging, manuring, planting, gathering crops, curing peats — and during those months school rolls dropped dramatically. These variations are recorded in greater detail in the survey of 1834[7] where, in one parish, attendance of 72 in winter dropped to 20 in summer.

With Shetland's population at 26,145 in 1821 the 393 attendance indicates that approximately one child was in attendance at parochial schools for every 66 persons in the community.

At the same time there were 13 Society schools with 604 scholars and, information from eight parishes indicate that 29 Adventure schools had 554 scholars in attendance. If the latter figures are extrapolated to 12 parishes we would have something like 44 private schools with 831 scholars. And if we combine the three types of schools — Parochial, Society and Adventure — we arrive at a total of 69 schools with 1,828 scholars, or one person at some form of school for every 14 members of the population.

This suggests a fairly satisfactory state of affairs but, apart from its crude mode of calculation, it fails to account for the great variations in standards and attendance. Many of the Adventure schools hardly merited the title of school. They were often conducted by elderly pauper women moving from house to house in the district and receiving their keep and 5d or 6d per quarter for their services.[8] Attendance was also spasmodic and often amounted to little more than two to three winter months.

A recurring note which emerges is the strong desire among parents for education for their children. An illustration of this comes from the small, remote island of Skerries with a population of 73.[9] In 1825 the laird and minister were persuaded to send in a young lad to teach for half a year. "The School was attended by about 25 Scholars of whom a good many were well advanced in years, and the people were so well pleased with the teacher, that they kept and paid him for three months longer." Public support could no longer continue and Skerries was again without education.

In the early 1840s the lack of a school in Skerries came to the attention of the local Baptist preacher, Sinclair Thomson and for a few years he found sufficient money to maintain a small school. He found it difficult to maintain the costs and applied to the Free Church in Edinburgh for help but the church could not provide funds unless the school became their property. Leaflets were printed and distributed appealing for assistance to the Skerries. Arthur Anderson, in London, became aware of the need and, with help from some of his acquaintances, raised sufficient money to build a new schoolhouse. Anderson personally undertook to pay a school-teacher £20 annually. William Peterson was appointed in 1850 and continued until his retirement in 1881. His salary ceased with the death of Arthur Anderson in 1869 and for a few years Peterson had to rely on contributions from the Skerries folk with some assistance from the Lighthouse Commissioners.[10] In 1871 an appeal was sent to the SSPCK who agreed to an annual grant of £10. Later, responsibility for Peterson's salary was taken over by the Education Committee of the Church of Scotland

Many of the Adventure schools offered little more than a very minimal introduction to reading of the Bible, and in very primitive surroundings. One old lady in the middle years of the century taught the alphabet and basic reading by smoothing a bed of peat-ash in front of the fire in the middle of the floor, and inscribing the letters with a stick. Another, when asked to help with a difficult word in the Bible would examine it closely then say: "Never leet you yon ane, my jewel — yon's Latin." Or another who kept a school in Lerwick "where a number of youths were initiated into the mystery of the alphabet, and for the modest sum of one penny a week a class was taught 'the Shorter Catechism and to read the Bible'. Barbara [Blair] was most peculiar and eccentric in her manner, but it was said she always claimed her place among the 'upper ten'".[11]

For all their limitations these little schools helped to give the population a basic literacy. A survey carried out between 1822 and 1825 by the Inverness Society for the Education of the Poor in the Highlands, revealed that, in Orkney and Shetland, 88 per cent over the age of eight were literate, a figure well in advance of any other area.[12] This result has to be set beside the fact that the other Highlands and Islands areas were Gaelic-speaking despite many of them having had Society schools for almost a century. The results from Orkney and Shetland are, nonetheless, impressive, although in many cases the degree of literacy would have been very low. The emphasis on reading in school is revealed in statistics obtained from the 1834 Enquiry where, from the seven parishes which supplied figures, 2,176 are recorded as being given instruction in reading, whereas only 640 were receiving teaching in writing. In his response, the minister of North Yell and Fetlar reported that there were 32 children over 15 who could not read but 559 who could not write.

Greater numbers of boys were taught than girls. In the 1834 enquiry, seven parishes provided numbers of scholars receiving instruction in reading and writing, divided into male and female. The difference in numbers being taught reading was not considerable — 54 per cent boys and 46 per cent girls — but there was an obvious tendency to consider writing as a skill girls could do without. Twenty-two per cent of Boys were taught writing but only 4.6 per cent of girls. The Unst minister crystallises the bias against girls receiving education when he comments that a graduate has been appointed parochial teacher but because of lack of proper accommodation he can only take 53 scholars: 40 males and 13 females.

The common refrain running through both the 1818 and 1826 responses is of the inadequacies of one school per parish and the great need for more schools in scattered areas. One respondent — the parish minister — says[13] that he is "inclined to think with the greater body [of parishioners], nearby three-fourths of the people, that it is extremely hard, not to say unjust, to assess them for the support of a school to which they can have no access or receive the smallest benefit."

In another widely scattered parish — Northmavine — the minister describes a proposed variation of the parochial school system which had been mooted. The local parochial teacher had died in 1823 and at a meeting of heritors shortly afterwards, the minister and a committee of local people proposed that the parochial school salary of 600 merks (£33.6.8) should be divided between four teachers in different districts. The heritors readily agreed to this proposed division of the salary and further agreed to provide the four sites for the schoolhouses, but with the important proviso that the people be responsible for the building and maintenance of the schoolhouses. The minister concluded: "owing to the poverty of the people, no progress has been yet made in the building of these schoolhouses." And in 1825 the post of parochial teacher was still vacant.

These surveys highlighted the comparatively small part parochial schools played in Shetland's educational provision — 393 scholars in attendance compared with 1,158 at other types of school — and illustrates the partial failure at least of the educational blueprint which emerged from the 17th century reformers.

Accommodation

The Act of 1696 required that the heritors should provide "a commodious house for a school". This vague requirement left heritors to provide their own interpretation of "commodious" and the schoolhouses of the 18th century varied from badly lit, cramped hovels with earthen floors and thatched roofs to fairly roomy houses with flag floors and slate roofs. The Act of 1803 made little progress towards ensuring that terminology such as "commodious", "sufficient", or "proper" was backed up by specific standards. The new Act merely required heritors to provide a proper schoolhouse together with a room and kitchen dwelling-house and a garden.

The surveys of 1818 and 1826 give us a general picture of early 19th century schoolhouses. They followed a pattern of about 30' long, by 13' wide, by 8' high, usually with a schoolroom of 15' x 13' and open to the inside roof. The majority had two floors with the schoolroom and master's kitchen (about 14' x 13' x 6') below and one or two garret bedrooms upstairs.

A classroom 15' x 13' must have been very overcrowded when, as two schools indicated[14], 72 children attended during winter. Allowing for the teacher's space at the front, little more than two square feet would have been available for each child. Forty years later the Argyll Commission regarded eight square feet per child as "Sufficient school accommodation."

The worst aspect of the teacher's accommodation was the miserable allocation in the garret where they had barely 2' of side wall plus the roof pitch. In Delting it was even worse with only 15" above joists. In most cases the teacher's sole living space would have been the kitchen downstairs where he and his family had to conduct all their affairs as well as prepare and eat meals.

An extreme example of tardy and inadequate provision was North Yell and Fetlar which had the dubious honour of being the last local parish to establish a parochial school — in 1827.

What had bedevilled the situation in North Yell and Fetlar was the separation of the two parts of the parish by sea requiring a journey of two to three hours. Since Fetlar had a Society school the assumption was that the parochial school should be situated in North Yell. One can well appreciate the reluctance of Fetlar heritors and people to contribute to a school which their children could not possibly attend. Even a site in North Yell, however strategically chosen, would involve children from some townships having to travel two to three miles over "mountains and peat-bogs". Over a period of 60 years heritors had met several times to consider the building of a school, come to a reluctant decision, then allowed nothing to happen. Eventually, in 1824, a grudging agreement was reached that a school be built to "as limited dimensions as the law allows"[15] and that the heritors should assess themselves for its cost at 1/- per merk which would produce a building costing about £90. They also made the proviso that if the Society school were to be removed from Fetlar the parish schoolmaster be bound "to reside and teach in that island every alternate year."

In 1825 the minister reported[16] that "The heritors have, during the last 60 years, several times met, and resolved to furnish accommodation for a teacher; but nothing has been done till a few weeks ago, when the building of a schoolhouse commenced... But the accommodations now furnishing will be so small and comfortless, that it will be difficult to find a person possessing those qualifications, which a parochial teacher ought to have, to inhabit them."

Despite the shortcomings of the buildings, William Craigie, Society teacher in Fetlar decided in 1827 to move to the parochial school in North Yell — presumably attracted by the increase of salary from £15 to £25. On 7th November he wrote to his colleague in South Yell, Andrew D. Mathewson: "I arrived here Friday last having taken a final farewell of the good people of Fetlar, and whenever it shall please the great disposer of every event to place me at any further period of my life I never again expect to be placed among a set of people more inclined to oblige than I found many individuals in that island. I have got my furniture, my cattle, and some potatoes brought over, but as yet I have got no corn. I have had the use of the old house at Cullivoe where my furniture etc. have been placed until I can conveniently bring it up to the house."

Craigie had already in Fetlar experienced poor accommodations in the Society school as well as lack of support from the principal heritor, Sir Arthur Nicolson. Charles Cowan, the Fetlar and North Yell minister, "regretted that the Heritor on whose property the [Society] school is established has for some time neglected to keep the house in repair, and to furnish the fuel required, so that it is probable the Society will either withdraw the salary of £15 per annum or the teacher will be obliged to leave the island as his health has already suffered considerably from the deficient state of the accommodations."[17]

He was not long in discovering that the parish schoolhouse was as "comfortless" as that of the Society, but as parochial teacher he had a course of action available to him which he did not have as Society teacher. On 19th May, 1828, he took the line of last resort which the Act of 1803 provided, and petitioned the Quarter Sessions of the Justices of the Peace in Lerwick representing the "incommodious and inadequate state of the schoolhouse and schoolroom" and craving that an extension to the buildings be authorised.

He claimed that:

> the roof, when in its best state, could not keep out water; and during the very first winter some of the ridge slates were blown off and your petitioner was under the necessity to cover the holes with pones (flakes of turf), with a view to preserve the rest of the roof and to keep out water, but every succeeding winter has made it worse, so that it is now in a very ruinous state, for, even where the slates are lying on, they have so shifted as to produce openings in every direction.
>
> The small upper room allotted for the teacher's accommodation was lined with wood so ill seasoned that the boards have separated, so that the sky can be seen through the ceiling and roof. Your honours may easily conceive that in such a place your petitioner's health must be endangered, and his comfort destroyed. When snow falls it lodges between the ceiling and the roof, and is melted by the heat of the fire, so that the water runs down in his bed and over the floor the same as during the heaviest rain, and your petitioner has no other place to resort to. In the report of the masons, the height of the wall is said to be from 8½ to 10 feet, in which case the floor must either be 18 ins. off the level or the given height be 8½ feet, which, after deducting for joists and floor, scarcely leaves 8 ft. of wall for both lower and upper room. The whole length of the schoolroom is only 17 ft, and part of this must be used as a passage along the foot of the room. Only one table — 11ft. 10 ins. by 2 ft. 2 ins. — was provided, which being flat can only admit of one scholar to write on the breadth of it, and your honours can easily conceive how many writers that table can accommodate. Two benches or forms of the same length were also furnished, but of such flimsy material and bad workmanship that they soon went to pieces. The schoolroom is lighted by only two small windows, which are so low in the wall, and placed in such a position that the back part of the schoolroom has no light, and the scholars who are obliged to put up with the dark side must unavoidably lose much time as they cannot see to read unless when brought to the side which is lighted. The present schoolhouse, had it been well lighted and properly furnished, would accommodate about thirty scholars, yet the average number that have been admitted is thirty-eight, but of these your petitioner had to place some in the kitchen. Twenty-eight in the schoolroom were learning to write, and as the table can accommodate so few of the writers at one time it is impossible for your petitioner to describe the bustle and confusion which is produced in his school in a dark winter day in consequence of the perpetual changing which must take place and although boys may submit with reluctance to be removed from place to place in order to accommodate one another as far as possible yet they cannot make that progress which they would were better accommodations provided for them, but grown-up lads will by no means submit to such treatment.
>
> Many in this place are still deprived of the inestimable blessings of education, though a school has been built for the purpose, as will be seen by the accompanying representations from heads of families in the district and by a letter addressed to your honours by the late Rev. Mr. Cowan, minister of this parish. It is impossible for your petitioner to remain in the house another winter

as it now is, but must be under the necessity of giving up teaching and removing himself and effects to some other lodging until the accommodations provided for both teacher and scholars are made suitable and sufficient.

Such is the state of the parochial schoolhouse of North Yell, yet your petitioner has been informed that it cost £90 sterling, and if such is the case he is persuaded that were it sold this day for the very purpose for which it was erected it would not fetch above half of the original cost: nor is this to be wondered at when the carpenter and slater work was executed by men who neither understood their business nor could they execute work to any purpose, as would appear, were the house to be inspected by competent workmen, it never having been reported by any other person than by the very individuals who did the work.

From the following short description of the house it may be inferred how little regard has been paid to the comfort of the teacher and scholars in devising the plan when the place allotted for the teacher's kitchen has the same number of windows and of the same size as the schoolroom, while the teacher's own room has only one small skylight, with one square of glass in it and at the end of the room too, so that in sitting at the fireplace one can scarcely see to read at midday.

May it therefore please your honours that your petitioner, with all due submission, earnestly requests that your honours will be pleased to take the above facts and circumstances under your serious consideration, and if necessary allow your petitioner to withdraw his petition of the 19th of May, 1828 so far as it respects the building of a new schoolroom, and decern and ordain the Heritors of Fetlar and North Yell to meet in the said schoolhouse and along with them workmen who are disinterested and well qualified to inspect and report to them the present ruinous and unsuitable state of the above schoolhouse so they may be the better enabled to determine what alterations and repairs will be found necessary for the accommodation of scholars the local situation of the parish will permit to attend, as also to consider what additional accommodation is absolutely necessary for the comfort of the teacher, by lengthening the house to at least 36 feet, inside measure, as was agreed at a meeting of Heritors held for the purpose Sept. 8th, 1820, and which has not yet been rescinded by any subsequent meeting — putting in two or three additional windows in the schoolroom and raising the wall of the house to 3½feet above the joists — the roof having to be taken off at all events — so that there can at least be one plain furnished but comfortable room above stairs for the use of the teacher, and either a window at the gable of the room or a folding skylight on the roof, with four panes of glass.

And failing the Heritors doing so by the space of three or four weeks your honours will be pleased to appoint competent workmen to inspect the premises and report to your honours that you will be more fully able to judge of the facts above stated, and appoint one or more qualified persons to put your honours decree in execution with full powers to assess the Heritors in such sums as may be required for defraying the necessary expenses and to have the same completed before next winter so that your petitioner may not be under the necessity of removing to another lodging, which must be inevitable if things remain as they are.

The J.P.'s gave the Heritors the opportunity of answering Craigie's charges and on 28th May, 1830, Sir Arthur Nicolson submitted to James

Greig, a Lerwick lawyer, a response[18] signed by every resident heritor in Fetlar. Despite their recorded agreement that the building be as limited as legally possible, Nicolson claims disingenuously that "the schoolhouse is one of the best built and most comfortable… in this country." He echoes the old complaint that the school will be of no benefit to Fetlar which contains more than half the people in the parish, and argues that the North Yell heritors, in agreeing with Craigie's request for improvements to the schoolhouse, do so "at our expense". He does indicate, however, that he would be anxious to undertake limited repairs.

The Justices decided on 13th December 1830 that Craigie's complaint was justified and instructed the heritors to carry out the necessary extension and repairs to the schoolhouse. The heritors met in North Yell on 24th February, 1831 to consider the decision. Nicolson did not attend but sent a draft resolution[19] to the effect that the extension and repairs should be carried out "by constraint".

The improved schoolhouse still remained too remote for children from the south part of the parish and, writing for the New Statistical Account in 1841, the minister found that there were "upwards of 130 scholars betwixt five and eighteen" who could attend a school if provided but "nothing has been done to supply this deficiency, and nothing can be done by the parish on account of its poverty. Unless subscriptions can be obtained in the south for a school and schoolhouse, the parish must still suffer."

Other parishes in Shetland suffered from the poverty which was endemic to the area during the 18th and 19th centuries but the heritors of North Yell and Fetlar did not have a good record of fulfilling their legal obligations. North Yell Church was ruinous from 1737 and the minister was "obliged to preach either in the open air or in an old house where his books were soaked in Rain." He claimed he has "stood in Rain, Water, Snow and Slush for hours…after coming off the sea bedaubed with salt water in two to three hours crossing from Fetlar."[20] When the Rev. Gordon was inducted in 1754 and came to Fetlar, he found the Manse was not habitable.[21] The heritors refused to build a new one and Gordon was left with no alternative but to build his own. During the building operations he lived in a barn. He also complained that there were no proper kirkyard dykes and the swine were getting in and tearing up corpses.

Such blatant disregard of legal obligations is difficult to countenance but Yell was a particularly poor island and it was reckoned that half the entire rental in the 1830s was not sufficient to "build churches, manses and schoolhouses, and to pay the minister's and schoolmaster's salaries."

REFERENCES

1. Traditional Fetlar story told by James J. Hunter, Uyeasound, Unst
2. Shetland Times, 2/3/1878
3. Digest of Parochial Returns made to the Select Committee appointed to enquire into the Education of the Poor, Session 1818, Vol. III, Printed 1819, PP
4. Returns from Sheriffs of the several Counties of Scotland, relative to the Parochial Schools of Nine Hundred and five Parishes, showing the State of the Establishments for Parochial Education in Scotland, PP, 1826, xviii, 95
5. Education Enquiry: Abstract of the Answers and Returns made pursuant to An Address in the House of Commons dated 9th July, 1834, PP
6. Answers made by Schoolmasters in Scotland to Queries circulated in 1838 PP, 1841, XIX 64
7. Education Enquiry, 1834, PP
8. Answers to queries by Sheriffs, 1826, Lunnasting Parish, PP
9. Ibid.
10. Out Skerries, An Island Community by Joan Dey, Lerwick 1991
11. Shetland Times, February, 1895
12. Moral Statistics of the Highlands and Islands of Scotland compiled from Returns received by the Inverness Society for Education of the Poor in the Highlands, Inverness 1826, SRO
13. Answers to Queries by Sheriffs, Lunnasting Parish, PP
14. Education Enquiry, 1834, PP
15. Minute of Meeting of Heritors of North Yell and Fetlar, 28 July, 1824, Nicolson Papers, SA
16. Answers to Queries by Sheriffs, 1826, North Yell and Fetlar, PP
17. Ibid.
18. Answers by Sir Arthur Nicolson and other heritors, 28th May, 1830, Nicolson Papers, SA
19. Nicolson Papers, SA
20. ZPM 24/6/1778, SA
21. ZPM 25/6/1802, SA

Chapter 11

Society Schools Inspected, 1835

DR JOHN KEMP's visitation of Shetland's Society Schools in 1799 was the first occasion when these schools were inspected by a representative of the Society. Patrick Butter made a further inspection in 1824 and, in 1835, a comprehensive survey was made by Mr John Tawse, secretary to the Society, and Mr John Bonar, a Committee member.

They left Edinburgh for Aberdeen by Union coach at 5am on Monday 13th, July, arriving at 6.30pm that evening. The sloop *Fidelity*, mail packet to Lerwick, had been damaged on its journey south and was delayed in Peterhead for repairs. She did not leave until 25th July and anchored in Bressay Sound on the morning of the 28th. The inspectors were welcomed by William Hay, one of Shetland's leading merchant lairds of the time, who offered them the hospitality of his home during their stay.

They began their visitation of the 13 Society schools on the following day at Cunningsburgh, and in the next 12 days visited a further eight — Scalloway, Burra, Lunnasting, Fetlar, Eshaness, Skeld, Weisdale, and Whiteness. Sandness and Sandsound were both vacant and the accommodation so sub-standard that the inspectors declared the Society was unlikely to appoint teachers to them unless there was substantial improvement. The Papa Stour teacher, James Irvine, had gone to the mainland for medical assistance for his sick child but the visitors received good reports on his capabilities from minister, heritors and people. The weather prevented a visit to Foula but the parish minister and the laird reported that the teacher, John Fraser, was diligent and the schoolhouse acceptable.

Bonar and Tawse's Report[1] is the first comprehensive account of one type of educational provision in Shetland. The Society schools were, in some respects, less well endowed with buildings and teachers than the parochial schools but their wide range of provision, from the excellent to the miserable, provides a good cross-section of what a dispersed and impoverished community could attempt.

At the 11 schools visited they rated Fetlar, Scalloway, and Weisdale excellent, both for buildings and classroom attainments; Cunningsburgh and Eshaness were regarded as adequate but the teachers could have shown more energy; and they were appalled at the deplorable standards at Burra and Lunnasting. In Burra they found accommodations which were "in every respect bad. The dwelling house and School room form the same building or rather hut, and are only separated from each other by a slight partition not reaching to the roof, indeed it seemed to consist of the back of the beds or sleeping places. The School is dark, ill furnished and not water-tight, and the dwelling house consisting of a single room, being the other half of the building is a miserable dwelling, dark, gloomy, and neither roof or the walls sufficient to keep out the rain. The whole is disreputable…". The teacher did not impress either. "Magnus Thomason has been here since 1820. He is a sickly looking man seemingly possessed of no energy, but at the same time capable of teaching the most ordinary branches. He has a wife and large family, all of whom looked sickly, indeed it could scarcely be otherwise from the miserable manner in which they lived." The report observes that this was the only means of education in the island and the visitors were therefore reluctant to recommend closure. The school continued under Thomason until 1846. He had found enough energy to secede at the Disruption and continued to preach in the School until he was investigated by Presbytery that year.[2]

The school at the head of Skeld Voe in Sandsting parish was equally miserable. The schoolroom was small and dark, with scarcely any forms in it, the only writing desks being rough boards placed on loose stones. The teacher's accommodation, consisting of one apartment at the other end of the schoolroom, was in such bad repair that in wet weather the family had to move into the schoolroom, which was slightly more watertight. The whole building was scarcely safe and could well become ruinous in a very short time. The visitors were no more impressed by the teacher and scholars. The 18 children who were present that day "could read a little, but by no means perfectly and this, imperfect as it was, formed the whole amount of their attainments — they were very defective in the catechism, and seemed to have very little knowledge of what they were about, further than going through a certain mechanical operation. What questions were answered, were plainly a mere exercise of memory without any apparent intelligence, or their mind apparently at all engaged in the work, but they were taken by surprise and some allowance must be made for that." These comments seem to sum up all that was unsatisfactory in the poorer schools of the period.

The teacher, George Henry, possessed of no real qualifications and lacking in energy, was a rather pathetic specimen. He had succeeded his father in 1824 and inherited the antagonism which had existed between old Henry and the parish minister. Henry Sr. had, for conscientious reasons, not attended church and, as a result, John Bryden, the minister, had announced publicly from the pulpit that he would never visit the school. This situation continued after son succeeded father, despite the fact that Henry Jr. regularly attended church.

The visitors sympathised with the present teacher, recognising that he had a large family depending upon him, but at the same time could not see the community making any real effort to improve the accommodations so long as he remained teacher. He appears to have remained a Society teacher in Skeld into the early 1850s.

At Vidlin, in the parish of Lunnasting they found William Pole, schoolmaster, his wife and eight children, living in appalling conditions — "The houses are perhaps the most miserable that can be conceived. It is impossible the Society, had they been aware of their state could have permitted any of their teachers to remain in them", and, the report continues, we "were astonished how the teacher with a large family could have remained there even for a few weeks." All they had for living and sleeping space was a kitchen and one small garret.

The visitors regarded the school as totally unsuitable but discovered a further reason why it should not be continued by the Society. Quite recently the heritors had placed the parochial school a quarter of a mile away at Quiness, thus rendering the Society school unnecessary. Messrs Bonar and Tawse realised the parish was large and with a scattered population and felt the school would be extremely useful either in Nesting or Whalsay where there was a great need for education. The teacher was well qualified.

The school at Still, Fetlar, under Robert Bayne, was the next to be visited and a welcome contrast it must have been to Burra and Vidlin. The accommodations were small but in very good repair, and the dwelling house consisted of three rooms. It was in the classroom, however, that the visitors were "very much pleased". The day was wet and stormy with only 35 scholars present, whereas normally there would have been 96. The children "read and spelled very accurately" and "it was quite evident that they were made to understand what they were reading, and that the exhibition was not a mere mechanical one." Classes were also available in Navigation and work-books were shown, with neat diagrams and solutions "worked out with considerable taste."

In general terms the visitors found the Society's Shetland schools much better than they had expected. They had previously shared the idea held by a number of influential people in the south that, somehow or other, Shetland required only a very elementary education, and that teachers of most moderate attainments were all that was required. This misapprehension, acquired through lack of knowledge of Shetland and the comparatively little communication it had with the mainland, had led to the Society appointing teachers to schools in Shetland who would not have been regarded as qualified for posts on the mainland. Messrs Bonar and Tawse now reject this erroneous idea, stating that "We found the common people in general intelligent. They are simple in their manners, a kind, hospitable, and moral people. Crimes are little known among them. But they are an enquiring people, anxious for information."

The report gives us a broad outline of the operation of Society schools at this time. The accommodations were provided by heritors or parents, or a combination of both. The parents were generally responsible for maintenance of buildings which mainly involved regular thatching of roofs, and also were expected to pay modest fees and keep the teacher supplied with peats. This latter responsibility was not always carried out, especially, as in Papa Stour, Fetlar, and Weisdale, where the peat-hill was distant and difficult of access. The Weisdale parents initially provided £3 in lieu of peats but this had declined and, in 1834, Laurence Henderson, the teacher, received only 10/-, leaving him with an outlay of almost £7 for peats — just about half his salary. The situation was discussed with the parish minister who undertook to read from the pulpit a letter on the subject from the Society pointing out that supply of peats to the teacher was one of the conditions upon which the school was continued.

The requirement that the teacher should have a garden and sufficient grass for a cow was carried out at every station apart from Whiteness.

The report states that parents do not seem unwilling to pay fees "when they have it in their power to do so" but points out that because of the prevailing poverty "little can be expected in the shape of fees. The average collection at many of the Country churches on Sundays is 1d or at most 1½d." The Papa Stour teacher states in a letter to the visitors that because the schools are known as charity schools the parents think they are entirely free and refuse to pay fees, provide teacher's peats, or repair the roof of the schoolhouse. A contributory reason for this, James Irvine, the teacher, explains, is that his predecessor, an old man who resided in Papa and had no family apart from a servant, obtained his own peats, thatched the roof himself, and took no fees. Notwithstanding this, Irvine adds that "he was easy and indolent".

All the schools seen in action taught the basic subjects of reading, spelling, arithmetic, and the Catechism, while about half had teachers capable of teaching the higher branches, particularly book-keeping and navigation.

All the teachers had organised Sabbath evening schools which were well attended and, when the minister was preaching in other parts of the parish, several of them read a sermon in their local church.

The report made two key recommendations regarding future appointments — that teachers with higher qualifications should be sought after for Shetland and that they should not be paid less than on the mainland. The visitors point out, in support of this latter recommendation, that the cost of living in Shetland is higher than in Scotland, with meal bought in Leith or Peterhead for 18/- costing at least 22/- in Lerwick.

A further recommendation was that the school day should not exceed five-six hours, with a sufficient interval. They had encountered too many schools operating an eight-nine hour day with only ½ hour interval.

They also recommended several districts which should be considered for Society schools in the future — Gulberwick, four miles from Lerwick and with a population of nearly 900, Uyeasound in Unst, Burravoe in Yell, population 900 and no school, North Roe, population 1,000 and no school, Quendale.

The patchwork nature of educational provision in Shetland during the first half of the 19th century was accentuated by the introduction of General Assembly Schools from the 1830s and Free Kirk schools after the Disruption in 1843. The New Statistical Account of 1841 mentions five assembly schools — at Bressay, Gruting (Sandsting), North Unst, Tingwall, and Trondra. There was also one at Brae, Delting from 1827. These schools, organised by the General Assembly of the Church of Scotland, proved very popular, because of the quality of accommodation or teacher, or both. The Bressay minister makes the telling observation that "The institution of the Assembly school has excited a desire for education in Bressay beyond what existed before, and the people appear sensible of the great advantage of having a teacher so well qualified as the present." [3]

The church obviously still wanted to be at the centre of education in the land and, aware of the mounting concern and involvement of the State, was anxious to strengthen its influence

REFERENCES

1 Scottish Record Office, GD95/9/5
2 ZPM 25/3/1846, SA
3 New Statistical Account, 1841

Chapter 12
Schools of Advanced Education

Lerwick Subscription School

AS MENTIONED in Chapter 3 there is evidence of spasmodic attempts in Scalloway and Lerwick during the 17th century to operate grammar schools, i.e. schools where Latin was taught. In 1700 Brand recorded that "The Ministers there (in Shetland) are very desirous that… a Latine school be set up either in Lerwick or Scalloway". Nothing substantial appears to have been achieved in this direction and, in 1743, Thomas Gifford of Busta took steps to give some financial basis to a grammar school. He undertook a bond to pay annual interest on a sum of £600 Scots on behalf of a Master of a Grammar School in Lerwick.[1] This initiative does not appear to have established a regular grammar school for, in the early 1790s, the Lerwick minister notes[2]: "There has not, as yet, been any established schools in the parish; but there are always one or two teachers of English, writing, arithmetic, book-keeping and navigation, in it, who depend entirely on the quarterly payments. Those, therefore, who wish to give their sons a grammatical education, are under the necessity of bringing teachers from the continent of Scotland, upon salaries paid according to their respective subscriptions."

These so-called subscription schools appear to have operated in Lerwick during the latter part of the 18th century, making use of Gifford's bond as a built-in subscription. On 10th October, 1775, a group of 10 subscribers engaged a Charles Macnab to teach Latin grammar, together with English, writing, arithmetic, book-keeping and church music. His contract was for three years and he was to be paid an annual salary of £30 sterling, £2.10/- of which was to come from interest on Gifford's bond. The subscribers undertook to find a schoolroom adequate for 25 scholars, and to provide fire and candle. The quarterly fees were of the order of £1.10/- per scholar, and as an extra encouragement the teacher was allowed to take five additional scholars who would pay their quarterly fees to him. He was allocated two vacations annually — 14 days at Christmas and 14 in June.[3]

Continuity of teachers would appear to have been a problem. In 1783, James Malcolmson, Sheriff-Substitute in Shetland, wrote to his superior in Orkney stating that his 15-year-old son had been a scholar at the Lerwick school but that the teacher had "foolishly deserted office a year ago contrary to his agreement".[4] He therefore enquired whether the boy might continue at Kirkwall Grammar School, adding that he had been studying *Caesar's Commentaries, Sallust,* and *Ovid's Metamorphosis,* but had not yet started Virgil or Homer. The Orkney Sheriff replied that the Kirkwall schools were good at the moment, the Grammar in Latin and Greek, and the English school in reading, writing and arithmetic; that the fee for the language course was 10/- per annun and lodgings for the boy could be provided for £7 per annum, including washing.

The next we hear of the Lerwick subscription experiment is in 1817, when a well qualified young teacher — John McMorine, the same who was the teacher of A. D. Mathewson — was appointed at a salary of £80.[5] Convenor of the group of subscribers was Andrew Duncan, Sheriff-Substitute, and the other 12 were business men and landowners. The Articles of Agreement signed by the subscribers included an undertaking that the teacher be appointed for seven years, that he should teach English grammatically, writing, arithmetic, and the common branches of mathematics, with Latin and French; that the number of scholars be limited to 30; that the parents determine the particular branches of education to be taught, and that they should have the power to appoint the teacher and determine "everything relative to the interests of the school". A room was obtained from the Freemasons in the Tolbooth, the only public building in the town at the time.

The school was regularly inspected by the parish minister who had authority over certain aspects of the curriculum. In 1820 a meeting of Subscribers instructed McMorine to change his methods of teaching Latin in accordance with the recommendation of the minister.

The schools called into being by the subscription process appear to have been relatively short-lived. As a student of theology McMorine was anxious to continue his studies and in 1820 requested leave of absence to do so, recommending that his brother undertake his duties. He continued at his post, however, until at least 1823 when he wrote to A. D. Mathewson saying he was about to leave Shetland.

Moravian Teachers

A subscription school which began in 1835 had a remarkable impact, not only on its scholars, but the entire community. Miss Catherine Stafford Spence, whose father, Dr William Spence, was Convener of the Board of Directors for a period, recalled that "... in 1835, a lasting impulse had been given to the mental activity of Lerwick by the opening of a school for the sons of those able to pay a higher fee than that exacted by the parish teacher, to receive in return more individual attention than was possible with the number this teacher had to instruct."[6] A young

Englishman belonging to the Moravian sect or United Brethern as they termed themselves, came as teacher. He had been educated at a seminary in Saxony, Germany, which was supported by the sect.

At the outset he declared that 10 or 12 boys were as many as he could undertake to teach as thoroughly as he would wish, and recommended that a Moravian friend of his come as assistant.

The school continued for about three years with a number of different teachers, all Moravians, one being a native German. "These young men," Miss Spence states, "were received with open arms by the community, and German ideas and literature held thenceforth a measure of attention in the place which they had never had before."

The school operated until about 1838 but its success was such that, almost immediately, plans were afoot to establish another, also staffed by Moravians.

On 1st February, 1839, the new school was launched with 16 subscribers who each paid two guineas as his share in the school. Almost half of them were merchants, with three members of the legal profession, two doctors, one parish minister, and one Lieutenant of the Royal Navy. Only two, a joiner and a bootmaker, could be regarded as from the artisan class.

A Code of Regulations was prepared which, among other things, laid down that a headmaster and one assistant teacher be engaged, and that a third master be employed if the number of pupils exceeded 32; the four quarterly terms should begin on 1st May, 20th August, 1st November, and 1st February; the summer vacation should be six weeks and Christmas not more than 10 days.

School fees were:

Division 4 — reading and writing (English) — 10/- per qr.
"... 3 — Above plus arithmetic, book-keeping and geography — 20/- per qr.
"... 2 — Above plus Latin, French or mathematics — 30/- per qr.
"... 1 — Above plus Greek, German or Italian — 40/- per qr.

In addition to school fees, each pupil had to pay an equal proportion of the expenses incurred for room rent, servant's wages, light and fuel, pens and ink. (This was approximately 4/3d per pupil.) Also 5/- per qr. had to be paid to defray the costs of establishing the school — books, maps, and furniture. Individual books and stationery were to be paid for by the pupils.

A pupil attempting an education which could lead to university would have to pay about £2.10/- per quarter. Only the upper layer of people in Lerwick at the time could afford to meet such expenditure. A haaf-fisherman's total earnings for his summer season of 10 weeks at the fishing generally came to about a quarter's fees.

The first headmaster — Mr W. L. Wünsche, a German Moravian — received £80 per annum as salary, and his assistant — Mr Hull — £50. The school opened in February, 1839 with 21 pupils and a let of premises in the Subscription Rooms — a building formerly the Auld Kirk but recently modified. The furnishings were basic — four large tables with eight forms for the pupils, a square table and two chairs for the masters.

Everything seemed set for a successful venture but within a year the usual staffing problems arose. Mr Wünsche gave notice that he had to return to Germany as the Moravian schools there were in great need of teachers. He retained a keen interest in the Lerwick school and corresponded with a number of German teachers seeking their interest in succeeding him as headmaster. No one applied and Mr Hull was offered the post, although he too gave notice of his intention to resign in July 1843. Eventually, in August, 1842, Mr John G. Glass commenced duties as assistant, although with Mr Hull's departure he was soon to find himself the sole teacher. In view of this the Subscribers increased his salary to £64.

The arrival of Mr Glass, which might well have consolidated the staffing situation in the schools, coincided with a severe local crisis which was to materially affect the future of the school. In the late 30s and early 40s the local economy was ravaged by a series of disasters. The haaf fishing had not recovered from the disaster of 1832 when 18 boats and 105 men were lost. Between 1835 and 1839 three harvest failures had precipitated the population into famine conditions with the inevitable recourse to increased credit from the merchants. In 1840 the herring fishery failed with severe losses in men, boats and equipment. The Corn Laws were in full swing with a boll of meal in Lerwick costing £2. Then, in 1842, came the financial bombshell. The Shetland Bank, operated by the two leading Shetland merchants, James Hay and Charles Ogilvy — both subscribers to the school — collapsed, leaving the local mercantile system in even greater chaos. The major firm of Hay & Ogilvy, with a finger in most of Shetland's economic activities, was declared bankrupt and this in turn led to commercial paralysis locally.

Several of the Subscribers had withdrawn their children from the school where the numbers had declined from 21 when the school opened in 1839 to a mere nine in 1844. The school funds were in deficit with no prospects of any improvement and in May, 1944 the directors informed Mr Glass that the school would close in July.

Fortunately the post of headmaster at Lerwick Parochial School was vacant at the time and Glass was appointed there with the responsibility for teaching reading, writing, arithmetic, book-keeping, English grammar, mathematics, navigation as the basic courses with, in addition, the elements of Latin, Greek, French, and German. The fees were considerably lower than had pertained in the subscription school: reading — 1/6d per quarter; writing, arithmetic, and English grammar — 6d each extra; geography or book-keeping, including all abovementioned branches — 5/- per quarter; geography and book-keeping, together with all abovementioned branches — 7/- per quarter; navigation — 18/-. In the higher department Latin, Greek, French, German, mathematics — 10/6d for any one per quarter; for any two — 12/6d; for three — 14/6d; for four — 16/6d; and for the whole five subjects — 18/-. All or any one of these five branches to include book-keeping and geography, and the four elementary branches (if so desired).[7]

J. G. Glass was an an able and committed teacher who, by all accounts, was a strict disciplinarian, more feared than loved by his pupils.[8] One of them, Arthur Laurenson, recalled:

> The first day at school made a pretty strong impression on my mind. When you stood on the landing outside the door, before entering, you might have supposed the room empty, save for the occasional scrape of a pencil, scratch of a pen or the brief questions of the master. Inside, utter silence reigned.... No military discipline could have been firmer or more uniformly carried out. One voice at a time alone, was allowed in these precincts: the faintest attempt at a whisper was caught up with: 'Johnson, come to me after 12', or 'Anderson tertius, stop behind'. No wonder a legend arose that he could see behind him, and that he had something in his ears that made him hear anything. This was a new experience to that generation who had been accustomed to do very much what seemed good in their own eyes at school, and at times even to diversify the dulness by an open row, or a concerted mutiny.
>
> I joined the Senior Latin class, which was then called the First Latin, and was also directed to attend on certain evenings at the master's lodgings, at 7 p.m. there to study under his eye, and prepare the next day's work. This night work was a grievous burden upon us all. There for two hours, seated around a table, while Mr Glass sat at the head, we ground away with the consciousness that his eye rested on each separately and individually and in terror lest one should accidentally kick his neighbour under the table, and be, of course, instantaneously detected in the act. Then as our orders were to appeal only for help if we were stuck, and not to trouble him with trifles, we were always in anxiety as to what was a 'trifle', knowing that next day would bring swift retribution if we made any mistake. (He worked meantime on German editions of Virgil.)

It was, however, as a musician that he impressed himself upon Lerwick. Arthur Laurenson describes how

... gradually he [Glass] drew about him all the voices in the town suitable for a choir.... In 1848 he began a series of practisings which ceased only with his life. Every night in the week — but Saturday — he devoted to this work. Monday, Tuesday, Wednesday, Thursday he met the voice-parts separately; on Friday there was general rehearsal. Every other spare moment was occupied with his own practising, music-copying, and other details of his work. Far on in the morning his light was seen. He never wearied, never grumbled, never stopped in his way onwards: taking all the labour and expense on his own shoulders and content only that his choir should give attendance and do their best. His temper never failed him: blunders did not irritate, carelessness did not provoke to censure.... Nothing but perfection could satisfy him, and the torture which he underwent under blunderings might easily be estimated by the sudden changes which passed over his face.

The first work he set his choir to — after long and, to them, tedious preliminary exercises of a bar or two at a time, repeated and re-repeated till their patience gave way — was Mendelssohn's 'Elijah', then newly published. It is curious to think of, that 'Elijah' was put in rehearsal in the Shetland Isles the same year it was performed at Birmingham, and I question whether it was then known at all in Scotland. After the 'Elijah' came the 'Messiah', 'Judas Maccabeus', 'Dettingen Te Deum', Haydn's 'Creation', Mozart's 'Twelfth', and latterly the 'Requiem Mass', Beethoven's 'Mass in C', 'Mount of Olives', and Mendelssohn's 'St. Paul', with other occasional smaller pieces. The 'Requiem Mass' was the last thing he took to hand, and it is a somewhat strange coincidence that he did not live to hear it performed.

In the spring of 1854 he became seriously ill and died shortly afterwards. Aged only 40, his 10 years in Lerwick left a great imprint on the community, particularly its cultural life.

Lerwick Instruction Society

The Anderson Educational Institute, Shetland's first and only academy, was founded primarily as an elementary school and any account of its origins has to take into consideration the basic educational facilities in Lerwick in the middle years of the 19th century.

Lerwick continued to grow throughout the century and the parochial school established in 1816 for a population of about 2,000 was totally inadequate for a population in 1851 which had increased by about 50 per cent. In 1841[9] there were four schools — the parochial school, the subscription school, and two small adventure schools. The parochial school, situated on the site of the present Baptist Manse on the Hillhead, could at best accommodate about 100. Mr Glass had found it so unsatisfactory that he transferred the school to two rooms in the Subscription Rooms.

By 1862 the utter inadequacy of school accommodation was highlighted in an editorial in the *Shetland Advertiser*,[10] which stated that between 180 and 200 children capable of receiving education were debarred from doing so because their parents were unable to pay for even the most rudimentary instruction. And there were just as many belonging to working people who could afford to pay a small fee. The large numbers of children running around the streets, some of them getting into mischief, even into jail, roused concern among the clergy and city fathers. Looking back on this period, Thomas Manson, editor of the *Shetland News* echoes criticisms of society today when he writes:[11] "Even among a section of those children who attended school in an off-and-on way, there was abundant evidence of a deplorable want of oversight and discipline. The parents either did not exercise or did not possess any real authority over their children; teachers had little or no opportunity to do so, and the clergy… seemed to possess little influence among the more turbulent spirits… ". In the summer of 1855 the Rev. Andrew Macfarlane of the United Presbyterian Church preached a sermon on the theme of duty to one's neighbour. He concluded with an appeal to the young men he saw present to come to the help of the many children and young people of Lerwick who were not being taught even to read and write because of the lack of school accommodation. Six young men volunteered and were the pioneers of a remarkable movement, which lasted for six years, whereby hundreds of young people received a basic education.[12]

They formed themselves into the Lerwick Instruction Society, its object being "the gratuitous education of poor children." and undertook immediately the task of finding the necessary resources for their task — principally money to rent a suitable room and acquire books, slates, stationery, etc. Its constitution included the provision that the Society should "consist of 31 members of good moral character, competent to teach Reading, Writing and Arithmetic"; that it should meet quarterly; that a Superintendent be appointed who would be responsible for allocating the teachers to their respective classes, have oversight of school furniture, books, etc., and "have a discretionary power to dispose of cases of insubordination, etc. of Scholars without bringing them before the Managers"; that "candidates for admission as teachers should be examined as to their competency before a Board consisting of President, Secretary and Superintendent; and if found competent, the President shall immediately call a Meeting of the Society when he shall recommend the applicants; and a majority of the Members and Mandatories who must be Members then present shall either admit or eject them"; that teachers should "make it a matter of honour to attend their respective evenings and at the hour appointed precisely so as to prevent disorder and delay, and when absence is unavoidable they must provide substitutes, but failing that, they shall subject themselves to be tried at a meeting of the Society called for that purpose, when they may be either reprimanded fined or expelled from the Society;" that "the School should be open on Monday to Friday evenings from 8pm to 10pm, and be concluded by one of the teachers repeating the Lord's prayer and every scholar on leaving bowing to the teacher at the door."[13]

To qualify for entry to the school the pupil should not be attending any day school or have parents capable of paying day school fees. This rule was regularly enforced, particularly as the numbers attending increased from 150 to 190, which placed enormous pressure on their accommodation in a single room in the Subscription Rooms.

The core of this remarkable enterprise was the availability of a sufficient number of teachers at 8pm every evening from Monday to Friday, and this at a time when shops frequently remained open till 10pm. The committee regularly stressed the importance of the Early Closing Movement which was attempting to persuade shops to close at 8pm. Even so, these volunteers, mainly shop-keepers, shop assistants and clerks, were showing remarkable zeal in undertaking the tuition of large classes of children after a 12 hour working day. But that did not deter others from joining. The original six volunteers increased to 30.

The Society came to realise that it was not suitable for younger children to attend school up to 10pm and in 1859 they decided to commence a day school for five to seven year olds, which would be conducted by ladies. This development would also ease the unhealthy overcrowding of the single classroom. It proved to be as successful as the night school and within a year 106 young children were attending, although the prejudices of the day were revealed in "abominable letters" written by a local clergyman criticising the ladies for their involvement.[14]

Examination of the report for the year 1858-1859 gives some indication of the task undertaken by these volunteers. Eighty-eight boys and 82 Girls were admitted, the average attendance from October-February being 120, and from February-May 70. The reasons given for the falling off of attendance were that some of the scholars had gone to the Greenland whaling, while others had obtained labouring jobs in country districts during the voar period. Of the 170 admitted, about 60 could neither read nor write, while of that number about 30 knew little more than the alphabet.

An inventory of the school property on 2nd June 1857 indicates the materials which these committed people used in their arduous task, and gives a flavour of the classroom:

    2 large double-sided writing tables each 15 ft. long
    1 hanging desk complete 9 feet long
    Superintendent's desk and stand
    Small desk and stand

1 Form 16 feet long 10 inches high, 4 legs
1 " 10½ " " 10 " " 3 "
1 " 15⅓ " " 18 " " 3 "
1 " 15¹⁄₆ " " 18 " " 3 "
1 " 15¹⁄₁₂ " " 18 " " 3 "
1 " 12 " " 18 " " 3 "
1 " 9 " " 20 " " 2 "
1 " 6 " " 18 " " 2 "
– found in school room
1 " 6½ " " with half round end belonging to Mr S. Henry
1 blackboard 3¼ft x 2½ft found in school room
1 hat board with 8 hooks
3 double gasaliers
23 lesson boards
4 slates left by scholars
1 bottle ink. 1 box steel pens. Quantity of blotsheet
50 Bibles. 49 Testaments
4 large pictorial lesson books
50 arithmetic books. 4 Third lesson books
1 prize book *Light out of Darkness*. 1 do. *The God of Glory*
18x½d lesson books. 1 round roller
145 copy lines. 48 pen holders
6 pulleys. 3 screw hooks. 2 gimblets. Some nails

Arthur Anderson

The Society's sole income was from donations and in the accounts for 1857 the sum of £10 — almost half the total — came from Arthur Anderson, London, the Shetland-born lad who was a co-founder of the P&O Shipping Co and sponsored several philanthropic enterprises in his native islands. He became interested in the efforts of the Lerwick Instruction Society which helped to sharpen his intention to improve the educational facilities of the town. "A few years ago", he wrote in 1861, "I was informed that a large number of children belonging to the town… were growing up in a state of ignorance, their parents being either too poor or too negligent to procure instruction for them, the parochial school affording no accommodation for them.

"That this lamentable state of things was being attempted to be partially remedied by the laudable exertions of a few young men (assisted also by some ladies), who had devoted their evening's leisure to the gratuitous instruction of these children.

"I at once became desirous to assist in that movement; and after co-operating pecuniarily in it, I proposed that a properly trained master and mistress should be engaged, for the purpose of establishing an elementary school in the town, offering to defray, for a time, the cost of their salaries."[15]

Anderson Educational Institute

It was from this comparatively modest intention that, within a few years, the Anderson Educational Institute was to materialise. From the outset Anderson obviously anticipated significant local commitment, but he was to be disappointed. His proposal to engage and pay, for a time, a master and mistress was countered by the objection that there was no suitable accommodation for either school or staff. He then offered to build a schoolhouse at his own expense, provided a suitable site could be found. No immediate reply to this generous gesture was forthcoming but eventually a site on town property was offered. Anderson regarded this as quite unsuitable and the story might well have ended there. But he was not readily deflected from an enterprise when he had a possible solution in his sights. In 1859 he decided to make a personal visit to Lerwick, along with an architect, William Smith, from Aberdeen. He found a suitable site on the outskirts of the town, purchased it, and set about building a school.

In the meantime his vision of an elementary school for Lerwick had expanded. He now envisaged an academy as well as an elementary school, to be housed in a building of architectural merit, which would also provide accommodation for community needs. This more ambitious provision meant considerably greater expenditure, but he was happy to undertake this although, as he indicated in a letter of 20th November, 1861 to the Shetland Literary and Scientific Society, he expected a significant local response by way of "sympathy and active co-operation". The only conditions he attached to his gift were that the main object was the establishment of an elementary school, and that it was to be open to children of parents of any Christian denomination. He did, however, make a few suggestions for consideration by local management once it was instituted. He recommended that the school should be placed under Government inspection which would necessitate the appointment of a certificated master and mistress. This would, in his opinion, kill two birds with one stone: obtain revenue from the Government based on results, which would contribute towards the running expenses and thus reduce fees and local subscriptions, and which in turn would act as an incentive to the teachers. He envisaged that an academy be established in the building and that it should also accommodate local societies and organisations of a community nature.

Anderson's plans were again rebuffed. The Literary and Scientific Society considered his letter and, after praising the "patriotic motives which must have led [him] to erect, at so great an expenditure, the spacious and elegant edifice which now adorns the town in order to supply the blessings of education to his countrymen, not only in Lerwick, but throughout Shetland," they made the extraordinary statement that he could expect no contribution from the local community. They were even more explicit in indicating that, to operate and maintain the school as he had envisaged, would require an endowment yielding at least £250 annually, a sum they considered to be beyond the reach of local people. The Society did, however, pledge to continue to co-operate with Anderson "in the furtherance of his philanthropic designs, and act as the medium of communicating his further intentions to the community."[16]

For all their protestations and praise, the Society couldn't have been more unhelpful. While no doubt it would have been unlikely for local sources to find a capital sum capable of producing £250 annually, there could at least have been the offer of some manner of contribution to set against Anderson's munificent benefaction.

Anderson's response on 15th January, 1862 conveyed his disappointment. He observed, he said, "with regret, not unmixed with some surprise, that the Society was unable to point out any means of raising such a sum, even temporarily, and that, consequently, it would form an insuperable difficulty to the carrying into effect objects so desirable and important." He then proposed a step which the Society could, at least, have initiated, i.e. that a subscription sheet, copies of which he enclosed, be circulated in Lerwick and throughout the islands, inviting donations towards the running of the school. In the meantime he wasn't going to allow the apathy in Lerwick to blunt his purpose or hold up his plans. He informed the Society that he was going to look out for a teacher or teachers who could start the scheme and engage them at his own expense, and with regard to the academy, he requested that parents interested in having their children attend an advanced school, should inform him.[17]

On the 29th February, 1862, a meeting was held of parents and others interested in having "The Means of a Higher and more Select Education than presently exists in Lerwick". It was stressed that such a school was "the great educational want in Shetland" and that investigations had established that 59 boys and 21 girls would be ready at once to enter it, with prospects of more to follow from all over

Shetland. Obviously pleased at this very clear indication of support, Anderson moved in his typically positive manner. On 16th April he wrote to say he had engaged a Principal to take charge of the Educational Institute — the Rev. G. W. Ellaby, presently headmaster of the Grammar School of St Helens — who would be assisted by his wife and her sister in undertaking "the female educational department... for imparting useful domestic instruction and accomplishments."[18]

Anderson's original conviction that an elementary school was the prime requirement for Lerwick had now changed. He realised that the Education Bill then going through Parliament would probably result in joint funding of elementary education by Government grant and local taxation and that it would be premature to launch a school at that stage from private sources. Furthermore, it became increasingly obvious that he could expect little local support for elementary education. His subscription sheet had lain exposed in the Union Bank and the Institute for several weeks and the princely sum of £16 had been offered from three individuals! Where were the local merchants, lawyers, ministers, who had lauded Anderson's scheme? Where the local response to Anderson's £6000 building? No wonder the local newspaper, *The Shetland Advertiser*, exploded: "We are proud of our *countryman*, but we blush for our *countrymen*". The editor launched a fierce attack on the obstructiveness of the Lerwick establishment. "Can it be possible", he asked, "that they see looming in the distance, the labourer's son raising himself by means of the education obtained at the Institute, and that they tremble at the thought that their own children, if exposed to competition, might very possibly sink in the social scale?" He also claimed that Anderson had been mislead by the statement that at least 59 boys would attend higher grade classes and that Mr Ellaby would be disgusted "when he finds he is expected to keep a sort of higher and more select dame-school for boys from five to ten".[19]

Anderson's persistence in the face of the shabby response he received from Lerwick's city fathers is remarkable. Even during the erection of the school building he was subjected to petty opposition. No sooner had building operations begun than the Town sent an account of £3 to him for alleged damage to roads caused by the carting of building materials.[20] When public response to Anderson's appeal for funds for the running of the school proved so meagre, there were sneers to the effect that if Arthur Anderson chose to build a monument to himself he should not come to local people for subscriptions.[21]

REFERENCES

1. SA, Register of Bonds, SC12/53/6
2. The Statistical Account of Scotland ed. Withrington and Grant, vol xix, p. 446
3. SA, Register of Bonds, SC12/53
4. SA 2/69, Letters by James Malcolmson, Sheriff-Substitute, Lerwick to Patrick Graeme, Sheriff-Principal, Lerwick, 1780s
5. SA, SC. 12/6/1823/20
6. The Memoirs of Arthur Laurenson by Catherine Stafford Spence. T. Fisher Unwin 1901
7. Minutes of Heritors of Lerwick and Gulberwick, 5 Nov. 1844, SA
8. Shetland Times, "The Passing of the Auld Kirk" Part IX, 27/7/1907
9. NSA, Lerwick, Rev. Thomas Barclay, 1841
10. Shetland Advertiser, 23/6/1862
11. Thomas Manson, Lerwick During the Last Half Century (1867-1917), 1991
12. The Memoirs of Arthur Laurenson, ed. Catherine Spence, 1901
13. Reid Tait Papers, SA
14. John o' Groats Journal, 25/9/1860
15. Lerwick in the Last Half Century, Thomas Manson, pp 142-143
16. Ibid. 144-145
17. Ibid. 145-146
18. Ibid. 149
19. Ibid. 152-153
20. SRO, Edinburgh, ED13/208
21. Shetland Advertiser, 16/3/1863

Chapter 13

The Beginnings of State Education

THE EDUCATIONAL surveys conducted between 1818 and 1838 had shown that the parochial system was transparently inadequate. In 1834 a pamphlet entitled "Scotland a Half Educated Nation", by the Rev. George Lewis, focussed on the evidence that, in Scotland, only one child in every 12 attended school. He argued that "it was the duty of government to provide schooling for the rising generation in 'useful knowledge and religious principle'". Shetland's statistics in an 1867 survey[1] showed a much worse situation with only 32.5 per cent of children aged four-15 attending school compared with 64.1 per cent in Orkney. This survey identified certain areas with specific needs:

Quarff — School indispensably necessary... Parish Minister for some years has given instruction to all who are able to attend.

Delting — Great need of additional accommodation

Bigton — population 800-1,000 — no school — five miles from nearest

Sandwick and Cunningsburgh — two districts — population 400 each — in need of schools — two adventure schools in one of these districts but open only four months of year

Fair Isle — No school for more than a year — population 300 — 50 children ready to attend — poverty of people means they cannot support school without assistance

Fetlar — Another school required — population 253. About 35 children not at school

North Yell — Two districts without schools — population 70 each — four miles from any school — no roads

Mid and South Yell — Great need of additional and better accommodation

Nesting — population 500 — no school

Northmavine — General want of schools

Sandsting and Aithsting — Do.

Unst — One district with at present an adventure school, needs efficient school

Sandness and Papa Stour — Sewing school for girls needed

A visit by a Church of Scotland deputation in 1862[2] revealed Whalsay's plight. They found a population of 780 which, for upwards of

20 years, had had no school apart from a Sunday school. Of the 486 people aged eight to 30 only 181 could read, 78 could read and write, and a mere seven could read, write and count. The proprietor offered a sum of £50 towards a school building but made a condition that the people of the isle should demonstrate their desire for a school by doing their part. A public meeting was held where evidence of strong commitment was shown. Twelve men offered to act as collectors and before the deputation left Shetland they learned that, despite the poverty of the people, the sum of £40 had been subscribed. At the time the wages of men were 8d. per day, women 5d., and boys 3d. As the meeting was breaking up one old man came to them and said: "God knows, sir, our need is sair," and he broke down and cried like a child.

As a result of this visit a General Assembly School was established not long afterwards.

The situation was little better in Nesting, the landward part of the parish containing Whalsay. A report in 1826[3] stated that at least two schools were required — one for the north part of the area with 48 families and another for the south part with 50 families. In the absence of any official provision the people were driven to seeking makeshift solutions. About 1830 a very basic house was constructed of turves in the Laxfirth area at the north end of the district. Old people recalled their grand-parents referring to it as "da faelly skule" where, it was said, "You were laek ta die o reek." Laurence Johnson and a Miss Wishart were spoken of as teachers. About 1820, in the south end of the district, at Skellister, the community built a stone schoolhouse measuring 24'x12'x 6' high. In the fall of each year they would select as teacher a young man from the district who was educationally a little in advance of the majority. During the three winter months the school was in operation a few forms to be used as seats were borrowed from the kirk.[4] In the 1840s the building was appropriated by the laird for a tenant. Another school was conducted in a barn at Skellister by Walter Sutherland and, later, Adam Arthur and Gilbert Gray. A woman, Belle Leask, taught in another barn in Upper Catfirth.

As in so many Shetland parishes geography was an unrelenting enemy to education. The parish of Nesting and Lunnasting contained the islands of Whalsay and Skerries separated by miles of sea. Even in the landward part — Nesting and Lunasting — long voes running deep into the land made travel all the more difficult. In 1831 when Quiness, Vidlin was being considered as a central situation for a new parochial school building, it was argued[5] that "the population of Laxfirth and Billister in Nesting" could have access to the proposed school "in good weather by Boat across the sheltered Voe, when they have among them scholars of sufficient age to direct the Boats." It is a reflection of the thinking of another age when children of 12 and 13 are to be put in charge of a boatload of pupils crossing even a sheltered Shetland voe.

As the century progressed and books and newspapers became more available the hunger for education increased. The grand-daughter of a local minister, the Rev. James Pottinger (1815-1895), recalled him saying that the people would collect the scraps of newspapers wrapped round their messages from the shop and bring them to him to read for them.

Even in the late 1870s the school board had not provided proper schools in Nesting. In the north part of the district a disused lambhouse measuring 14½ feet by 11½ feet was used as a school.[6] This proved too far for the Grunafirth people and accommodation was found there in the ben-end of a croft. The teacher, William Pottinger, taught in both schools on alternate weeks, pupils often following him from the one to the other. At last, in 1887 the board opened a school in Laxfirth with William Pottinger as teacher. A board school had already been operating at Vassa in South Nesting since 1876. The Nesting situation was typical of many Shetland parishes at this time — a great hunger for education with only the barest of provision. Even General Assembly schools, usually well-built and commodious, were bursting at the seams by the 1870s. A report of 1871[7] stated that the school at Burra had 96 children packed into 252 sq. ft. of floor. In fine weather the "youngest after lessons outside" could lie down. Inside they had to stand but were "wonderfully orderly and quiet."

The sheer diversity of organisations involved in Scottish education eventually became a problem in itself. In 1867 Shetland had 24.8 per cent of those in attendance at parochial schools; 37.85 at Undenominational or Other (mainly SSPCK) Schools; 14 per cent at Church of Scotland Assembly Schools; 9.3 per cent at Free Kirk Schools; 3.6 per cent at Episcopalian Schools; and 10.2 per cent at Private Adventure (often Dame) schools.[8]

By the 1860s the clamour for a national system of education with greater government participation surfaced in parliament and the Argyll Commission was set up to examine the existing system and recommend improvements. The Commission's 2nd Report of 1864 took a progressive but cautious line. They recommended that new public schools be built, financed partly by government grant and partly by a local rate. But these new schools were merely to fill gaps in school provision. The commissioners were reluctant to lose the financial support from churches and other voluntary organisations such as the Society for the Propagation of Christian Knowledge. Government support meant annual inspections and the introduction of a code indicating curricular standards. They also recommended that the provision of education in every parish was to be the responsibility of school boards elected by the owners or occupiers of property worth at least £4 per annum.

With these recommendations in mind, the Duke of Argyll introduced an Education Bill in 1869 which was severely modified in the Commons and returned, with many amendments, to the Lords. There it was allowed to lapse. In the following session, in 1870, the English Education Act was passed. Much of the opposition to the original Scottish Bill emanated from the churches who were alarmed at the prospect of religious instruction in schools being diminished.

In 1871 a revised Bill was placed before parliament and eventually emerged in 1872 as the landmark Education (Scotland) Act. A national system of education was created, controlled from London by the Scotch Education Department and, at the parish level, managed by locally elected school boards; attendance at school was to be compulsory until the age of 13; the school boards were to take over all parochial schools, and arrangements were made for church schools to be transferred to the boards; religious teaching, which was to be confined to the Lord's Prayer and Scripture reading, was to be undertaken at the beginning or end of the school day so as not to interrupt the secular instruction, and there was a conscience clause to enable pupils to withdraw from these sessions if their parents so wished.

Elementary education in Scotland had moved decisively from church control into the hands of the state, but the centralisation of its management in London created much Scottish opposition. The Duke of Richmond pronounced that "It means simply a room in Whitehall, with the word 'Scotland' painted on the door. It is a sham, and can be nothing but a sham." To appease the critics the Act contained a provision that a Board of Education be set up in Edinburgh for three years to supervise the establishment of the new system, advise on the setting up of school boards, provision of new accommodation, and conditions for grant assistance. Strong Scottish demand persisted for a permanent headquarters in Scotland and the Edinburgh Board was allowed to continue until 1879.

The 1872 Act was a major step forward in Scottish elementary education, and influenced its progress for the next century, but it failed to provide for the future of secondary schools. This failure arose, to a great extent, from the Scottish parochial tradition which regarded the parish school as the means of providing a full education from early years to university entrance, whereas the new Act specifically stated that the new national schools were to provide only elementary education.

School Boards 1872-1900

The Act was welcomed in Shetland with enthusiasm but without the sectarian rancour aroused in other parts of Scotland. "We are pleased to observe", said a *Shetland Times* leader, "that everywhere a repugnance to mere denominationism is being manifested."[9] and went on to recommend that lay people should stand for the new school boards.

As it turned out, boards in Shetland generally included a local minister and the principal heritor with the landed interest solidly represented. Lerwick School Board comprised the parish minister, a merchant laird, two doctors, a solicitor, and two merchants; while Dunrossness had, unusually, three ministers, two lairds, and two others. John Walker, factor for the Garth Estate, was returned to no less than five boards and appointed chairman of three, despite his notoriety in these areas as the person responsible for the eviction of many crofters. Such are the vagaries of democracy.

Like all previous educational legislation the 1872 Act failed to take account of the geographical and economic condition of the Highlands and Islands. The Argyll Commission had recommended a rate of 2d in the £ in most areas, but 2½d in the Highlands. They were well short of the mark. By 1877 the average Scottish rate for education was just over 4½d with the Highlands ranging from about 7d to 10d. Shetland's low rentals placed it in an infinitely more difficult situation. The Scotch Education Department sent Professor George G. Ramsay to Orkney and Shetland as an Officer of Inquiry and he produced two valuable Reports in 1873 and 1876 which portrayed starkly the local situation. His conclusion was that the Act of 1872 "if it be carried out as in the other counties of Scotland, will prove altogether intolerable", and "will be at once unjust, impolitic, and in some cases, preposterous."[10]

In 1873 Ramsay calculated that there were 5,649 children aged five-13 in Shetland but satisfactory accommodation for only 1,445. In Orkney he found the majority of the buildings "in a miserable condition" with "… damp floors, or rotten boarding resting on or even below the ground, walls green with wet, low ceilings of eight, seven, or even six feet in height, crazy roofs, chimneys that will not vent, windows that will not open, and in general dirt, untidiness, and wretchedness, are the order of the day."[11] And, as he went on to state, Shetland schools were in even worse condition. Lerwick, with the excellent new provision at the Anderson Institute, had good accommodation for 512, which meant that rural Shetland had to face the enormous task of building new accommodation for 4,516 children. What it amounted to was a building programme of about 60 schools and schoolhouses costing up to £1000 each — an enormous undertaking for an impoverished community.

Ramsay illustrated Shetland's problem by comparing it to a parish in Inverness-shire which had a rent-roll of £13,000 and 200 school-children — resources amounting to £65 per child — whereas some Shetland parishes had little more than £2.10/- per child. He specifically mentioned Unst, an example of one of the better-off parishes. There, he pointed out, four new schools and two schoolhouses were required for a total of 440 children. The estimated building costs would be £3330 of which Government grants would meet half, leaving £1665 to be raised by the parish — or three-quarters of the entire net rental of £2200. If the parish borrowed the £1665 at the current interest rate of seven per cent for 25 years there would be an annual charge on the parish of £115.10/, amounting to a rate of just over 1/- in the £. And running expenses, including salaries, were on top of that.

Ramsay claimed that the shadow of these heavy financial burdens was resulting in increased immigration. Yet little was known of this in Westminster with Sir Leonard Lyell, Member for Orkney and Shetland, strangely silent on the question.

Ramsay was sympathetic to local conditions but his outlook was coloured by an over-zealous desire to protect the public purse. And that at the zenith of Britain's imperial wealth! Although the new schools to which the Act gave birth were designed to last — as many have done for well over a century — Ramsay saw them only in the short-term. He argued that Shetland weather and poor or non-existing roads would continue to limit attendances and recommended that schools should be designed to accommodate only three-quarters of the children in the district.[12] He took no account of the fact that, during the better months and with compulsory attendance, the buildings he proposed would be impossibly overcrowded.

School boards procrastinated and for three years there was no building. Argument raged over the necessity of erecting good, solid buildings or more economical structures with the bare minimum of facilities. Letters to the local press dismissed playgrounds, lavatories and wash-hand basins as unnecessary luxuries, declaring that generations of former pupils had washed their hands in the nearby burn, and that lavatories were superfluous since children could do what was needful before leaving home in the morning. The new regime was lampooned by George Stewart, previously teacher of the SSPCK School at Dunrossness. In a poem entitled "The Trials o' Granny Thule" he includes the new educational requirements among Shetland's "trials":

> *Then the schule when she speaks o' it she loses her breath*
> *And Lord kens, if it is no sent for her death;*
> *For she's now on the Board an clean oot o' siller*
> *Yet the State sends a message that's helping to kill her;*

Says they — now listen old Mrs Thule,
The lear o' your bairns is no what it should be,
You maun big a great school and house for the master,
And plenish and finish wi lath an wi plaster,
An pay Dominie a hunder a year
An be roupt at da Cross if ye fa in arrear.

The New Code of 1875 introduced more generous grant support for the Highlands and Islands whereby, apart from the original grant of £300 the government would meet half the costs beyond that figure. This meant that if a school cost £1000 there would be the initial grant of £300 plus half the balance, i.e. £350, making a total grant of £650. This proved a more manageable allocation and between 1875 and 1880 the bulk of Shetland's 60 new board schools were erected.

The school boards are to be commended in taking the longer view and building schools capable of accommodating attendances which improved communications would make possible.

The new board schools were a vast improvement on many of the older parochial buildings. The parochial school at North Yell, for example, measured 15' x 13' and was replaced by three new schools — at Gutcher, Cullivoe, and Colvaster. Cullivoe School had two classrooms measuring 20' x 16' and 19' x 16'; Gutcher had similar provision, while Colvaster measured 18' x 16'. All rooms were high and airy, with large windows. Roofs previously thatched were now covered in blue slate. The new class of school buildings represented a social advance not previously seen in the rural areas of Shetland. A report by an E.I.S. visiting Commission in 1912 speaks very favourably of the standard of buildings and general classroom conditions: "We found the school buildings, as a rule, clean, fresh, and well-equipped. Indeed, some of them were models for more favoured localities to strive towards."[13]

The new building programme, however, involved considerable borrowing which burdened the parishes with disproportionately heavy rate-bills.

The Curriculum in the Elementary School

It is a commonplace criticism of modern education that "da bairns nooadays canna coont and write laek dey did i da aald days." Certainly some pupils from board schools were well grounded in the 3Rs and capable of writing a fine copperplate hand but closer examination reveals a very narrow, rigid curriculum which must have produced a boring diet of education for many pupils.

Inspectors' reports regularly reveal evidence of stilted, uncomprehending reading, together with poor results in arithmetic. Long

22. Class 6 Anderson Educational Institute 1932. Back row: Elsie Durham, Minnie Leask, Norman Sutherland, Florence Hughson, Isa Stewart. Middle: Wm. Christie Pr. Teacher of English, Violet Duncan, Mary Sutherland, Andrew Johnson, Maisie Robertson, Walter MacPherson, Wm. Rhind Pr. Teacher of Mathematics, Andrew T. Cluness, Rector. Front: Jas. Eunson, Marion Taylor, Geo. Jamieson, Bessie White, Robert Wishart, Gertie Halcrow, Rhoda Hunter, Pr. Teacher of French.

23. "Byre" school at Laxfirth, Nesting – small felt-roofed building to left of photo.
Courtesy of Shetland Museum and Nesting Local History Group

Senior Department.

FEES, 10s 6d PER QUARTER.

SUBJECTS—

Religious Knowledge, English, Writing, Arithmetic, Composition, History, Geography, Elementary Mathematics, Latin, French, Vocal Music, Drawing, and Elementary Science.

Pianoforte Music 10s 6d per Quarter.
Pencil, Pens, Ink, Coals, and Copy Books, 2s per Quarter.

Higher Department.

FEES, 10s, 12s 6d, and 15s PER QUARTER.

SUBJECTS—

Religious Knowledge, English, Writing, Arithmetic, Composition, History, Geography, Mathematics, Algebra, Greek, Latin, French, German, Vocal Music, Drawing, Science, Book-Keeping.

Pianoforte Music 10s 6d per Quarter.
Pencil, Pens, Ink, Coals, and Copy Books, 2s 6d per Quarter.

Preparatory Classes.

Infant Department.

FEES, 7s 6d PER QUARTER.

SUBJECTS—

Religious Knowledge, Reading, Writing, Arithmetic, Object Lessons, Lessons on Form and Colour, Kindergarten Lessons, Musical Drill and Vocal Music.

Juvenile Department.

FEES, 9s PER QUARTER.

SUBJECTS—

Religious Knowledge, English, Writing, Dictation, Arithmetic, Geography, History, Grammar, Drawing, and Vocal Music.

24. Prospectus for Anderson Educational Institute 1888.   *Courtesy Shetland Archives.*

25. Old Vidlin schools shown on Quiness peninsula with Board School on left and Parochial School and Schoolhouse on extreme right.

Photo J. D. Ratter, courtesy Shetland Museum

26. New Vidlin Primary School 1996. *Photo John Coutts*

27. Classroom in Burra Public School, Hamnavoe, c.1910.
Photo: John H. Smith, courtesy Shetland Museum.

28. Pupils and teacher engaged in French lesson in new school, Vidlin.
Photo Norma Smith.

sessions at the slate produced, in some cases, a good hand but at what cost in terms of time and interest? Much good, conscientious work was accomplished but in the face of great difficulties. The most intractable of the problems teachers struggled against was poor attendance. School log-books of the 70s, 80s, and 90s are littered with complaints about poor attendance — from illness, bad weather, inadequate clothing or footwear, or parents simply keeping children at home to help with croft work, especially at voar, hairst, and peat-curing times. Sometimes more than half the class would be absent and this must have plagued teachers trying to progress class-groups and reach a reasonable standard. The most common source of absenteeism, and the one most annoying to teachers, was staying at home to help parents. This was very apparent in Lerwick and Scalloway schools where high rates of absences persisted despite the schools being within reasonable walking distance. In both these centres during the 1890s the herring boom was in full swing and children could always find, what was for them, lucrative jobs. Making kipper boxes at 6d per hundred was attractive and then loading the full boxes on ships earned for them 2d per hour. Sometimes they worked through the night when the more diligent ones would then go off to school.[14] But many would have spent most of the school day catching up on sleep.

Lack of roads was a major factor in the poor attendances of the period. During the years of great distress and poverty in the 1840s a government scheme to assist the poor in the Highlands and Islands, involved the construction of "Meal Roads" in Shetland using local labour. Between 1848 and 1852, under the supervision of Royal Engineers, roads were constructed from Lerwick to Mossbank, Dunrossness, and Walls; Olnafirth to Hillswick and Dury Voe; and Burravoe to Cullivoe.[15] Shetland's geography meant that many communities lay several miles from these main roads with only paths or cart-tracks at the best. During the 1870s and 80s inhabitants of these areas frequently petitioned the local Road Trustees to build roads to enable children to attend school.[16]

In 1887, for example, the Northmavine School Board petitioned the Trustees for a road in Ollaberry to pass from the Post Office, across a hill to Leon. Children were having to walk over a mile through boggy hill-ground. The petition was turned down because of lack of funds — a mile of road cost, at that time, about £360. The children in the districts of Gluss and Bardister had to walk about three miles over hill and rough ground to the Ollaberry School.

The Act of 1872, in making attendance compulsory, gave boards the power to prosecute offending parents. Compulsory attendance officers were appointed to visit defaulting families and give them due warning of the consequences of their actions. Some of these men acquired formidable reputations and their very presence on the doorstep was enough to prise out the truants. But the process of taking parents to court was seldom activated. It was a costly as well as a sometimes protracted process, and boards generally resorted to local action by summoning parents to appear before them at a specially convened meeting to receive a warning to the effect that if they persisted in not sending children to school they would be reported to the Procurator Fiscal.

A single teacher in charge of a huge class, sometimes over 40, and ranging from Standards I to VI, was caught up in an impossible situation. Classes had to be gathered together for group sessions, leaving others to silent reading or copying from a book. Generally, a class had a reading book for a year and this was read over and over until it was imprinted on the memory. The 3Rs occupied the greater part of the school day. Advanced subjects such as English literature, history, geography, mathematics, French, Latin, could be included in the curriculum but a single teacher school, even with the support of a pupil-teacher, could only do justice to senior pupils at the expense of the junior standards, and it was from there — the lower and middle orders — that the bulk of the "results" income would materialise. An Inspector's Report in 1894 for Happyhansel indicates the extreme pressures some teachers were working under. The school roll of 98 had to be squeezed into two classrooms arousing the Inspector to comment: "How anything like efficient teaching can be carried on is a mystery. There seems barely room for the children to sit tightly together. It says much for the intelligence and kindly tact of the Master [Mr George Andrew] that order and results are what they are. The large proportion presented in the higher standards must make the work very laborious." He threatened that if the accommodation was not extended grants would be "seriously endangered". George Andrew was in poor health and resigned three years later — just before the board extended the accommodation.

A snapshot of a Lerwick Infant School classroom in 1899 is provided by a pupil.[17] "We were given slates. It was considered unmannerly to spit on your slate and wipe it with your sleeve. A damp sponge in a small tin box was more seemly. Our slates were engraved with pairs of widely-spaced lines with narrow spaces between each pair. Our very first exercise was to inscribe a row of slanting hooks between the wide lines, and my first of many scholastic inaptitudes was to place the inscriptions in the narrow spaces.

Reading began by learning the ABC. The modern phonetic method lay far ahead in the future. We went on to the construction of sentences of 'the cat sat on the mat' type... Gradually, learning to repeat the prescribed arithmetical tables, and to sing-song the spelling of words indicated by the teacher's pointer on the blackboard, we ascended to 'The Fivepenny Book'. (The price paid for this particular Reader)."

Classrooms in those days were usually places of silence broken only by the teacher's voice or pupils reading aloud in rotation round the class. Pupils were rarely encouraged to speak beyond brief responses to the teacher's questions. Verbal skills were rarely developed and Inspectors frequently criticised pupils' mumbling, indistinct speech, and monotonous delivery. In one Northmavine school HMI Muir was constrained to state: "It is pitiable to see boys and girls of 13 and 14 about to go out in the world hardly able to stammer through their reading book" — and he blamed poor attendance.

The pupils Muir was commenting on were native dialect speakers struggling to express themselves in a language in which they had no confidence. The speech of their homes was tabu once they crossed the threshold of the school. A considerable number of teachers during the half-century after 1872 were from the South and, apart from their genuine desire to suppress any non-English form of expression, would have had some difficulty in understanding the dialect. From the age of five or six, children had their natural mode of expression stifled and were left to communicate in an alien tongue. They came to regard their native tongue as socially suspect and when they mixed later in life with people from other areas they often displayed lack of confidence and insecurity of speech. Even when Shetland teachers began to enter local schools in numbers — after the First World War — they too tended to suppress dialect in the classroom, regarding it as an obstacle to "proper" speech in English. The parish ministers who conducted the annual inspection of religious education often displayed as little sensitivity to the pupils' linguistic problems as, for example, the Dunrossness minister's report on Boddam School: "The senior section answered well on the first Book of Samuel, but some of the boys were slow in answering questions that they seemed to know. Recommended that the habit be dealt with in strict discipline."

Discipline

The silent classrooms of the old schools, with pupils rooted to their desks, grinding away at repetitive tasks, called for great self-discipline. The culture of the classrooms of the 18th, 19th and for part of the 20th centuries, had at its core respect for authority, reinforced by the teachings of the Bible and Catechism. The importance of discipline was a basic doctrine frequently stressed by Inspectors and regarded as self-evident by a Department statement: "The intimate connection between discipline and efficiency is clearly recognised by most persons."[18] Children were regarded as passive learners. John Ross, parochial teacher in Bressay, reporting on the progress of 10 poor boys maintained by the Parochial Board,[19] described them as "ingenious, regular in attendance, docile and tractable." — qualities obviously ranking high in his estimation.

The teacher's authority was absolute and many resorted to intimidatory language.[20] One Northmavine teacher struck fear into the hearts of his charges by bellowing: "Boy! I'll jump down your throat with my boots on!" A colleague from Skeld used to patrol the classroom chanting: "Cow-hide, good and tough — good for idle boys." Various punishments were used, such as detention, lines, loss of privileges, but the ultimate was the belt or expulsion. The latter could be resorted to for almost frivolous reasons, as in one instance[21] when a boy was expelled for insubordination which amounted to failure to account for a pencil passed to him. When listening to old folk reminiscing about their schooldays it is interesting to note how frequently the belt is mentioned. Some teachers used it to sadistic excess. In Skeld the abovementioned teacher belted a boy severely about the face and head, and threw him upon the floor — and all for not knowing the meaning of a word. When the boy tried to escape from the classroom the teacher caught his head between the door and the doorpost to the extent that his face and ear were cut. A Bressay teacher selected a switch from a willow tree and, on one occasion, gave a boy such a severe licking about the legs that the boy had to stay at home till the weals healed.

Parents generally accepted the rule of the belt and tended to praise the firm teacher. An expression often heard was: "Man, he [or she] could fairly drive it in." Occasionally when the belt had been applied cruelly to their children, some parents resorted to the law. Sheriff Court records contain evidence of a number of these, including cases at the Anderson High Elementary School, Boddam, Firth, Scalloway, and Skeld. Sheriffs tended to reflect the current educational philosophy that control in the classroom was all-important and that the tawse, handled with moderation, was an appropriate deterrent. Fines of £1 for severely assaulting a pupil with the tawse were commonly imposed. In the Skeld case abovementioned, Sheriff Rampini took a more serious view.[22] Addressing the accused, William Robertson, he said: "I have pointed out before, and I desire to impress it upon you, that there are two ways by which a school can be governed — the one is by way of kindness, the other is by way of severity. The first is by the force of moral influence, the other by brute force; and the man, I need scarcely say, who is able to govern his school by moral influence is a better man all round than he who does so by brute force... I am going to say, and it is my judicial opinion, that you are unfit for the place you hold." Strong words considering the climate of opinion at the time. The Sheriff concluded by stating he had been contemplating a custodial sentence but had decided to fine him heavily — £10. Robertson resigned a few months later but, strange to relate, the school board, despite a local petition protesting against the proposed move, appointed him to another school in the parish — Gruting — where he taught for a further seven years.

The Skeld case and another at Boddam about the same time were reported at length in *The Shetland Times* and no doubt highlighted for both teachers and parents the need for moderation in school discipline.

The use of the belt in Scottish schools continued, although less rigorously, well into the middle of the 20th century. As teaching became more pupil-centred the belt was regarded as an alien instrument in classrooms and in 1986 was proscribed by law.

Payment by Results

With the launching of a national system of education supported by government grants there came the parallel development of school inspection to monitor standards in schools and, more crudely, to check if schools and teachers merited the payment. Thus came into being the notorious "Payment by results" system.

To ensure that inspectors operated consistently and within a framework of standards, a Code was introduced which laid down the requirements which schools should follow. It was based on the Code which had operated in England since the early 1860s but with specific Scottish variations. The principal conditions included the requirement that before pupils could be put forward for testing they had to have at least 250 attendances out of a possible 400. This would entitle the school to a grant of 4/- for each such pupil, augmented by 1/- if music was part of the course, and a further 1/6 if organisation and discipline were considered excellent, or 1/- if merely good. Then in the "payment by results" category there was a sum of 3/- for each scholar who passed in each of reading, writing, and arithmetic, with a further 2/- per head if Standard II and Standard III pupils showed an intelligent and grammatical knowledge of passages they had to read. Senior pupils in Standards IV to VI were allocated 4/- each for a pass in up to two "specific subjects" including English literature, history, geography, Latin, French, mathematics, mechanics, chemistry. If, however, the inspector considered the school inadequately staffed, in unsuitable premises, or faulty in teaching, discipline, or registration, he would impose deductions on the grant.

The grant, when finally calculated, was passed over to the school board and became the board's principle item of annual income from which teachers' salaries were paid, together with maintenance of buildings, and school equipment such as blackboards and wall maps.

There was no national scale of salaries for teachers beyond the minimum of £45 per annum which was generally augmented by a share of the grant obtained and also by half the fees paid by pupils. The "payment by results" philosophy impinged closely on the teacher's income and the annual inspection became, inevitably, a highly stressful testing-ground. If the teacher and his pupils failed to produce good results and the grant was reduced or removed, the balance would have to be found from the community via the educational rate. And the teacher's job could be at stake.

The early days of board schools gave inspectors much to criticise. In 1874, Gott Public School failed to impress. "Instruction in this School," ran the report, "is very elementary, more so than it should be. Though organisation and discipline are, on the whole, satisfactory, there is a want of life and spring in the general management. The Standard work, with the exception of Arithmetic, is creditable within the limited range preferred. Numeration is weak and meaning of words should receive more attention." Under the headmaster, Charles C. Beatton — previously assembly teacher at Laxfirth — little improvement, if any, was noted in subsequent years. In 1886, with Beatton on the point of retiring because of old age, the inspector reported that "The School is still in an unsatisfactory state of efficiency, there being little that can be said in its favour. The attendance is extremely irregular, but after making great allowance for that the work is very poor... All over the school wherever a pencil can reach the walls and woodwork are literally covered with scribbling. The furniture is cumbrous and antiquated and what does for duty as a map is simply a tattered rag with part of the northern division of the country alone visible. It is hardly necessary to add that the answering in Geography was practically nil."

James Hunter, the well-respected teacher of Lerwick parochial school from 1854, was ill-at-ease under the new regime. He was particularly critical of the new regulations concerning religious instruction and confided his frustration to the school log-book: "... A decree from the school board — Catechism banished. Paraphrases as hitherto committed to memory proscribed. Prayer on behalf of myself or Scholars in School laid under ban... Asked the Scholars whether they were glad for these changes. All who are, hold up right hand. Not one. All who are vexed... hold up. Every hand up in a moment."

The presentation by the school of pupils for a series of arbitrary tests with the object of obtaining a maximum pass and therefore a bigger grant invited mechanical teaching, with pupils, especially the slower, subjected to a grinding repetition of basic skills.

The general pattern of inspection was for the inspector to take the pupils in one standard, dictate a passage for writing, set some arithmetic sums and then, after a suitable interval, line them all up and hear them read, one by one, while marking their writing and arithmetic at the same time. This would be followed by a few questions on meaning or grammar and then he would move to the next standard and so on until the school was completed. The inspector also had to check registers, progress of pupil-teachers, listen to class singing, and examine the condition of the building. It was a full day's work with little if any time for the giving of positive advice to the teacher. On occasion the visit could be traumatic.

Robert J. Muir was HMI for Shetland from 1873 to the turn of the century and acquired a reputation for being inconsiderate and ill-natured. In 1880 Peter Williamson, teacher at Gulberwick Public School wrote to the Lerwick and Gulberwick School Board complaining of Mr Muir's conduct during a recent inspection. The letter was subsequently published in the *Educational News*.[23]

> In your letter which I duly received along with Mr Muir's [Inspector's] report on Gulberwick School for this year, you ask me if I have anything to say in reply. I certainly have something to reply, and respectfully hope for the Board's forbearance, should my exasperation at the injury done me shew itself more strongly than may seem to your calm judgment advisable. I am, as you know, a person of a usually good temper, but it is not easy to stand by & say nothing while one's character as a teacher is thus publicly degraded....
>
> "Mr Muir promised to inspect my scholars on Monday and Tuesday & did not come at the time fixed. I expected him on Wednesday, but still he did not put in an appearance; on that day however, he sent me a note intimating that he was unwell; on Thursday he came a short time before Noon, and told me that he had taken only two mouthfuls of bread for a very considerable time — in short, that he had not got his breakfast. He looked rather sickly and nervous. The officer had been kept waiting at the school on the three days afore mentioned.
>
> "Mr Muir began the inspection pretty slowly, but he began to lose patience and hurried the 1st and 2nd standards through the arithmetic with undue rapidity. I believe that very few scholars in these standards would have failed if they had had the usual amount of time for doing the work. The whole time occupied with the inspection, such as it was, did not exceed two hours — about half the time I think it should have been. I was requested by him to assist by summing up figures, dictating exercises, & and thus the work was quickly got through. The inspection had not proceeded far till Mr Muir lost his temper, & after that there was very little good done. All of a sudden he gave a yell which made every scholar in the school, as well as myself, to start. The oldest girl in the school — perhaps the second best scholar — had asked the girl next to her, in a whisper, a particular word which she herself had missed in the dictation. For this

offence he made her stand upon the top of a seat for a long time — thus taking upon himself the task of punishing scholars, which was no part of his proper business as Inspector. He soon had two or three more scholars standing up similarly for offences which, in my humble opinion, were mostly imaginary, as I observed only one case of copying or attempting to copy. No sooner had he broken out into a fit of violent passion, accompanied by great vociferation and action, such as stamping, than some of the scholars set up a frightful crying such as was never heard in the school before — expecially one girl who persisted in crying for a considerable length of time. All my efforts to calm her being fruitless, I need scarcely add that the more timid of the scholars became paralysed with fear, and the more bold and firm-nerved were inclined to smile. In fact, the whole machinery of the school, as I had arranged it, was thrown out of gear, and many of the students were rendered incapable of doing the prescribed work as well as they otherwise would have done. At this stage, he seemed incapable of explaining clearly what it was that he wished the scholars to do; and when I interfered by explaining matters to them, I got the tide of passion turned furiously against myself for attempting, as he said, to take the work out of his hands. In the geography class, I was ordered to turn the face of the map to the wall, and then the pupils were asked to point out places on the blank side.... When the noise of the people crying was at its highest, the scholars in the fourth standard were reading. Only one of them passed in the reading, in which I had expected they all would have passed. The best reader in the school — a girl in the sixth standard — failed in reading, and in geography and history, in which I heard some of them answer pretty well, not even one seems to have passed.

A year or two ago I was told by a Teacher that he himself had lost his school a whole year's grants, and also a premium to which he was entitled for length of service, solely because Mr Muir, in examining his school, lost his temper to an unusual extent, and frightened the scholars to such a degree that they were unable to pass creditably. The school referred to is in the Mainland of Shetland, and the Teacher referred to has taught for upwards of fifty years; he has for many years been an elder in the Free Church, and is well known to be a man of veracity.... He told me that a year before the examination above mentioned, he had earned £27 of grants, whereas on this occasion... he did not earn a farthing.... The consequence was that the teacher had to leave the school without having got the Grants for his year's labour, with his character as a teacher ruined, & a pension which, according to his own account, he would otherwise have got, not obtainable.

I now come to the Inspector's Report on the school taught by myself for the present year, & ... it appears to me to be unfair in the highest degree — even untrue. The writing and spelling of the scholars, of which he complains, will contrast very favourably with his own — a specimen of which is enclosed.... He degrades me as a teacher to the lowest position. He did not always do so. In 1876, after inspecting my school. he asked me to stand up, and in the presence of two clergymen, expressed a highly favourable opinion regarding me.

Of all educated men that ever I knew, he is, in my opinion, the least qualified to be an inspector of schools, for an inspector of schools requires to be possessed of judgment, discrimination, self-command, & impartiality, in all of which he is deficient.... Indeed I cannot imagine a greater burlesque on the Education Act than the existence of Mr Muir as inspector, justifying his eccentricities, inconsistencies, and absurdities by quoting the articles A, B, C, of the Code. These articles he uses like so many pieces of artillery to demolish all opposition.... His inspections would in many instances be laughable, were it not for the important pecuniary interests involved in them, the amount of individual suffering caused by them, and the feeling of uncertainty which is, in every case connected with them.

As regards myself I should be a better teacher now than I was in 1876, [having] had more experience and having always tried to do my best, but according to the Inspector's shewing, my skill and ability must have diminished very greatly.[24]

Even making allowances for Peter Williamson's injured feelings the atmosphere in the Gulberwick classroom during Mr Muir's inspection cannot have been conducive to a fair examination of the pupils. And it would appear that this was not an unusual occurrence. Muir's irascible behaviour was exposed again in 1887 when Robert Fairbairn, teacher of Twatt Public School, wrote to the *Shetland Times*[25] complaining that Muir conducted himself in a "rude and bullying" manner, had terrified the children and, when a junior pupil's pencil had made a scratching noise on her slate he had banished her from the group and refused to examine her even when she was armed with a softer pencil. He had also stood in front of a class with a watch in his hand while the pupils were doing arithmetic sums. Fairbairn's letter drew three other local teachers to defend Muir but there is no doubt that he, on occasion, transgressed the general guidance given to inspectors that "it is incumbent on an Inspector to show by his manner in examining... that the main object of his visit to a school is to elicit what the children know, and not to prove their ignorance. That object is entirely defeated, if by a harsh, impatient, or indistinct manner of questioning the scholars, he frightens or confuses them."[26]

It would appear that Muir was a competent inspector but prone to moods. He could be generous in his general assessments and reported to the department in 1876 that he had found "Shetland children showing greater sharpness of comprehension in reading than agricultural parishes on the mainland and also various town schools." He conceded there was a feeling in government circles against helping one part of the country more than another but argued that the national community should take an interest in the welfare of the community at large and, in doing so, take account of poorer areas.

Many inspectors undoubtedly adhered to the Department's principles but, even so, the tension inherent in the inquisitorial situation could not be eased. The system distorted classroom teaching and, as John Kerr, one of the more enlightened inspectors wrote: "The highest function of the teacher is not to produce, nor of the inspector to record, certain mechanical results."[27] Everyone in the educational field was relieved when in 1886 and, again in 1890, substantial relaxations of the Code were introduced. Individual testing was dropped in favour of a general assessment of the class. In 1892 a Certificate of Merit was introduced for pupils who stayed on at school beyond the age of 13 and who satisfied the inspector that they were competent in the 3Rs, two class subjects (English, history, geography, needlework, elementary science, drawing) and one specific subject (Latin, French, mathematics, etc.).

Teachers after 1872 — the Move to Professionalism

Before 1872 there were no specified qualifications for teachers. The traditional Scots dominie was often a graduate, frequently qualified for the church. But, especially in remote areas, teaching posts were generally filled by able young men who had been selected at school as pupil teachers. Of the 12 parochial teachers in Shetland in 1861, two were graduates, six had some training at a Teachers' Training College, and four had no professional training.[28] Teachers of General Assembly schools had usually received training but Society teachers were generally home-grown. Many of these were talented men who made unique contributions to remote communities.

The 1872 Act stipulated that teachers entering the profession required a certificate from the Scotch Education Department. Teachers in post received certificates upon examination by Inspectors. There was no ban on uncertificated teachers but their lack of qualification affected their emoluments and the grants which were so important for the operation of the State system.

The general practice in paying teachers was at the board's discretion. When the Dunrossness School Board advertised in 1879 for a sole teacher for Sandwick, with well over 100 pupils, the salary was fixed at £35 per annum, paid quarterly, plus half the school fees and half the government grants awarded annually to the school based on the pupils' performance. In 1877 the estimated income from fees at Sandwick was £17.5.3, to be collected by the teacher, and the Government grants £48.17.2[29]. Half of those would amount to £33.1.2, which would make the salary £68.1.2. The Dunrossness Board Conditions of Service, which the teacher had to sign in accepting the post, stated that "Should any part of the grant be forfeited by neglect or misconduct of teacher such as irregular keeping of books, or having premises dirty or in bad order, the loss will fall to be made good out of his [teacher's] half [of the grant]. Other conditions included provision of sewing instruction; keeping school, house, and offices clean at all times; airing premises for at least an hour before and after instruction by opening windows and ventilators; collecting from children cost of books and stationery. Three months notice of departure had to be given, and the board could dismiss immediately for gross immorality or drunkenness, or conviction of a criminal offence.

Pupil teacher

From the middle of the century increasing numbers of teachers attended training colleges (or Normal Schools as they were termed). Among these were numbers of pupil teachers who, having served their four year apprenticeship in schools, were now ready to acquire their teaching certificates. The pupil teacher system, introduced in 1846, engaged children at the age of 13 to assist in schools for an annual payment of £10 rising to £20 over four years. If the period of apprenticeship was concluded satisfactorily they were eligible for the competitive Queen's Scholarship award which was made to the top 25 per cent of applicants for entry to a Training College.

These pupil-teachers were invaluable in assisting hard-pressed teachers faced with large classes, often well over 50. For example, Virkie Public School with 70 children on the roll had one certificated teacher and a pupil-teacher — the teacher with a salary of £25 per annum plus half the fees collected from parents and half government grant paid to board, while the pupil-teacher received £5 per annum. It was a gruelling apprenticeship and only the dedicated stuck it out to the end. Miss M. J. Henderson of Noss, Scousburgh, Dunrossness, was a pupil teacher at Boddam Public School from 1894-1898. She outlined her activities for a typical day.[30]

    6 a.m. — Revising work done previous day — 1-1¼ hours
    7.15 a.m. — Breakfast
    7.45 a.m. — Leave home to walk 2½ miles to school
    8.30 a.m. — Questioned by headteacher on work done on previous day. Also given tuition
    9.30-12.30 — Teaching Infants — Standards I and II
    12.30-1.30 p.m. — Dinner interval (Cold milk and beremeal bannocks)
    1.30-2.30 p.m. — Teaching classes as above
    2.30-4 p.m. — Studying. Assisted by headteacher for short period after 4 p.m.
    about 4 p.m. — leave school to walk 2½ miles home
    5.30 p.m. — Meal
    6-10 p.m. — Studying

Salary for 1st year — £6; 2nd year — £7.10/-; 3rd year — £9; 4th year — £10.10/-

Text books provided by School Board. Prize of £10 offered to pupil-teachers passing Scholarship Examination in 1st or 2nd Class. Three winners in 1898 — T. Finlay, Sandwick; Jeremiah Halcrow, Cunningsburgh; M. J. Henderson, Quendale.

Miss Henderson subsequently returned to Boddam as headteacher where she remained for most of her career — a dedicated and efficient teacher. But there is no doubt that the pupil-teacher system with its endless treadmill of teaching all day followed by long periods of study every evening inevitably narrowed the educational outlook of those young entrants to the teaching profession. J. J. Haldane Burgess, local writer, began as pupil-teacher at the Anderson Institute Lower School in 1875 but obviously found the work uncongenial. He is recorded in the School Log in 1878 as showing little energy. He subsequently was pupil-teacher at Bressay Public School for a time before proceeding to Edinburgh University in 1886.

Women Teachers

Until pupil-teachers appeared on the scene, teaching was very much a male domain, except, that is, in the dame schools where elderly women, often of very limited ability, kept small schools as a means of livelihood.

With the rapid growth of new schools and increased attendance the 1870s and 80s saw growing numbers of women attend training colleges. In small schools in rural areas women were increasingly appointed as headteachers. In 1892, in the 62 elementary schools in Shetland, there were 25 women headteachers. Only one of these was a Shetlander, although there were 15 Shetland women teaching in Shetland schools at that time. During the period up to the First World War, Shetland-born teachers were in short supply and it was difficult to recruit Scottish teachers. A considerable number of the teaching staff during this period came from England. Many of them proved excellent teachers. A report by a visiting Commission of the E.I.S. in 1912[31] stated that "... among the brightest and most effective teachers in Shetland are teachers who hail from England".

Women teachers were consistently discriminated against, and some school boards paid them only half as much as their male colleagues. The increasing demand for teachers in the period following 1872 had driven salaries upwards. In 1877 newly qualified men were averaging £84.15/- a year and women only £65.13.6. Women had a long fight ahead of them to obtain equality in educational circles. In 1901 Lerwick School Board drew up salary scales by which a trained certificated male teacher received

£80 rising by biennial increments to £115, whereas the equivalent woman teacher received only £70 rising to £85.[32] They had strong allies in the inspectorate who based their support on what they found in the classrooms, claiming that women teachers, "having no family cares — were able to give their whole heart and soul" to their work.

Junior Students

The Junior Student system, introduced in 1906, integrated an element of teacher training into secondary schools. Students had to have completed three years of a secondary course, and passed the Intermediate Examination.

Elizabeth J. Smith from Bressay began her secondary course at the Anderson Institute in 1910 and during her senior years joined the Junior Student system. "For those of us", she wrote,[33]

> "who intended to take up teaching there was a scheme whereby we went to the Central School one day a week, heard a lecture by the headmaster, and applied ourselves to teaching a lesson on some subject selected by him or suggested by ourselves; being given a criticism of our efforts written by the teacher on whom we were inflicted; handing the 'crit' to the headmaster and hearing his comments.
>
> In the last summer, with the herring fishing at its height, we prepared lessons on boats and fish, illustrating it by herrings and other fish begged from here and there. The lesson over, and we released, we walked to the point of Victoria Pier and threw the fish as far as we could, thankful to be finished with our stern, if just, master, whose advice and training helped us to avoid being quite so diffident when confronted by new children, new teachers, and new examiners.

Security of Tenure

Parochial teachers had virtually absolute security of tenure. Officially, they held their posts *ad vitam aut culpam* — unless guilty of misconduct. The process of dismissal was handled by the Church Courts — Kirk Session, then Presbytery, with final confirmation by the General Assembly. There is little evidence of many of Shetland's parochial teachers appearing before the Church Courts but Tingwall appears to have had rather more than its fair share of problems.

John Tulloch was appointed Parochial Teacher of Tingwall, Whiteness and Weisdale on 1st May, 1780[34]. By 1789 he was regarded with such disfavour by William Mitchell, the minister, and the Kirk Session that he had been dismissed as Session Clerk and refused baptism of his children.[35] Tulloch appealed and his case was heard before Presbytery on 11th March, 1790. There he was charged with disobedience of Kirk Session instructions, neglect of duty as schoolmaster, using blasphemous language, breach of the Sabbath, and being a liar and slanderer. His neglect of school duties included poor attendance, being in Lerwick frequently during school hours, cursing scholars, and failing to conduct morning prayers. A number of parents testified to his unsatisfactory conduct as teacher. As the evidence mounted against Tulloch he decided to flee the country and was officially dismissed from his post on 1st July, 1790.[36] The process had gone through Kirk Session, Presbytery and finally, on 30th June, 1791, the General Assembly.

Some teachers, safe in their cloistered security, clung to office despite physical and mental frailty.

Alexander Sutherland, appointed schoolmaster of Tingwall parish in 1801 at the age of 49, found himself at 80 to be incapable of teaching because of ill-health. The Tingwall parents, in a petition to the minister and heritors, stated that in

> Consequence of his declining years our Children were reaping little or no benefit from his School. Yet in consideration of his long and faithful past service and unwilling to deprive him of his Salary, House & Glebe in his Old Age. We at our own expense erected a small School house in the Town of Swinister [about a mile away] that we have supplied with teachers out of our own Pockets — an Expense very Inconvenient for many of us & that we cannot longer support.[37]

The parents' petition, implicitly recognising Sutherland's security of tenure, does not ask that he be removed from his post and accommodation but merely requests that John Thomson, the young man they have placed in the temporary school at Swinister be appointed "assistant and successor to Sutherland and allowed to share the schoolhouse with Sutherland, thus leaving the old man and his family during his life the old salary, Glebe and remainder of the end of the house."

The only case I have come across of a Shetland parochial teacher's tenure of office being seriously challenged through moral misconduct was that of James Halcro Johnston, schoolmaster of Sandwick 1846-1850.

In 1850 he was charged by Zetland Presbytery[38] of ante-nuptial fornication, a charge described as being "of a very heinous nature, calculated if proven, entirely to destroy his usefulness as a schoolmaster as well as produce the worst moral effects in the parish." Before Presbytery could take the matter any further, Johnston resigned and emigrated to New Zealand.

The parochial teacher lost his security of tenure with the 1872 Act which stated that any teacher appointed after 1872 held office "during the pleasure of the School Board." This dramatic curtailment of teachers' rights meant that teachers could be dismissed without any right of appeal, and without the board requiring to give reasons for doing so. It was all part of the "payment by results" regime. Failure to produce satisfactory results meant reduced income for the board and therefore the necessity to look for a teacher who could perform more effectively.

The school board's power of arbitrary dismissal does not appear to have been used to any great extent but there was a growing unease in the profession over the vulnerability of teachers under this system. It so happened that the key issues crystallised in a historic case in Shetland when in 1899 Robert Young, Headmaster of the Anderson Institute, was dismissed.

The Robert Young Dismissal

The Anderson Institute, financed largely from the founder's endowment, remained outwith the national scheme until 1889 when it came under the control of Lerwick School Board. The roll at that time of 170 consisted mainly of elementary pupils and the board, with the "payment by results" regime in mind, saw the Lower School as the key part of the organisation. Then, in 1892, the government decided to devote funds to the improvement of secondary education. Thereafter secondary departments would be examined by inspectors in the elementary tradition and paid according to results.

The board looked at the situation in the institute and were worried. They realised that the Upper School, under the then headmaster — Mr A. McDonald Reid — was unlikely to earn many grants. Reid, appointed in 1876, succeeded Mr John Allardice who had acquired a reputation in presenting pupils for University Preliminary Examinations. In one year alone he had presented 33, whereas Reid, while receiving very satisfactory reports from the inspector for the Lower School, had presented during the previous six years only eight candidates for the Higher Leaving Certificate instituted in 1888.[39] The academic decline of the institute resulted in able pupils enrolling at a private school in the town, and in 1889 13 of them passed University Preliminary Examinations.[40]

The board decided to obtain a headmaster capable of restoring the academic standing of the school and advertised for one at a salary of £350 — a figure well in advance of any other being paid locally. In 1894, Robert Young was appointed. He came with glowing testimonials from the Free Church Training College who described him as "one of the best students we have ever had" and who "distinguished himself highly both here and in the University."[41] McDonald Reid's activities were curtailed to the Lower School. To herald the beginning of a new era the Upper School acquired an identity of its own as Anderson High School, and Young was given the status of Rector.

The new Rector was faced with a challenging situation: a school whose elementary department had, four years previously, been described in an HMI's report as "simply deplorable", with almost half Standards IV and V failing in two or three subjects; whose senior classes had been consistently under-achieving and depleted in numbers; and whose previous headmaster, now demoted, would have naturally harboured a measure of resentment. Not only that, but some influential members of the school board regarded his appointment as unnecessary, and his salary an extravagance.

Four months after Young's arrival an inspector's report reveals that all was not well: "The school has suffered from changes of staff, illness of teachers and the friction attending reorganisation."[42] The following year the inspector gave a gloomy report on the High School: "English, history and geography taught to classes beyond the standards are decidedly disappointing. Mathematics of the first stage are weak. Latin of the first stage is very good, but in the second and third stages the translation of English into Latin is too often poor. French is good, and domestic economy is very fair. German and Greek are very satisfactory."[43]

McDonald Reid left in 1896 for a school in Peterhead and his place as Senior Master, in charge of the Lower School, was taken by Robert Millar. With this move, the friction appears to have increased, particularly between the Rector and Millar, until in 1897 Young complained to the board that, among other things, Millar had repeatedly declined to carry out his instructions. The board's response was extraordinary. They went over the Rector's head and invited Millar to report on the organisation of the Lower School. As Lord Balfour of Burleigh, Minister for Education, was to state later in a sharp letter to the board: "Instead of supporting the authority of the Headmaster, the Board passed a resolution, severely condemning his appeal to them, and called for a report upon the school from the... teacher implicated... It is impossible to conceive any course more likely to interfere with the efficient organisation of the school...".

The board had already challenged the authority of the Rector in another area. Following a complaint from a parent that his child had been forced to take a foreign language as part of his course, the board instructed the Rector "that no subject be forced on a child against the parent's desire." Young was not to be bludgeoned. His reply to the board was polite but firm: "Gentlemen! May I be allowed to take this opportunity of stating that, in my opinion, it is impossible to conduct any school successfully on the lines indicated...".

Inside the board all was not plain sailing. Two factions had emerged, each led by a member prominent in local affairs. Leader of the anti-

Young group was John Leisk, a merchant and current Provost of Lerwick, while the minority group, which supported Young, was led by the Chairman, A. A. Porteous, pharmacist, undoubtedly the board member with the best understanding of educational issues. Controversy raged and some idea of the hysteria and pettiness which entered into the debate can be gathered from Leisk's remark: "Can any good thing come out of Paisley?", to which Porteous retorted that: "The wisest man the world ever saw is presently the Headmaster of the Institute."[44]

The Leisk group contended that Young had not effected the improvements in the school which he had been appointed to secure. Certainly the roll had not significantly increased — from 57 when he was appointed to 61 in 1897. But, as the *Shetland News* pointed out, there had been a distinct improvement in the school's performance in the Leaving Certificate examinations since Mr Young's appointment. During the four years since he arrived there had been 62 Higher and 170 Lower passes compared with eight and 74 respectively during the previous four years.

Young's opponents on the board were determined on his removal. Events came to a head in September 1898 with a motion "that the Board resolve to terminate the present agreement with Mr Young." The mover agreed to postpone his motion but the press publicised it and public outcry ensued. The press was as divided as the board, with the *Times* strongly anti-Young and the *News* hotly defending the Rector. Newspaper comment in those days was extremely robust and some of their statements make today's editorial fulminations seem mild by comparison. The *Times* declared Mr Porteous to have been "A gigantic failure" as Chairman of the Board,[45] while the editor of the *News* opened his Yuletide leader with a blast to the effect that: "As an element of discord in the community, as an influence of evil, it [the school board] has been one of the worst features of our municipal life during the year that is drawing to a close."[46]

The majority of the board remained unmoved and in March, 1899 the motion was again raised. So were tempers, and the *News* reported that the meeting — conducted in private — became so heated that shouts of members could be heard in the next street. The motion was eventually carried by five votes to three, despite strong arguments from Porteous that the criticism of Young's running of the school should be put to the test by asking the Scotch Education Department to arrange a special inspection. Leisk and his group would have none of it. They wanted Young out and would brook no further delays. On 7th April, the clerk to the board was directed to give official notice to Mr Young in terms of the finding of the meeting: "… It is the belief and firm conviction of the majority of the Board that under more systematic and harmonious management the school should have made more progress during the past three years, and it is only by showing progress and efficiency in the Higher Department of this school that this Board can hope to retain the... grants and endorsements by which the school is at present supported."[47]

The local branch of the Educational Institute of Scotland had previously written to the board regretting their actions, emphasising Young's successful record at the Institute, and claiming that the steps being taken by the board would be injurious to the best interests of education in Shetland.

On 15th April, 1899, a petition signed by 582 of the 740 local electors, parents and guardians, declared that "... we the parents and guardians of the pupils attending the Higher Department of the Anderson Educational Institute desire hereby to express our satisfaction with the education given at the school, and our strong disapproval of the action of the school board of Lerwick in seeking to terminate his [Young's] engagement."

The controversy reached the columns of the *Aberdeen Journal* on 22nd April, 1899 where it was stated that... "It is evident that the local community have full confidence in Mr Young and that popular sympathy is overwhelmingly in his favour... Thus we would say there is a strong prima facie case in his favour against the school board majority, who have put forward no tangible reason for their action. It seems indeed, a very bad piece of local tyranny, activated by personal hostility...".

By this time questions had been asked in Parliament about the dismissal. The Government, well aware of the powers of school boards to appoint and dismiss teachers, were very circumspect in their response. The board was requested to send the department full details of the situation. At first, the board appeared to question the department's right to interfere, and asked for copies of the representations which had been made to "My Lords of the Committee of Council". The Secretary of the Department pressed the issue and the board decided to respond. They obviously could not all agree on the terms of the reply and eventually a majority report was submitted along with the views of the minority.

In his reply, Lord Balfour, Minister for Education, said that he had given full and careful consideration to the board's report, the minority's statement, and also inspectors' reports for several years back. He said he had:

> neither the power nor the wish to interfere with the discretion now vested in the School Board with respect to the dismissal of teachers, but as the question of that discretion is one of serious public discussion and as the Department had that

question before it and given deliverances thereon upon representations made by the teaching body, [he considered it right] to state the conclusions to which he is compelled to come regarding the present case. It is the more necessary for him to do so because the large subsidy paid to this school from the County Grant requires the Department, before sanctioning such grant, to be satisfied that there is nothing in the management of the school which militates against its efficiency as a place of higher education.

Balfour went on to consider the charges levied against Young by the board:

1) He was not convinced that Mr Young had support from the board in his dealings with members of his staff. Mr Young had felt one of his assistants to be incompetent and there was no evidence to refute this claim.

2) Mr Young had stated that another assistant had refused to carry out an instruction. The board did not back Mr Young but requested the assistant to present a report on the school. Balfour concluded *"It is impossible to conceive any course more likely to interfere with the efficient organisation of the school."*

3) The position of Mr Young had been rendered untenable by frequent adverse motions and by an entire absence of the reasonable support from the board which he was entitled to expect.

4) While the inspector's report pointed out certain defects, it was not on the whole an adverse report and the inspector indicated that really good work was being done.

5) It was not fair to judge Leaving Certificate examination results by small variations from year to year.

Balfour summed up by declaring that *"in his opinion the School Board have not exercised their authority in the way most likely to contribute to the efficiency of the school, and that the difficulties which have culminated in Mr Young's dismissal are not of a kind for which he can be held responsible."*

When the board met to hear the department's response, Porteous said the letter was the most severe condemnation of the action of a public board that one could conceive and that if there had been a court of appeal, Young would have been reinstated. He went on to say that what made it all the more telling was that previously Lord Balfour had always sided with boards against teachers, and this was the first instance a teacher had been vindicated. Porteous and his supporters endeavoured to have Young reinstated but the majority carried the day by simply having the department's letter minuted.

The damage had been done. Young's dismissal proceeded and he left that summer, his career blighted, and with bitter memories of his experiences in Lerwick. The local branch of the E.I.S. publicised the scandal of the dismissal throughout Scotland and advised members against applying for the vacancy. As a result there were only 19 applicants as against the 47 when Young was appointed. On 30th June, 1899 Joseph D. Kirton, a non-member of the E.I.S., was appointed rector.

The Young case was a historic one in terms of teachers' security. It undoubtedly influenced Lord Balfour to include in his 1900 Education (Scotland) Bill a clause to prevent a teacher from having his professional reputation destroyed through no fault of his own by unjust dismissal. The clause empowered the department to grant a certificate asserting that, despite a teacher's dismissal, his work had been satisfactory. Scottish teachers had campaigned for the introduction of appeal machinery but the Government was reluctant at that stage to undermine powers of local school boards. The high-handed and unjust actions of Lerwick School Board, however, did edge forward the case for greater rights for teachers.

REFERENCES

1. 2nd Report by H.M.'s Commissioners appointed to enquire into the Schools in Scotland, PP1867, xxvi
2. Shetland Advertiser, 29/12/1862
3. Returns from Sheriffs of the Several Counties, PP 1826, xviii, 95
4. Shetland Times, 12/4/1879
5. Minutes of Committees, No 3, Wed 26 Jan 1831, SA D8/327/23
6. Hunter, Robert, Things Seen and Heard, The New Shetlander, No.6, Oct.,1947
7. Cowper, A. S., SSPCK Schoolmasters 1709-1872, Scottish Record Society Publications, 1997
8. 2nd Report by H.M.'s Commissioners appointed to enquire into the Schools in Scotland, PP1867, xxvi
9. Shetland Times, 17/3/1873
10. Ramsay, Professor George G., Education in Orkney & Shetland, 1876
11. Ibid. 1873
12. Ibid.
13. Annual Report of Educational Institute of Scotland for 1912, Appendix III, EIS Library
14. Gray, Walter J, The Life Story of an Old Shetlander, Lerwick 1970
15. Reports by the Committee of Management... for Relief of Destitution in the Highlands & Islands of Scotland, 1852, SA
16. SA, CO2\2\3
17. Sandison, Tom, Lerwick Schools Seventy Years Ago, The New Shetlander, No 114, 1975
18. Scotch Education Department, Education (Scotland) Reports 1874-75
19. Minute Book of Fund in Lerwick for Education of Poor Children, Barclay Papers, Mid Yell, in possession of Barclay family
20. Local informants
21. Whiteness School Log Book, 1887, SA

22 SA, AD22/2/18/08
23 The Educational News, 4th December, 1880
24 MS in hands of granddaughter H. L. Langhaar. Copy from T. Goudie, Gulberwick
25 Shetland Times, 30 July, 1887
26 Scottish Education Department Report, 1877-78, p.78
27 Ibid. 1880-1881, pp126-127
28 Duncan, W. Rae, Directory of Shetland, 1861
29 School Board of Dunrossness Minute Book, 19/12/1877, SA
30 MS obtained from relative by author
31 Annual Report of Educational Institute of Scotland for 1912, Appendix III, EIS Library
32 Lerwick School Board Minutes, 12/2/1901, SA
33 Smith, Mrs. Elizabeth J, Schooldays Seventy Years Ago, The New Shetlander, No.100, 1972
34 ZPM 1/5/1780, SA
35 ZPM 17/6/1789, SA
36 ZPM 1/7/1790, SA
37 MS in possession of author
38 ZPM 13/11/1850, SA
39 Shetland News, 22/1/1898
40 Shetland News, 8/1/1898
41 Shetland News, 15/4/1899
42 School Log-book 1889-1899, SA
43 Shetland Times, 18/8/1895
44 Ibid. 13/11/1897
45 Ibid. 10/4/1897
46 Shetland News, 25/12/1897
47 Ibid. 8/4/1899

Chapter 14

Anderson Institute — The School in Operation

THE BUILDING, an elegant structure in the Scots Jacobean manner, standing on the slopes of Twageos overlooking Lerwick Harbour, was completed in late 1861 and on 4th August, 1862, the High School (as the 'academy' part of the Institute was named) opened. Almost 40 boys enrolled, many of them quite young, certainly well short of the 59 boys Anderson had been led to believe would attend. A number of girls also enrolled and were taught separately from the boys.

The fees were:

Scholars under 10 —	15/-	a quarter
" 10-12	20/-	"
French —	5/-	
Music, German, Drawing	10/-	
Stationery & Coal	2/-	

The headmaster was prepared to receive boarders at £30-£40 per quarter according to age, inclusive of tuition. This was an obvious attempt at boosting the school's income and when there was little response from Shetland, Anderson sent north several sons of senior employees of P&O. Shortly after the school opened there were seven or eight boarders staying in dormitories adjacent to the Rector's accommodation in the school building.

The fees were very similar to those charged by the Lerwick Subscription School. There a basic curriculum including one foreign language had cost 30/- per quarter compared with the Institute's 25/-. The parochial school was considerably cheaper at 10/6 per quarter.

Ten days later, on the 14th August, Arthur Anderson was present at the official opening of the Anderson Educational Institute. There he was received by 70 local gentlemen and as he listened to the plaudits showered upon him one wonders what thoughts passed through his mind. Whatever they were he allowed nothing vindictive to mar the cordiality of the moment and spoke at large about the future of the school. He announced that his previous reservations regarding the impact the proposed Education Bill might have on the funding of an Elementary Department had been removed with the abandoning of the Bill and that this key part of the school would soon be established. He stressed, however, that he wished to retain fees, "for I am averse to destroying the self-respect of parents by an entirely gratuitous teaching of their children."[1] On the basis of his own experience and achievements he appears to have erected self-help into a sort of dogma. During his speech he commended the Rev. Ellaby as an Englishman whose "training of our youth to English habits, and a correct pronunciation of the English language, will be of no inconsiderable advantage to them, in the country where most of them must go to seek their career in life."[2]

In October, Ellaby announced that pupils attending the Elementary School would pay fees of 1d., 2d., and 3d. weekly, depending on the subjects studied, and that Arthur Anderson had instructed that each year, five of the best conducted and most advanced pupils to be promoted to the Upper School were to receive their first year's instruction free.[3] The editor of the *Shetland Advertiser* did not accept Anderson's self-help theories and condemned the charging of fees. He claimed that a large group of children in Lerwick were unable to receive elementary education except by some charitable organisation such as the Lerwick Instruction Society whose termination was a sad blow to education of poor children in Lerwick. A poor labourer in Lerwick, he argued, could, if lucky, earn 1/3d. per day during the summer but would often be unemployed during winter and living on the sillocks he could catch.[4]

On 28th November, 1862, the Elementary Department was opened and 60 pupils enrolled, under Mr James Bryan from Liverpool as headmaster. His father was assistant to Mr Ellaby in the High School.

The building consisted of four large classrooms, each 42 feet by 18 feet, each capable of containing 100 pupils comfortably. The fact that the sole classroom of Lerwick Parochial School was a mere quarter the size of each of the Institute's main rooms gives some indication of the scale of Anderson's contribution to the local educational scene. There were also two small classrooms, one subsequently used as a library, the other a science laboratory.

The Institute comprised four different schools — Upper Boys, Upper Girls, Elementary Boys, and Elementary Girls.[5] Although all under one roof the four groups were clearly segregated. It was not possible to move from the Elementary School at the south end to the Upper School at the north end without going through the Rector's house in the centre. A former pupil recalls that "no law of Medes and Persians operated more rigidly than that which separated Upper from Lower Schools. No one from Lower School dared walk up by the wall path, and no desecrating foot dare pass above the sacred terrace."[6] The girls had a different curriculum from the boys, consisting of subjects deemed more appropriate for females, such as domestic skills, music, art. The philosophy of segregation and social division was put unequivocally by Ellaby when replying to a suggestion in the *Shetland Advertiser* that there should be a greater mix of pupils: "When another disapproves of the arrangements at the Institute, because all the pupils are not mixed together — because boys and girls, rich and poor, do not receive the same education and descend, I presume, to the same average level of manners and everything else — I believe absurdity can go no further."[7] Ellaby here demonstrates his failure to grasp the comprehensive nature of the Scottish parochial tradition where all pupils from the one district were taught together and where elementary and advanced instruction were given in the one building.

Anderson handed over the operations of the schools to trustees, with an endowment of £6666.13.4 designed to provide an annual income of £200, considered adequate for teachers' salaries, running costs, and maintenance. Deployment of this sum was placed in the hands of the trustees who were to be responsible for school finances. They appointed the headmaster but otherwise had no involvement with the staff who were appointed and paid by the headmaster. He, in turn, was responsible to a local committee of managers, appointed by the trustees. The headmaster was wholly occupied with the teaching of the upper school for six hours daily, apart from half an hour spent visiting the Lower School.[8]

The formalities of the Opening Dinner had obscured the underlying tension between Anderson and the local establishment but the Rev. Ellaby, as Anderson's representative in Shetland, was inclined to perpetuate the edgy relationship with local leaders.

During the early stages of Anderson's correspondence with the Shetland Literary and Scientific Society, they had suggested that the Institute might accommodate a community library and museum, the Society having already amassed a collection of exhibits. Anderson welcomed the suggestion, regarding it as in harmony with his concept of the building as a centre for "intellectual, moral and spiritual improvement." His only stipulation was that the museum fittings should be in keeping with the architectural style of the hall, in which they were to be incorporated. After the opening in 1862, Mr Ellaby was left to negotiate with the Society regarding the proposed library and museum but from the outset there is a certain coolness in the correspondence. Ellaby wrote in November, 1862 reminding the Society of Anderson's views and requesting the Society to provide suitable boxes for the exhibits. The Society replied curtly that they had placed the exhibits in the County Rooms (the original Auld Kirk). And that was the end of an interesting proposal which would have drawn the community and school closer together.

About this time Ellaby was engaged in a ponderous and pedantic exchange of letters with Dr G. W. Spence in *The Shetland Advertiser*.[9] Ellaby, in one of his letters, had quoted: *Parturient montes: nascitur ridiculus mus* (Mountains will be in labour; a ridiculous mouse will be born) which, in his reply, Spence had translated: *Mr Anderson promises great things for Shetland education: he sends the Rev. Mr. Ellaby*. A few months later,[10] Ellaby let fly at the local establishment in a speech where he spoke of how "Mr Anderson had suffered ingratitude, detraction and misinterpretation." His brief but contentious period as the Anderson Institute's first Rector reached a climax in June 1863 when he was charged with assaulting a seven-year-old boy boarder by striking him with a cane on his naked limb to the effusion of blood.[11] In his defence Ellaby stated that the boy, who showed "greater depravity than could well be supposed possible for his years," had persisted during evening divine service in "determined restlessness", and accordingly he had given him five strokes of the cane. He stated that he was "no advocate for flogging [and] never as a rule administer[ed] more than one severe flogging", and that "the boys I have flogged most as a rule love me best."

One of the two medical witnesses testified: "I am of the opinion that the boy was subjected to very severe punishment"... "that such punishment would probably be attended with dangerous consequences, although not in this case, the boy being remarkably strong and vigorous for his years." There is no record of the conclusion reached by the Court but Ellaby left Shetland shortly afterwards, to be succeeded by his assistant, James Bryan, Sr.

In the 40 years after the school was founded, the Upper School never attained the number of pupils Anderson had been persuaded might attend. The Elementary School averaged about 100 but the Upper School rarely, if ever, rose to over 60. In 1885, one of the trustees, giving evidence to an Education Commission, stated that the school, with accommodation for 500 and one of the finest buildings in the North of Scotland, had a roll of 107 elementary and 45 higher department pupils, to which the chairman, Lord Balfour, responded: "I'm afraid your building is very much of the nature of a white elephant." And George Bain, the trustee, replied that he was inclined to agree.

Arthur Anderson, in building and endowing the Anderson Educational Institute, set in train a process which not only opened unlimited horizons to thousands of young Shetlanders but helped to break down the very class barriers so openly and crassly proclaimed by its first headmaster. But Anderson must have wondered, in the school's early years, if he had seriously over-estimated Shetland's educational needs, especially at the senior level. In fact, before his death in 1868, he was so bitterly disappointed at what he regarded as a failure of his aspirations, that he contemplated disposing of the building.

Elementary Department

The first recorded visit to the Institute by an HMI on 28th June, 1870[12] indicates that the elementary part of the School was already receiving government grants. From 1840 the Committee of Council on Education gave limited grants to assist with buildings and acquisition of teaching aids, such as blackboards. In 1870 the AEI, with an average attendance of 48, received £7.10/-. In the same year Lerwick Episcopalian School, associated with St Magnus Church, received £60.10/- for 85 pupils; and Lerwick Parochial School £79 for 127 pupils.

The small average attendance of pupils at the elementary department, due largely to poor attendance, is remarkable considering the large numbers of children of school age in Lerwick. A census in 1873[13] revealed that there were 693 children of school age in the area but, excluding the AEI, accommodation for only 209. The AEI headmaster, Robert Whiteford, informed Lerwick School Board in 1873[14] that he could provide elementary education for 200 children. The board communicated with the trustees in London regarding transferring the entire school, with endowment, to the board. The response is not recorded but it presumably took the line advanced subsequently by the principal Trustee, Captain George Bain, when giving evidence to the Endowed Schools (Scotland) Commission of 1874. There he opposed the transfer of the endowment to Lerwick School Board on the grounds that the founder's aim had been to promote the education and intellectual improvement of children and adult inhabitants of the whole of Shetland, not just one part. Bain's argument was sound in respect of the Upper School but, at the same time, he was overlooking the fact that Anderson's initial inspiration to help education in Shetland was directed towards the poor children of Lerwick.

Compulsory attendance resulted in substantially increased rolls with 100 on the roll in 1874 and 182 present for the HMI's examination in 1876.

The Log Book from 1868 through the early years of the Elementary School complains regularly of poor attendance and indiscipline. In the days before compulsory education the onus was very much on parents to send their children to school but Lerwick parents seemed reluctant to prod the unwilling. In 1868 there is a rueful entry in the log: "Find that being severe with the children here will not do as their parents have little or no command over them and unless they are willing to go to school they never think of forcing them." Some pupils appear to have been rowdy and ill-behaved, with evidence of uncouth behaviour. A boy was punished for chewing tobacco in class and spitting on the floor. In 1878 there is reference to Standard 3 being "in a state of anarchy" and that the headmaster had to quell mischievous boys. Up Helly Aa — "that heathenish saturnalia" as one headmaster described it — was regarded as a baneful influence having "a marked immoral tendency on the children", resulting in "noisy, self-willed, quarrelsome behaviour, disinclination to work, general indifference and apathy", with "swearing amongst youngest children". All in all, it was reckoned that the festival set the school work back by six weeks. For those who are prone to look back nostalgically on "the good old days" it would be salutary to note how part of today's Up Helly Aa is integrated into the school curriculum.

Frequent changes of staff were commented on in the HMI's report for 1871. For example, one teacher had left in December, 1870 and his successor had remained a mere four months. The inspector considered the school was suffering considerably from these changes. Unfortunately, this unsettling trend continued with six changes of senior master between 1871 and 1881.

An Inspector's criticism for 1877 highlights the casual attitude of the time to sanitary arrangements. His report ordered that separate toilets for the sexes had to be provided, adding that "the only one in existence is in a mess of filth which no decent boy will use." No concern was expressed on behalf of the girls, but it is astonishing to think that a fine new school could have been built containing accommodation for 200 elementary pupils, and with only one toilet. Ventilation was also a problem in the upper classrooms with their low ceilings amd poor air circulation. One school board member commented that "the atmosphere sickened him in a couple of minutes".[15] An outbreak of typhoid was blamed on the conditions at the Institute.

After the 1872 Act the elementary department followed the regulations of the Scotch Education Code in order to qualify for the various government grants. The curriculum comprised reading, arithmetic, grammar, geography, Bible history, drawing, singing, and needlework but in the early years of the school pupils did not follow specified courses, parents being allowed to select classes at any stage. This freedom of choice was regarded by Robert Whiteford, Headmaster in 1874, as an obstacle to the efficient running of the school.[16]

Apart from the annual inspection by an HMI it was the custom for a public examination to take place at the close of the session, where scholars were orally examined in front of an invited audience. Parents attended, as well as local dignatories such as the Sheriff, parish minister, and local business men, a representative of whom sometimes participated in the examination process. The occasion included a prizegiving.

Under School Board Control

The national review of education endowments, which heard evidence for the AEI in 1874 resulted in the Education Endowments (Scotland) Act of 1882. An executive commission then reviewed the various endowments in Scotland, the principal objects being the better distribution of endowed funds throughout the country, and standardisation, as far as possible, of administration of the various schemes. They met Captain Bain, representing the Anderson trustees, on 18th February, 1885, who reported that the rolls for the junior and senior departments were respectively — 107 and 45. When he went on to say that the school, with accommodation for 500, had one of the finest buildings in the north of Scotland, the Chairman, Lord Balfour of Burleigh, as has already been mentioned, commented: "I'm afraid your building is very much of the nature of a white elephant," to which Captain Bain replied: "I'm afraid so."

The main recommendations for the Anderson Endowment emerged in 1888.[17] In future its administration should be vested in a more representative governing body to be called "The Governors of the Anderson Education Trust" comprising two members elected by the Zetland Commissioners of Supply; one appointed by the Sheriff of the Counties of Orkney and Zetland; one elected by the Commissioners of Police of Burgh of Lerwick; one elected from the school board of Lerwick and Gulberwick; and two appointed by the existing trustees to hold office for life. The buildings were to be transferred to the Lerwick and Gulberwick School Board who were to receive from the governors the free annual income from the capital sum of £6666.13.4 — approx. £200 — and who were to be responsible for maintaining and keeping the buildings in good repair. The split nature of the school was to continue. The head of the higher department was to be a graduate, with a salary not less than £150 and the right to occupy the teacher's house. He could also be the head of the whole school if, in consultation with the governors, the school board made an appropriate addition to his salary. The school board was also instructed to give free education to up to ten needy children. Governors were empowered to establish bursaries of £20-£25.

The school board reluctantly assumed control of the AEI on 1 May, 1889. They were concerned at the dilapidated state of the building, which they estimated would require £1000 of repairs. Such expenditure, they felt, would be contrary to the interests of the "poorer classes" in that they would be spending a large sum of money on a building where very high fees would exclude many poor children. The board recommended to the Scotch Education Department that the AEI should continue to be regarded as an "Elementary School with a Higher Department". This was sanctioned by the department on 14th May, 1889 and the school remained so until 1893 when the higher department was transformed into a Higher Class Public School under the new Secondary Education Minute. It then became quite distinct from the rest of the school. The Lower School catered for Standards I to V and the Higher for Standards VI to X. Alex. McDonald Reid was appointed headmaster of the whole school, with Robert Millar second master in charge of the Lower School.

The newly integrated school could not have had a worse start. Despite a favourable report for the previous session, HMI Muir's Report for the session 1889-1890 was uncompromising in its condemnation. It began: "The condition of this large and important school is simply deplorable," then continues: "4th and 5th Standards make an utter breakdown in Standard work, nearly half of them failing in two or three subjects. The pass in the 6th Standard is very fair. Grammar and Recitation are so poor in 4th and 5th Standards that not even the Lower Grant for English can be recommended." Mr Muir was able to report the following year that "The school has made decided and surprising progress since last year."

In 1891 the government abolished school fees for all pupils under 14 but Lerwick School Board resolved to charge 9d. per quarter for coals and pens. The custom in Shetland for children in rural areas to bring a peat as their contribution to the heating of the school, continued for a short while then died out.

Secondary Department

An educational return for 1874[18] provides a glimpse of the secondary curriculum of this time. The highest English class not only read Gray's Odes but, in the analytical manner of the period, parsed, analysed, and explained them. Other English textbooks used were Dalgleish's *Grammar, Analysis and Composition,* and Graham's *Etymology.* The highest Latin classes read Livy; and one Mathematics class were doing the Fifth Book of Euclid, and quadratic equations. The highest French class read *Telemaque* and used Schneider's Grammar, while the highest German class read Tiark's *Progressive Reader* together with Tiark's *Grammar.* Greek, music and drawing were also taught.

John Allardice (1876-1883)

The early years of the Institute were not marked with any great academic achievement. From 1871-1876 only two pupils had proceeded to university but the arrival in 1876 of John Allardice as headmaster galvanised the school into intense scholastic activity. A young man of 32, he came with a distinguished university record and glowing testimonials. He was not long in putting his stamp on the school. In the Orkney and Shetland Examinations Institute pupils had three first places in three years, and in the Society for the Propagation of Christian Knowledge annual examinations for the Highlands and Islands gained four top bursaries. In the 1880 Aberdeen University local examinations four Institute pupils obtained top prizes, with higher average marks than any other school in the North-east. In 1881, 15 AEI pupils entered for Glasgow University examinations, obtaining first places in English literature, political economy, Latin, and the first three places in logic. James J. Haldane Burgess, later to make a name for himself as a writer and scholar, came first out of 607 candidates and 47 marks ahead of the second place candidate.

A Scottish educational journal of the time, *The Schoolmaster*, commenting on the Institute's achievements, quoted the school managers' statement in 1871: "It is hoped that under the provision of the new educational system... and with the liberal and wise co-operation of an intelligent school board, the Anderson Institute may speedily realise the far-seeing intention of its patriotic founder and become a sort of insular university."[19]

Allardice certainly produced pupils of high academic calibre but not at the expense of the less gifted. Parents of Institute pupils, in a written tribute on his departure from Lerwick, testified that "you gave your anxious care equally to all the scholars with the result that your school throughout is a model of excellence."[20]

It is hard to believe that in 1881 Allardice, at the helm of a highly successful school in every respect, was summarily dismissed. Captain George Bain, principal trustee of the Anderson Endowment, made a lengthy visit of three months to the school in the summer of 1881. He and his wife stayed in the schoolhouse as the guests of the Allardice family and it would appear that the prolonged stay and Bain's interference in the running of the school led to strained relationships. On 12th October Allardice received a letter from his guest peremptorily dismissing him.[21] No reasons were given and the letter suggested that "it shall appear to the public as a voluntary act on your part."

Bain was exercising in the crudest possible manner his right as principal trustee to dismiss the headmaster of the Anderson Institute. When he appointed Allardice in August, 1876, the only terms of the engagement were 12 months notice by either party. He undertook the action of dismissal without even consulting the local management committee. Allardice, with no means of appeal and, despite having the whole-hearted support of the parents, left in 1883, his immediate career in ruins. He emigrated to New Zealand where he soon obtained a post as headmaster.

Between the 1872 Act and the Education (Scotland) Act of 1908 which gave them the right of appeal against dismissal, teachers were vulnerable to the whims of individuals such as Captain Bain. School boards, which at least had been elected by the community, were also guilty of unjust dismissals. One such was another headmaster of the Anderson Institute, Robert Young, who was dismissed by Lerwick School Board in 1899. His case has been described in the previous chapter.

National Development of Secondary Education

Virtually the entire emphasis of the 1872 Act was on elementary education, leaving secondary schools to exist on their own resources, consisting mainly of fees and endowments. The thinking behind the Scottish Act derived, to a great extent, from similar English legislation of 1870 which, based as it was on the elitist educational system there, saw secondary education traditionally supported by lavish endowments and not really in need of state aid. Eton, for example, had greater resources through endowments than the four Scottish universities and all the burgh secondary schools put together.[22]

The Scottish Act left secondary education in a confused state. Elementary schools, following in the old parochial tradition, were enjoined to take their brighter pupils into the higher levels of specific subjects, such as English literature, history, geography, etc, but teachers in the smaller schools found it extremely difficult to do justice to both junior classes and seniors involved in "Specifics". The obvious route was for separation of elementary and secondary to allow the necessary specialisation for older pupils.

This pattern was eventually mapped out by the Scottish Education Department under the guidance of Henry Craik, Permanent Secretary. Between 1885 and 1904 he introduced policies which set the secondary school firmly on its distinctive course, at the same time creating a ladder of opportunity for able children from elementary, through secondary, to university. In 1886 he introduced inspection of secondary schools resulting in more up-to-date and uniform curricula. He established in 1888 the Leaving Certificate giving schools a nationally recognised standard at which to aim, and in 1891 the Merit Certificate to mark the able pupils' completion of the elementary course. Then in 1892 he was instrumental in formulating a Bill which Parliament passed, giving grant aid to all secondary schools.

Anderson Institute — Secondary School for Shetland

The 1892 Act recommended that in each Scottish county a Secondary Education Committee be formed to administer government grants. Their first meeting took place on 2nd February, 1893, with Mr Hay Shennan, Sheriff-Substitute, as chairman and seven other members representing school boards, Town Council, and church.[23] They decided that the Anderson Institute higher department be made a separate higher class school for the whole of Shetland. The Government had allocated a secondary school grant of £60,000 to Scotland, Shetland's portion being £427.18.5. The Committee decided that, for the Institute to operate successfully and fairly as Shetland's sole secondary school, country pupils would require bursaries, and agreed that at least 10 bursaries between £10 and £15 be available, plus £5 to Lerwick pupils to encourage their parents to put them on "beyond the Standards". At a subsequent meeting the Committee received 72 applications for bursaries and decided to award them by competition.

These bursaries, although small, were of inestimable value in inducing rural parents to send children to the Institute. In 1900 there were 14 bursars from country districts; in 1907 — 23; 1908 — 38; in 1909 — 74. They came from all parts of Shetland. In 1910, 12 came from the North Isles; eight North Mainland; eight Westside; 10 Central districts; and 13 South Mainland.[24] In 1904 one of the 13 bursars was Andrew T. Cluness from Unst, a future Rector of the Institute. His father, a fisherman, would have been quite unable to support him in Lerwick for that period but for the bursary. The local bursaries, awarded for three years, left pupils who were anxious to continue towards a Higher Leaving Certificate stranded at the end of their third year and future progress towards university or college depended on their being awarded an Anderson Bursary or winning bursaries in the annual examination conducted by the Orkney and Shetland Association and the Highlands and Islands Educational Trust. Thereafter ambitious pupils had to enter the highly competitive national arena for University Bursary awards.

The transition of Lerwick pupils from the elementary to the secondary department of the Institute was relatively smooth. For their first three years they had been taught in the South Wing in Standards 4, 5 & 6; then those who were contemplating advanced studies moved, via the ex-sixth, to the Upper School in the North Wing. The academic transition may have been smooth but the physical change was dramatic. As already recounted, a pupil in the closing years of the century recalls the move: "The Upper School was attained rather than reached by way of the ex-sixth and no law of Medes and Persians operated more rigidly than that which separated Upper from Lower Schools. No one from Lower School dared walk up by the wall path, and no desecrating foot dare pass above the sacred terrace."[25]

The roll of the Upper School was heavily weighted towards the first three years. In 1904 there were about 60 pupils in the school with 47 in Class 1[26]. Pupils from country schools coming to the Institute tended to be older than their Lerwick contemporaries, and many reached the leaving age of 14 at the end of their first year. Rural schools were inclined to hold their senior pupils a year or so longer to enhance the school's performance in the annual inspection and thus increase the government grant. The introduction in 1893 of bursaries had encouraged more pupils from working-class homes to enter the Institute but most of these left by Class 3 for jobs in chemist shops, banks, post-office, civil service, and business.[27]

A full secondary education leading to a university course was a prospect which very few young Shetlanders could contemplate. In 1911, of 1,020 pupils aged 12 and 13, a mere four per cent attended the Institute. Apart from the few who obtained bursaries, the bulk of the population were too poor to consider the expense necessary in sending a child to Lerwick for five years. The London Trustees saw the school as failing to achieve the founder's ambitions and in 1903 one of them, Arthur Anderson Johnston, proposed to the school board that the Institute be sold and the funds devoted to the Widows' Fund.[28]

Although there was a strong desire in Shetland for education this was focussed almost entirely on the elementary stages and a good grounding in the 3Rs. Boys' ambitions were often directed towards the much-coveted skipper's ticket, and parochial and board schools produced many masters in the Merchant Marine. There was little or no tradition in Shetland of attending the Institute. The cost of "digs" in Lerwick and the outlay on text-books were beyond the purse of the crofter-fisherman. Even with the introduction in 1893 of £15 bursaries very few country pupils took the road to the Institute. The few who did were often responding to encouragement from their teacher who also tried to persuade their parents to make the financial sacrifice in the interest of "getting on".

REFERENCES

1 Shetland Advertiser, 18/8/1862
2 Ibid. 24/11/1862
3 Ibid. 27/10/1862
4 Ibid.

5 Statistics relative to Schools in Scotland collected by the Registrars of Births, Deaths, and Marriages, 1865, SRO
6 Centenary Booklet of the Anderson Educational Institute, 1962, article by Jennie J. Smith
7 Shetland Advertiser, 23/3/1862
8 Endowed Schools (Scotland) Commission, 1874, SRO
9 Shetland Advertiser, 8/12/1862
10 Ibid. 16/3/1863
11 SA, AD 22/7/23, Procurator-Fiscal Precognitions
12 A.E.I. Log-book, 1868-1889, SA
13 Lerwick School Board Minutes, 22/4/1873, SA
14 Ibid. 20/5/1873, SA
15 Shetland News, 13/2/1897
16 Return to Endowed Schools (Scotland) Commission, 1874
17 Minutes Anderson Educational Trust 1888-1932, SA, CO5/4/1
18 Evidence to Endowed Schools (Scotland) Commission, 1874, National Library of Scotland
19 Laurence, J.B., Letter to Shetland Times, 25/7/1896
20 SA, Testimonial to John Allardice
21 SA, SC12/6/1881/57
22 Osborne, G.S., Scottish and English Schools, London, 1966, p.18
23 Minutes, Secondary Education Committee, 1893-1894, SA, CO § 5/9/1
24 Institute Log-book, SA
25 1862-1962, Anderson Educational Institute, Jennie J. Smith, p. 35
26 Ibid. Andrew T. Cluness, p39
27 Ibid. pp 42-43
28 Minutes of Lerwick School Board, July, 1903, SA

Chapter 15
Some Remarkable Teachers

WHATEVER THE pattern of education produced by legislators, however sophisticated the educational aids in the classroom, the process of education depends ultimately on the teacher. In 18th and 19th century Shetland, with its widely scattered population and limited resources, the local teacher could often make a profound impression well beyond the door of his very basic classroom. These are some examples but there were many others who, through work and example, influenced generations of bairns and folk whose lives they touched.

Robert Thomson, Society teacher in Fair Isle from 1774-1780, was described by his parish minister as a man of many talents. He had built a small sloop "which goes to the fishing and also to other parts of the islands. He is now a farmer and a mariner, an excellent cooper, a wright, a mason, without ever having been an apprentice in any of these trades. His sloop was built from the keel and completely rigged by him."[1]

James Stout, teacher of the Wart School, Reawick in the 1840s and 50s, taught personal and social development over a century before it became a curricular innovation in secondary schools of the 1980s. A former pupil recalls James in his school: "Mr Stout is there before the scholars assemble; as they arrive, he addresses one and another, enquiring after his health and that of the family to which he belongs, just as if the teacher and scholar had been friends and equals. These questions properly answered, Mr Stout says, 'So you're a fine fellow,' which closes the conversation.

"In the meantime, the schoolroom is being put in order for the work of the day — each book, slate, and copy, being placed on the table where the owner sits whether present or not, so that, as each later one comes, he has only to take his seat quietly.

"These duties done, the school commences with a short devotional exercise — then reading, beginning with the Bible class, on which a few questions are put by the teacher, so as to give interest to, and fix the lesson on their minds — these questions, sometimes plain and obvious, sometimes odd and out of the way, but always tending to increase the knowledge of the scholar, and keep him cheerful. Then spelling, not by giving each a word, but by giving the class a sentence, each naming the letter which falls to him, he that names the last letter of the word pronounces it, and he that names the last letter of the sentence pronounces the whole. The effect of this system was extraordinary proficiency in spelling. Then follow the other branches, until each has had a share of attention; but all short.

"Again a class is called out into the centre of the room, so as to be seen by all, to get a lesson on positions, how to stand, walk and carry their heads and arms, in short, general deportment, accompanied with remark and anecdote to the delight of all. Then one is sent outside to knock at the door as a stranger, while another is appointed to say 'Come in' — both the knock and the invitation to be properly done, the 'stranger' then comes in with a 'Good morning' and a polite bow to the master and school. Should any part be stiff or awkwardly performed, the teacher goes through the whole before the class, and next sends one of his older scholars who can do it well.

"Then comes a lesson in music, begun with the scale, and ended with some choice piece, Mr Stout leading with violin and voice. Then the school is out for a little, after which the more important lessons are gone over again; the whole closed with prayer, and the school dismissed with a song. The above is a bare outline of one day in the school: but no two days were exactly alike, so that no part of the varied exercises ever became stale or uninteresting.[2]"

Another of his former pupils writes: "There was no fixed routine... and no tawse — the great symbol of authority. Mr Stout's object was not to teach the dry abstract lesson within as short a time as possible. His object was to form the character of the future man and woman, intellectually, morally and socially. In doing this, he was content to wait on the dullest, filling up the school hours with a variety of exercises and enlivening these by questions, remark and anecdote in such a way that his school was a happy home to all, instead of a "sore bondage".[3]

And yet another: "Dear old friend, with all your foibles you made the little circle in which you lived better, because you had lived there. It is well you passed before the new order of things made you impossible, and no one better for the changes."[4]

James Stout was obviously a natural teacher with a flair in presentation which enabled him to escape from the tedium of the 3Rs slog. A talented musician, he composed over 100 psalm tunes as well as a number of fiddle tunes, and conducted singing classes throughout Shetland.

When Arthur Anderson heard in the late 1840s of the continued lack of educational provision in Skerries he undertook to build a school and schoolhouse and provide a salary for a teacher. The teacher selected to take up this post could not have been better chosen. **William Peterson**, a native of Lerwick and a slater by trade, had been conducting an

Independent Sabbath School in the town and his qualities had come to the attention of the Bressay minister who recommended him for the post. He proved to be not only a gifted and dedicated teacher but a source of great strength to the island community. His parish minister writes of him: "He was one of the best men I have ever met. He was like those men of whom we read who live and labour not to amass wealth or acquire fame, but for the sake of doing good… In this remote locality he lived thirty years. This space of time was one continued round of labour for the welfare of the community over whom he presided. He taught his scholars during the week with the greatest diligence. He was patient, kindly, and earnest in imparting instruction; in short one of those who have been called heaven-born teachers. He was able to keep order without harshness or severity. On Sabbath day he preached twice in a most impressive manner, with a natural eloquence and persuasiveness which charmed and edified his hearers. He also taught a Sabbath School which old and young attended. As it was part of my duty to examine the Sabbath School, I had the opportunity of seeing the tact which he possessed in asking questions, and the kind and genial way in which he managed his school. He was well acquainted with the Scriptures, and was quite original in the illustration which he employed when imparting instruction… Most of the inhabitants had passed through his hands as pupils. Instructing their children was thus rendered comparatively easy. He had great difficulty, in beginning his work as a teacher, in enforcing habits of cleanliness… When such instances were only too apparent, and there was thus danger of others being contaminated, Mr Peterson sent them home, with instructions not to return until their clothes were washed. The mothers were in great wrath at this treatment. But it occurred to him that if such cases of temporary dismissal were accompanied with a present of soap this might mollify the resentment of parents, and be an effectual remedy for the evil. And it was so. In due course the children came to the school with clothes and person clean and neat. The reformation extended not only to the children, but to those of riper age."[5]

William Peterson, for 30 years at school and church exercised a firm but kindly influence on Skerries

In 1858 **Robert Jamieson** returned as Society teacher to his old school at Cruisdale, Sandness, imbued with the desire to bring the very best possible educational opportunities to the community. He was immediately confronted with a major problem. The school, built as a croft-house in 1790, was extremely dilapidated with the roof leaking so badly that rain stood in puddles on the floor.

Despite a disability from early youth which left him lame and in need of a crutch while walking, Robert Jamieson was a man of great energy and determination. He knew that the local people just did not have the means to contribute to a new building and that the heritors had no responsibility for the Society school. He decided that the only way forward was for him to try and raise the money by appeal through the national press.

He was already a regular correspondent to the *Scotsman*, contributing articles on Shetland, its Norse history, lore and language. He now proceeded to write hundreds of letters to the national press and people of influence. So successful were his appeals that £500 was raised within a few years, sufficient to build a new school and schoolhouse to his own specifications and later regarded as complying with the new Government regulations under the Education Act of 1872.

Dr R. T. C. Scott, RN, of the landed family of Scotts of Melby, gave an acre of land for the school and schoolhouse. One of the principal contributors was a successful merchant whose business had flourished in Madras. He stipulated that the school be named a "Madras" School, and on its completion in 1870 it was officially named "Sandness Madras School" and remained so until Robert Jamieson's death in 1899.

The school at Cruisdale was very much a family concern. Each of four sons and one daughter served in turn as pupil teachers, while receiving advanced instruction, including French and Latin, from their father. All four boys went straight to university from Cruisdale; all had distinguished careers — Frank as lecturer in classics at Edinburgh University and then Senior Chief Inspector of Schools, John as professor of anatomy at Edinburgh University, Edward as lecturer in anatomy at Edinburgh University, and James as a distinguished physician in New Zealand. Christina Jamieson remained in Shetland where she was noted for her scholarly articles on Shetland history and tradition. Mrs Jamieson taught the girls singing and sewing.

Jamieson's personal library, augmented by review copies of books which had accumulated in the *Scotsman* office and sent to Sandness by the editor, were available to pupils and parents. Also available were copies of the *llustrated London News, The Graphic, Punch,* together with the London *Times* and *Scotsman*. The teacher and his family did not live a life apart from the community. Friendships formed at school were continued into later life with regular correspondence between schoolhouse and seamen in the Merchant Navy or girls south in domestic service. Mrs Jamieson was described by one of her sons as being "far more to the people than the laird's lady or the minister's wife, for she was of themselves — *prima inter pares*."[6] Robert Jamieson had, from an unpromising start, created not only a fine new school but an example of community education at its best.

A visitor to Foula in 1867 found another talented man — **James Cheyne**, Society teacher, whom he described as "A very versatile genius indeed. He reads a sermon every Sabbath in the kirk; teaches the school through the week; is agent for the Poor Law Board, session clerk, and registrar. He makes first-rate shoes and splendid coats, having originally been a tailor by profession. He built his boat, he coopers, shoots, fishes, farms his croft, and is a most successful sheep-farmer; for a hardy breed of hungry sheep he brought once from Fair Isle have multiplied very rapidly, to the alarm of the natives, who are afraid lest they destroy the pasture on the 'scathold'".[7]

William T. Laurence was transferred as Society teacher from Vatchley, Dunrossness to Fair Isle in 1875. In 1878 he became the first board teacher on the Isle. During his 12 years there as teacher/catechist he was a vigorous campaigner for better communications between Fair Isle and the outside world, and also life-saving facilities for shipwrecked seamen. Many ships had come to grief on the savage coast-line of Fair Isle but there was no lighthouse, no lifeboat, no life-saving apparatus.

Laurence wrote regularly to the *Scotsman* presenting Fair Isle's case for improved life-saving services. In 1875 he petitioned the Prime Minister, Benjamin Disraeli and three years later the government responded with a lifeboat to be based on the isle — the first in Shetland.

Laurence thoroughly immersed himself in the life of the community. A visiting minister wrote: "The catechist and schoolmaster appointed by the Established Church is just the man for his post — intelligent, kindly, earnest. He is regarded with great affection by the islanders, and well may he be, for he has shut himself up to a life for which few would be qualified, and the isolation of which fewer still would bear. He administers medicine to the sick, teaches the children, conducts religious services, gives counsel to the perplexed, as J.P. settles any petty cases that might come before him; and, being an experienced seaman and officer in the merchant service, he is qualified to train any young men who may aspire to a position superior to that of fisherman or A.B. He has lately been the means of securing a fortnightly mail for the island, wind and weather permitting; more recently he has secured a lifeboat, cliff-ladders, and other life-saving apparatus, and he hopes that ere long a lighthouse will fling its friendly cheer across the dark and troubled water of these dangerous seas."[8]

Within a relatively brief period Laurence had been instrumental in acquiring for Fair Isle an impressive range of lifesaving facilities and improved communications. Sadly, the island lifeboat he had helped to procure was to carry him to Lerwick where he died of blood-poisoning in September, 1887.

The SSPCK, for over two centuries, made an enormous contribution to education in Shetland. Their charter allowed them to supply teachers' salaries and school textbooks but the local community had to provide the school buildings.

REFERENCES

1 Diary of Rev. John Mill, Scottish History Society, Edinburgh, 1899
2 Shetland Advertiser, 3/3/1862, Shetland County Library
3 Scottish Congregational Magazine, May 1862
4 Shetland News, article by Captain John Johnson, in 'Shetland Captains' series.
5 Russell, Rev John, "Three Years in Shetland", Alexander Gardner, 1887
6 Jamieson, Dr James P. S., letter to author, 17/6/1960
7 Reid, John T., "Art Rambles in Shetland", Edmondston & Douglas, Edinburgh, 1869
8 Shetland News, 30/6/1953

Chapter 16

The Twentieth Century

Lerwick — Pressure on Accommodation

AS THE century drew to a close, Lerwick's rapidly rising population put more and more pressure on school accommodation. The old parochial school building was sold to the Baptist Church in 1865 and replaced with a new building to become known as First Lerwick Public School — and in more recent times "The Old Infant School". Increased numbers after the 1872 Act led to the board building an infant school in Prince Alfred Street — presently housing the Shetland Times Printing Works. Two rooms in the south wing of the Institute, capable of accommodating 200, were used by Standards 4, 5 and 6. St Magnus Episcopal schoolroom, built in 1868, took about 80. It was open to children of all denominations, but with a priority for Episcopalians. Despite the variety of buildings available, school accommodation was still inadequate. The Rechabite Hall and basement of the Baptist Church, had to be brought into use.

A census in 1897[1] revealed that there were 1,308 children under 14 in the district with 473 under five years of age, leaving 835 of school age. Of these, 25 had left school and 36 were unfit to attend, which gave a total of 774 at school. These were allocated as follows:

Institute, Higher Dept.	—	64
Lower Dept.	—	190
Central Public School	—	160
Infant Public School	—	253
St Magnus School	—	80
Gulberwick Pub. School	—	27
		774

A contributory cause of the increasing numbers was that the children previously educated privately in Lerwick were now choosing free education at board schools. In 1890, 85 children attended private schools: in 1894 there were 51.[2]

Obviously more accommodation was urgently required. Just how this was to be done was the source of an extended and contentious debate in the school board. This coincided with the dispute over the dismissal of

Robert Young, Institute Rector, and made board meetings at the time lively, often acrimonious occasions. The more conservative members — their minds fixed on local rates — argued for extensions to existing buildings but the progressively minded — led by the chairman, A. A. Porteous — stressed the need to get away from the old solution of patchwork building and to build new for the foreseeable future. A new building, Porteous argued, would not only provide more space but would have better ventilation and lighting, a hall for physical exercise, and rooms for cookery, laundrywork, and technical subjects. A swimming bath was even suggested. Options discussed included selling the Institute and the First Lerwick Public School. It was claimed that the Institute was too far away from the core of the expanding town and that this affected attendance, particularly in bad weather. This brought a sharp reminder from the editor of the *News* of Lerwick's churlish attitude to Arthur Anderson's initial proposals for a school in Lerwick. The editor reminded his readers that Anderson had wanted the very site presently occupied by the First Lerwick Public School but influential Lerwegians had blocked his approaches to the Feuars and Heritors who owned the site.[3]

Finally, at a meeting in October, 1900, the board decided to build a school with accommodation for 900 including areas for practical subjects. Plans had been prepared by John M. Aitken, a local contractor with a successful record in erecting public buildings throughout Shetland. With Aitken as principal contractor, work began in the spring of 1901 and was completed in 18 months at a cost of £6550.14.5. Lerwick Central School was officially opened on 27th September, 1902 by Sir Henry Craik, Secretary of the Scottish Education Department. Pupils from the Institute's Elementary Department then moved down to the new school, leaving the Institute solely secondary. In 1904 the average attendance at the Central was 667.

A former pupil of the Central recalls his first day in the new school:[4] "What remains in the memory is the smell of new paint and varnish; the dual desks were an innovation. Bags of buns and cakes were handed out to us, and we were introduced to an entirely new and exotic fruit, the banana, which we all saw and tasted for the first time... Mr W. M. Wightman was the first headmaster."

In 1901 the Education (Scotland) Act raised the school leaving age to 14 and at the same time abolished the widespread practice of obtaining exemption for pupils over 10 years of age who had satisfied the inspector of their competence in the 3Rs. This meant a significant increase in the 12-14 age group and to cater for this group supplementary courses containing practical, vocational elements were introduced. At the age of

12 pupils sat the qualifying examination which determined whether they proceed to a supplementary course or a secondary course at the Institute. In the early years of the century the term "primary" came to be used instead of "elementary" implying that the early years of a child's education was merely the first of two stages.

In 1904 the new Lerwick Central School included book-keeping, commercial correspondence, and woodwork in its supplementary curriculum. An entry in the log-book for 1909 indicates the resources problem involved in introducing practical subjects: "A typewriter and sewing machine have been introduced into the school. Lessons in typewriting are given to two pupils at a time from 8.45-9 and 1.45-2 on Monday, Wednesday and Friday, and from 1.45-2 on Thursday. Pupils and staff were obviously prepared to work outside normal school hours to introduce these new subjects. Under W. Robertson Durham, headmaster from 1906 to 1936, the Central School went on from these tentative beginnings to establish a range of commercial, technical and homecraft courses, while the Institute concentrated on purely academic courses. The next 30 years saw the steady growth under George W. Blance of the Central School towards a roll of almost 1000.

Anderson Institute — A Solely Secondary School

Joseph Kirton

In 1902 the Elementary pupils at the Institute moved to the new Central. The Institute, now a purely secondary school, began to acquire a character of its own. Under the leadership of Joseph Kirton, a gritty little character from the north-east of Scotland, the school developed a happy blend of rigorous standards and informality. Small in numbers there was a family atmosphere about the place. A pupil from 1915-1922[5] has left a vivid portrait of Kirton. "No one seeing a back view of Joseph Kirton's diminutive but jaunty figure, clad in a shabby overcoat, narrow baggy trousers fitting but ill his short and bandy legs, and a bowler hat crammed down over his ears, would pick him out as an outstanding sample of the human race. But let him turn round and show that direct and commanding look, those frosty blue eyes and that determined small chin formally decorated with a pointed ginger beard, and nothing could be calculated to wipe off more quickly the silly grin on the face of the beholder. Here, it was obvious, was no ordinary mortal.

"… From him I not only learned Latin and Greek, and some appreciation of the beauty and nobility of classic literature, but, more importantly, how to use the mind. 'What d'you think I'm teaching you Latin for?' he would bark in exasperation. 'I'm not just teaching you to say *mensa, mensae, mensae, mensam*; I'm teaching you to think, boy, I'm teaching you to think!'"

The early years of the century saw the school moving in a slow, sometimes makeshift fashion, towards a modern curriculum. With the introduction of experimental science, taken initially by an English master in a tiny room, equipment had to be provided from a sparse budget. Pupils became involved: "... we constructed much of our own equipment, litre boxes of cardboard, gummed and dipped in paraffin-wax, slide rules of cardboard, thermometers; there was only one weighing machine and we made for it extra sets of weights... A heavy ball of iron was suspended from one of the massive cross-beams in the Hall and allowed to swing freely illustrating Foucault's Pendulum Experiment to demonstrate the diurnal rotation of the earth on its axis."[6]

The Inspector was not impressed. "Experimental Science", he reported in 1907, "was taught in conditions which render efficient work well-nigh impossible. There are two labs far apart from each other, both very inconvenient, unsuitably furnished and poorly equipped. In view of these serious disadvantages the pupils acquitted themselves with considerable credit under examination."

In 1910 shorthand and typewriting was introduced for junior classes but with only one typewriter available, "hands on" experience must have been limited.

The Leaving Certificate, instituted in 1888, was originally awarded on a single subject basis but this came under severe criticism as being contrary to the Scottish tradition of a broad-based education. The department responded by introducing in 1902 the Group Certificate to run in parallel for a time with the single subject award. It was designed for pupils who had completed five years of secondary education and consisted of four subjects, with English and mathematics compulsory. The Intermediate Certificate, introduced at the same time, was intended for pupils who had studied a two year advanced course. The Institute approached the Group Certificate cautiously, with one presentation in 1907, five in 1908 and four in 1909.[7]

Andrew T. Cluness

In 1924 Joseph Kirton was succeeded by Andrew T. Cluness, former pupil and veteran of the Great War, emerging from that holocaust with the M.M. and Bar. Under his leadership the Institute matured into a school with a reputation for scholastic attainment in a happy environment. Its ethos is captured by a former pupil: "... as a Shetlander, no advantage, either material or cultural, which could have been gained only at schools outwith the Islands, could have compensated for the loss of identity I would have sustained had I never been a pupil at the grey school which looks down on Bressa Soond and never come under the influence of its greatest Rector."[8]

The first 37 years of the school's history had seen seven headmasters come and go, some remaining for only a few years. With the arrival of Joseph Kirton in 1899 a period of greater stability began. For the next 71 years the school had three headmasters: Joseph Kirton (1899-1924); Andrew T. Cluness (1924-1953) and William Rhind (1953-1970).

The Long Plateau — 1900-1960

Many administrative changes altered the face of education from 1872 onwards but classroom life remained remarkably unchanged until halfway through the new century. In 1979 Samuel Polson, headmaster of Baltasound Junior High School, Unst, on the occasion of the school's centenary celebrations, recalled his predecessor, David J. White, moving one hundred years previously from the old parochial school buildings to the new board school, and said: "If Mr White had returned in 1946 he could have resumed without much difficulty. Education was without frills — the three Rs and little else."[9]

When set against the deluge of changes which have beset schools since 1966 the first half of the century was certainly a period of unbroken curricular stability.

Curriculum

The primary curriculum continued according to the strict letter of the Scotch Code as promulgated by the Department. In 1902 Haroldswick Public School Class III Junior were taught: reading, writing and dictation; long multiplication and short division; physical drill; sewing (for girls); singing; Scottish kings and queens: repetition of Wordsworth's *Lucy Gray* (for four months); simple analysis, parsing of nouns, adjectives and pronouns; study of the daffodil and the spider; solids, liquids, gases, crystals.[10] A substantial and, in parts unappetising diet for a 10 year old and one that continued very much unchanged for the next half century.

Much excellent and conscientious work was done by teachers but the learning process was largely passive, a relentless topping up of little pitchers, with not a great deal of consideration for the less able. The curriculum was, to a great extent, divorced from the local scene. Geography lessons began with study of the globe, then moved to Scotland, England, and other European countries where capes, rivers, towns and products, were studied and memorised. There was little or no attempt to move pupils' comprehension from the known to the unknown by taking as a starting-point the geographical aspects of their own surroundings in Shetland.

The great majority of primary teachers during the first half of the century were local women who had taken a course at Teachers' Training College in the south and returned to their native isles to carry out their career. They saw education as the gateway to opportunity and were imbued with the desire to help their pupils along that road. This they did with great diligence and dedication.

Side Schools

Shetland's geography and lack of roads at the close of the century meant that several pockets of population, including small populated islands, were without schools. Side schools were created, staffed by uncertificated teachers on low salaries of around £30 per annum. In 1920 there were altogether 83 schools in Shetland, 20 of them side schools. These were at Garth and Collafirth in Delting; Brettabister in Nesting; Tingon in Eshaness; Lochend in North Roe; Collafirth in Ollaberry; Gunnister in Sullom; East Burrafirth and West Burrafirth in Sandsting and Aithsting; Girlsta and Trondra in Tingwall; Pettister, South-the-Voe, Burrafirth, and Norwick in Unst; Dale in Walls; Gossabrough and Sellafirth in Yell; and the Isles of Uyea and Havera.

When the 18-year-old Annie Deyell went as teacher to the Isle of Havera at £30 per annum there was no school building available and for a time "The arrangement made for the teacher was that she should stay in one house a week for each child of school age and then move on to the next. The people were very kind and the children pleasant, but it was a very unsettled existence, with absolutely no privacy as I had to share bedrooms with my pupils. Later she acquired a house to herself but it was basic in the extreme. [It] consisted of the 'but' end which was used as the schoolroom, a sleeping closet with two built-in bunk beds, and a stair leading up to a loft. When school was over I swept the floor, moved the two big desks against the wall, and there was my living-room. I had a table and chair, my kist..., a wooden biscuit box with a lid for groceries, and another standing on its end with a shelf in the middle... Here I kept my few dishes and my bread and marge."[11] Annie wanted to become a qualified teacher and took lessons from a correspondence college to enable her to qualify for entrance to a teacher's training college. Her two rigorous years on the tiny island of Havera failed to blunt her enthusiasm and she eventually qualified.

Small island communities such as Havera, Papa, Oxna, Linga, Hildasay, and Uyea, did not survive long into the twentieth century and all fell victims to the blight of depopulation. As roads and communications improved, schools were gradually centralised until the 83 of 1920 were reduced to the 36 of 1996. And the process threatens to move on. The debate about the virtues of the small school as against the avowed efficiency and economy of the larger still rumbles on. The Dunrossness centralisation in 1969 when the schools at Bigton, Levenwick, Boddam, Quendale and Virkie were absorbed is set as an example of the success of the bigger school. But there are small single-teacher schools where children receive as rich an education.

Health

The biggest change in the concept of school education occurred early in the century with the recognition that education should not only develop mind and spirit but should be responsible for physical and social well-being. The poor physical condition of recruits for the Boer War had shocked Parliament and in 1908 an Act laid down that the larger school boards should provide for medical examination of pupils and subsequent treatment. Five years later a further Act made all boards responsible for the medical treatment of necessitous children. Two World Wars disrupted the full implementation of these acts but the Education Act of 1945 compelled all education authorities to provide medical inspection and appropriate treatment for school children.

In January, 1920 Shetland appointed Dr John Crawford as its first Medical Officer of Health and School Medical Officer. His early annual inspections revealed a reasonably healthy school population, personal cleanliness being the most controversial revelation. Almost 40 per cent had nits in their hair with 2.44 per cent verminous.[12] Subsequent inspections saw a steady improvement in these figures with none verminous in 1931 and 17.74 per cent with nits. Dr Crawford reported that in certain of the fishing communities typhoid fever was practically endemic but the shadow hanging over Shetland at that time was the threat of tuberculosis. Between 1920 and 1930 it was at epidemic proportions with 326 deaths. The school medical inspection of 1931 revealed 48 pupils suspected of having the disease. Its virulence can be gathered from the fact that 65 per cent of cases notified were dead within the year.

School Meals

Before the 1945 Act made the provision of milk at the mid-morning break and a hot mid-day meal obligatory for all authorities, Shetland children's only sustenance during the school day was a bannock or oatcake brought from home together with an occasional bottle of milk.

Many of these had to walk long distances, some well over two miles, existing for at least six hours on the bare minimum of food. When faced with the added handicaps of bad weather and poor roads it is not surprising that many parents kept their children home on bad winter days. In 1902, at 17 of the 63 schools the average attendance was less than 75 per cent. A few enterprising teachers organised hot soup for their pupils. In 1902 in Eshaness Miss Elizabeth McNicoll raised funds locally for plates and spoons then made and supplied soup at the mid-day break. Her successor did not keep up the practice but, a stickler for manners, insisted pupils said grace before eating the bannocks they had brought from home. His grace ran:

> Be present at our table, Lord,
> Be here and everywhere adored;
> Thy creatures bless and grant that we
> May feast in Paradise with thee.

The lady[13] who recalled this memory added wryly: "Paradise wis da ony wye dey micht faest for mony o wis hed naethin left ta aet efter da grace". Several had either consumed their bannocks before break-time or even during the grace.

Most schools from the 1920s served a hot drink, usually cocoa, at mid-day in the winter. Sometimes sandwiches were available for which pupils paid a penny per week. Lerwick Central, through its domestic science department, served hot soup and bread to necessitous children, identified as such by the school.

School boards, abolished in England in 1908, continued in Scotland for another 10 years but their parish basis was recognised as too fragmented to be efficient. The 1918 Education Act transferred responsibility for education in Shetland to a county-wide Education Authority to be elected by proportional representation and quite separate in operation from the County Council. To maintain local links with schools School Management Committees were formed comprising representatives from parents and teachers, with powers including enforcement of attendance, maintenance, and school cleaning.

Bursaries

The 1918 Act also empowered the new Authorities to award bursaries to able children proceeding to secondary schools and beyond to universities. To determine who should receive bursaries an entry examination known as the Control was instituted in 1920. Those receiving over 65 per cent were regarded as eligible for the Anderson Institute and Lerwick Central. The Central had just been created an

Intermediate School with provision for a Commercial Course. Bursaries were £24 per annum for country pupils and £7 for those from the town. Students at universities received £40 per annum.

These bursaries were important incentives to parents to send children for secondary and university education. Numbers at the Anderson Institute increased from 108 in 1920 to 144 in 1930. In 1939, 81 bursars were attending the Institute with 30 at the Central.

Control Examination

The annual Control Examination became an important event in the primary school year with results not only determining the future of their more able pupils but also the standing of the school in parents' eyes. Conscientious teachers found themselves irresistibly drawn into meticulous preparation for the examination and most pupils from 10 to 12 spent long hours on complicated arithmetical calculations, historical and geographical data, analysis of sentences, parsing, and writing of essays. The Control was a stiff test and those who passed certainly knew their basics. They were recognised as "academics" while those who either failed or did not attempt the examination were the non-academics. Lerwick Central developed a three year secondary course concentrating on practical subjects — shorthand & typewriting, book-keeping, navigation, woodwork — which together with English, mathematics, geography, history, French, science, gave pupils a wide-ranging choice.

Promotion Scheme

By 1947 it was felt that entrance examinations such as the Control were rather crude instruments to make the all-important assessment of a child's ability which would to a great extent affect his or her future. Research had been done on various methods of intelligence testing and this was to be the technique of the future for selection of pupils according to age, aptitude and ability. Each authority had to submit to the Scottish Education Department a Promotion Scheme based on a combination of intelligence and attainment tests. The Shetland Scheme consisted of two Verbal Reasoning Tests, Attainment Tests in English, arithmetic, and an essay, together with the class teacher's estimate of the pupil's ability, the headteacher's recommendation, and the parents' desire. This formidable battery of information was scrutinised by a local Promotion Board comprising 12 teachers and four members of the Education Committee. On the basis of their performance pupils were allocated to either Institute, Lerwick Central Secondary, or to rural secondaries. In 1950, 86 (27 per cent) were selected for the Institute,

105 (33 per cent) for Lerwick Central, and 127 (40 per cent) for rural junior secondaries.

The tests provided a reasonably accurate assessment of abilities but when a borderline decision had to be made on the basis of a single mark obtained from a battery of five tests, the validity of the whole operation is called into question. At the same time, however, the system allowed for parental appeals and these were given careful consideration by the Director of Education. The final decision was not inflexible and if, after a period at the selected school, a pupil was obviously in the wrong course arrangements were made for transfer. The Intelligence and Attainment Tests, based as they were on completion of a large number of questions within a given time, favoured the quick worker and counted against the more careful, methodical pupil. Speed of operation was critical and it was inevitable that teachers, in an attempt to help their pupils over this all-important hurdle, should give them plenty of practice in the type of questions they were likely to tackle. Indeed publishing firms produced work-books based on the Intelligence and Attainment Tests and these were used in many schools. This led to a distortion of the curriculum with more time devoted to the honing of arithmetical and verbal reasoning skills and less to creative writing, history, geography, art and music.

Hostels

Country children proceeding to the Anderson Educational Institute had to find accommodation in lodgings in Lerwick. Frequently the budding scholars shared their "digs" with working men and while this often added a new dimension to the growing-up process it could not always be described as a good learning environment. Then in 1923 came the generous gift of the Bruce Hostel for 44 girls provided by Robert Bruce, laird of Sumburgh, and in 1939, although not occupied by pupils until after the end of World War II, the Janet Courtney Hostel for 55 boys. Both hostels have, over the years, given country boys and girls an invaluable experience of communal living and learning to adjust to a wide variety of personalities and temperaments. Even with the hostels there were in 1963 about 130 pupils in lodgings in Lerwick.[14]

1960-1990 — Decades of Change

Few major changes affected Scottish schools during the first 60 years of the century. It was inevitable that the build-up of progressive educational thought accumulated during the years before and during the Second World War would eventually filter through to the top echelons of the S.E.D. A number of challenging reports began to appear. If the

1946 Education Act provided the political mechanism by which the education system was to operate for the benefit of all, it was the Reports by the Scottish Advisory Council on Primary (1946) and Secondary Education (1947) that presented a vision of what that education should consist of. Both Reports were extremely influential. Under the wise chairmanship of J. J. Robertson, Rector of Aberdeen Grammar School, the council produced an inspiring and enlightened document on secondary education. It argued, among other things, that the secondary curriculum contained an excessively high intellectual component and should be balanced with more courses of a practical and aesthetic nature. It pointed the way ahead to the comprehensive school by arguing that greater emphasis should be placed on the needs of the many than on the gifted few.

An inspiring document but one that did not find favour with the conservatively-minded leaders of the S.E.D., and little of a practical nature stemmed from it. What it did do was to become a sort of educational bible for many secondary teachers of the time who absorbed much of its philosophy into their teaching practice. But, notably, it laid the foundations for subsequent reforms.

The report had strongly recommended that Scottish children should be made more aware of the richness of their cultural and historical background. It emphasised "the fundamental truth that education must be rooted in reality, finding its material and its starting point in the environment of the child." It was recognised by an increasing number of teachers that one of the most fundamental parts of the environment is the language the child hears from early childhood. Zetland Education Committee acted positively. In the 1960s it commissioned two publications for local schools — *Nordern Lichts* — an anthology of Shetland dialect writing — and *The Shetland Book* — a textbook on Shetland history and environment. The long-established trend which had devalued the local dialect was gradually being reversed. Now in the 1990s there is a recognised place in Shetland schools for Shetland dialect. Poetry and prose collections have been prepared, many of them with taped recordings, and visiting dialect speakers bring Shetland poetry and traditional tales and traditions into the classroom. It is ironic that, at a time when the daily use of the dialect has declined considerably, its status has never been higher.

Curricular Change
Primary

A radical change in the primary curriculum took place following the publication in 1966 by the Scottish Education Department of "A

Memorandum on Primary Education". It advocated a basic change from passive to active learning whereby children found out by seeing, doing, and talking rather than passively absorbing in an atmosphere of chalk and talk. The classroom was to become a sort of learning laboratory with children participating in the process. The days of the silent classroom were over: the era of the project had begun. Greater emphasis was to be placed on communication, both written and oral, and art, music, and physical education were to be integrated more closely into pupils' work.

This new approach was a heaven-sent opportunity to the imaginative teacher but to exploit its possibilities fully required much preparation and organisation. It was natural that older teachers should find some of this an invitation to chaos in the classroom and a retreat from the well-tested traditional methods, but the majority of Shetland teachers responded positively to the challenge and an HMI Report in 1971 stated: "That the primary schools in Shetland are in the mainstream of educational advancement is a tribute to the calibre of the teaching staff".[15]

Secondary

Prior to 1950 primary schools had operated Advanced Divisions for those who had completed the primary course but did not go on to secondary education in Lerwick. In the small school the additional work involved in this arrangement imposed an additional burden on the teacher and it was recognised that the situation was not providing senior pupils with meaningful courses. In 1948 the government announced that the school leaving age would be raised to 15. In anticipation of the increased rolls Shetland Education Committee provided additional accommodation at Lerwick Central and nine rural schools — Baltasound, Mid Yell, Urafirth, Whalsay (Brough), Happyhansel, Scalloway, Sandwick, Aith and Brae. These rural schools became, in 1950, junior secondaries, and received local pupils of secondary age who had not gone to the Institute or Lerwick Central.

The conversion of these nine primary schools into junior secondaries involved considerable changes. What had been, for most of them, a two teacher school, now had five or six staff, with about twice the roll, and new subjects such as woodwork, metalwork, homecraft, and science. Schools could not justify full-time specialist teachers, particularly in the practical subjects, and had to rely on visiting teachers. Increased accommodation was provided through the erection of hutted classrooms of the H.O.R.S.A. (Hutting on the Raising of the School Leaving Age) type, but there were serious restrictions. In 1963[16] Scalloway was the only junior secondary to have a gymnasium and, apart from Brough in

Whalsay, a playing field. Art teachers had to make do with either the homecraft room or a room without water.

Despite the difficulties much interesting work was done during the three-year course but the lack of a terminal certificate tended to limit motivation which had to be supplied by the teacher, topic or project. The final year of the course was often vocationally slanted with instruction in subjects such as navigation and machine knitting.

Two-tier System

To operate the comprehensive system, new syllabuses had to be prepared which took account of mixed ability teaching groups. To keep the curriculum under review a national body, the Consultative Council on the Curriculum, was established in 1965.

From the mid-fifties to the early sixties there had been a sharp political debate on the question of comprehensive schooling and in 1965, under a Labour Government, the Scottish Education Department issued an edict stating that Scottish education would henceforth be based on a comprehensive secondary system. All authorities were instructed to prepare schemes for putting this decision into operation. Shetland Education Committee initially favoured a single comprehensive school in Lerwick which all children of secondary age would attend. This unleashed considerable controversy. It was argued that to remove all children of 12 and over from rural areas already suffering from severe depopulation would deal a body blow to these communities. The message came across clearly that centralisation should not proceed without careful consideration of the social implications. The widespread public concern and outright opposition from within the council eventually resulted in the committee changing its view and in 1966 it was decided that a two-tier comprehensive system should operate. The Anderson Institute and Lerwick Central Secondary were to amalgamate but seven junior high schools would be retained. Pupils over 12 at Happyhansel and Urafirth would attend Aith and Brae respectively. The Promotion Test was abolished and all pupils over 12 would go to their local secondary school for two years to study a Common Course which would include a foreign language. At the end of the second year parents had the right to select certificate courses at the Anderson High School — as the new six year school was named — or a vocationally slanted course at their local junior high school.

The Scottish Education Department gave this package a cool reception, expressing reservations about the problems of acquiring specialist staff for the new junior highs and maintaining comparable standards during the common course in all schools. They were eventually persuaded to accept the scheme but only on a trial basis. The new junior highs were thrown the challenge of proving themselves in action. Their response was positive. The wider range of ability in the first two years provided a new dynamism in the schools and gave an added incentive to both pupils and teachers. Close co-operation between staff of all schools resulted in an integrated approach to the common course and pupils from rural schools moved smoothly into the third year at the Anderson High School. In 1971 the Inspectorate was able to report[17] that "By the united efforts of policy-makers and practitioners the fine reputation enjoyed by the schools of Shetland has been maintained and enhanced."

The main problem in the junior highs lay in devising appropriate courses for those pupils who remained in Classes 3 and 4. Small numbers followed a limited range of certificate courses with considerable success and it became apparent that, if more certificate courses could be offered more pupils would decide at the end of the second year, to complete their education at junior highs. The Education Committee were eventually persuaded to provide additional staff and accommodation to make this possible and the 1990s saw the development of Brae Junior High into a six-year secondary and the other junior highs providing four year certificate courses with considerable success.

Anderson High School

Shetland was the ideal area for a comprehensive school and the combination of the Anderson Institute and Lerwick Central took place relatively painlessly in 1970. It was largely the historic identities of the two schools which had previously tended to keep them apart. The Institute had established a reputation for preparing young Shetlanders for the professions and for a long time its courses were directed along a narrow academic front, whereas Lerwick Central had developed successful commercial courses and was, in the 1960s, presenting growing numbers of pupils for O Grades in the Scottish Certificate of Education.

Shetland's social and educational background had been much less divisive than in England and, to a lesser extent, Scotland. Rural schools, in particular, had a fine social mix, children of crofters and fishermen often attending the same school as the children of ministers, merchants and teachers, sitting side by side, sharing the same games and activities, and building solid friendships.

In Lerwick the first experience of segregation began at the end of primary when the brighter pupils tended to leave for the Institute, breaking up associations and friendships. At the Institute the only significant social distinction was between town and country, with differences of speech and dress subjected to low-key banter.

The newly created comprehensive, the Anderson High School, had a roll of 679 and, until the extension to the old Institute building was completed in 1977, operated on two sites with staff and pupils commuting between Bellevue and King Harald Street. The integration of the two schools had only well begun when North Sea oil hit Shetland. The 1970s has been described as the most tumultuous decade in Shetland's history: 10 years that changed the face of the islands and launched the community into a period of unrivalled prosperity. It saw the population increase by an incredible 54 per cent and the Anderson High School roll by 48 per cent. The Anderson High School extension took five years to plan and six years to build at a cost of over £4½ million. Sullom Voe Terminal took three years to plan, four years to build and cost £1,200 million. It is ludicrous to compare the two projects but the degree of the disparity gives some indication of the sheer scale of the impact of North Sea Oil on a small community.

Educationally the challenge of oil fell into three main categories: the physical provision of school buildings to cope with increased pupil numbers; the smooth integration of incoming pupils to local schools; and the curricular exploitation of the fact that, for the first time in its history, Shetland had in its midst a major high technology industry. Shetland Islands Council launched into a remarkable programme of school building. In Delting, the main area of oil-related population, two primaries were built at Brae and Mossbank. The growth of Lerwick demanded a second primary school at Sound. New primaries were built in Whiteness, Cunningsburgh, and Hamnavoe, and an extension in Dunrossness. The roll at Anderson High increased to over 1,000 stretching the new accommodation to the limits. New secondaries were built in Brae, Sandwick and Aith. A remarkable programme of school building by any standards and one which, despite the scale of expenditure, received the full backing of the community.

Barrage of Official Reports

During the 50s and 60s it became increasingly evident that the existing educational system was not meeting the needs of the children who attended its schools. The Higher and Lower Leaving Certificate examinations catered for the academically inclined minority, with the result that many young people left secondary schools with a "Failed" label attached. In 1961 the Scottish Certificate of Education Ordinary Grade was introduced to replace the old Lower and cater for a wider range of pupils. The Brunton Report appeared in 1963 with its main recommendation that secondary courses should have a greater practical content and be more vocationally orientated.

The early 70s saw the beginning of a barrage of official reports recommending radical changes in content of courses and teaching techniques. From the Munn and Dunning Reports came major changes in curricula and certificate examinations. Although their recommendations were modifed in implementation the changes were considerable, involving the development of new syllabuses. Coming shortly after comprehensive reorganisation with its necessity to construct new courses for the new mixed ability class structures, considerable burdens were imposed on teachers. There is no doubt that this was an important factor in the teachers' strike in 1984.

The Munn and Dunning recommendations had considerable merit — principally the "certification for all" policy whereby the Standard Grade examination was divided into Credit, General and Foundation levels. Standard Grade examinations, introduced in 1961, had replaced the long-established Lowers — designed for a mere 30 per cent of pupils. The new examination, designed to cater for the great majority of pupils went a long way towards removing the divisiveness of the old system which had left a substantial number of pupils with a sense of failure.

Also to descend upon schools in the 70s were reports on the introduction of guidance to pupils; the Pack Report on Discipline in Schools; the Warnock Report on the Education of Pupils with Special Educational Needs; another on the Education of Pupils with Learning Difficulties; one on importance of teaching sound English across the curriculum; and then, as though the mandarins of St Andrews House felt a pang of guilt at imposing such additional burdens on teachers, they came with the Sneddon Report on Learning to Teach.

The long-running argument between those who advocated a broad, liberal type of education and those favouring the introduction of a vocational element surfaced strongly in the early 80s. As a response to high youth unemployment the Thatcher government, through a new agency, the Manpower Services Commission, launched the Technical, Vocational and Educational Initiative in 1983 aimed at the over-16s. It offered considerable financial incentives to authorities prepared to introduce training in technology and computer education into its schools. Scotland was initially cautious but the financial inducements were too attractive to resist and in 1984 the SED launched its action plan largely based on the TVEI. These initiatives were responsible for introducing an important new element into school curricula — short modular courses. These modules enabled greater diversification and flexibility of courses and were very appropriate for the less academic pupils who could focus their strengths on a variety of subjects with attainable goals.

TVEI heralded another new development in Scottish education — the direct intervention of government in the school curriculum. This trend continued throughout the remainder of the Conservative government with the Scottish Office Education Department tending to operate more by dictat than consultation. HMI's moved from a regulatory and advisory function to one more developmental. What happened in schools was now very much what was determined by the SOED, renamed in the 1990s Scottish Office, Education and Industry Department.

The 90s saw the tide of change reaching the upper stages of secondary schools. For over a century the Higher Leaving Certificate had remained the ikon of secondary education but the changes introduced further down the school in the 70s and 80s had left it more and more out of kilter with other courses. Higher courses remained strongly academic in emphasis and made no provision for the vocational element in many of the new modular courses. The SOED Report "Higher Still" which appeared in 1994 aimed at tidying up the fragmentation of courses and awards at the top end of the secondary school. It proposed a reorganisation of courses designed for all abilities up to university entrance. The certificate would be awarded at four levels — Access (containing a high proportion of practical elements), Intermediate (suitable for students who had performed well in Standard Grade Foundation and quite well in Standard Grade Intermediate), Higher and Advanced — bringing all post-16 courses into a coherent structure under the one certification umbrella.

Higher Still is being introduced at breakneck speed with the first awards initially planned for 1998 and later postponed until 1999. A more rational integration of courses and awards at the post-16 level was certainly desirable but the pace of change takes little account of the pressures imposed on school staff and the inevitable dislocation of the curriculum. Staff must always be satisfied that new approaches are both relevant and workable. Change in any institution has to be carefully initiated and managed and there does come a time when constant innovation frustrates the very process it sets out to achieve.

Despite the unsettling influences of constant change in the curriculum Shetland schools have continued to produce quality education. Supported by the traditional interest of parents in the education of their children, and the generous resources provided by an enlightened local authority, Shetland schools are, at the close of the twentieth century, equipping their pupils with a rich and relevant education.

Further Education

The 1946 Education Act outlined the blueprint of the brave new world which would follow the depression years of the 20s and 30s and the horrors of war in the 40s. Education was to be free to all children of school age who would also have their health and social welfare provided for. Furthermore, there was to be the opportunity for young people to continue their education beyond school, whether at university, college, continuation class, or properly organised vocational training.

Apart from navigation and book-keeping taught at some parochial and board schools, and commercial subjects at Lerwick Central, schooling in the nineteenth and the first half of the twentieth century contained little of vocational relevance. Education was, to a great extent, regarded as what happened within the four walls of the classroom between 9am and 4pm. There was little or no link between the school curriculum and the world of work. The 1908 Education Act strengthened the status of continuation classes or "Night School" as they were known, by making it obligatory for school boards to provide continuation classes for all people over 14 who wished to attend.

From an existing situation where further education in Shetland amounted to little more than sporadic "night classes", a vast new expansion was envisaged: there would be adults studying academic, vocational and recreational courses, apprentices attending Day Release or Block Release courses in their chosen trade; people of all ages attending community clubs to take part in a recreational pursuit or simply to meet his or her fellows in a relaxed atmosphere. A daunting prospect for a small island community but one which the council had to face up to. The Education Committee decided to appoint an Organiser of Further Education and in 1946 James W. Irvine, fresh out of army uniform, was appointed. He set about his task with enthusiasm and records[18] how, as he travelled through Shetland, he discovered "a tremendous fund of pent-up energy to be released". Community clubs were formed or existing clubs expanded. Accommodation did not match aspirations but a solution, temporary at least, was reached by the acquisition of army huts vacated on the exodus of troops at the end of hostilities. By the early 70s there were 75 community clubs in Shetland supported by a number of youth and community workers. In Lerwick the Education Committee moved positively and in 1946 acquired for £4500 Islesburgh House as a centre for community activities. Time has proved the wisdom of that move. For over half a century now, Islesburgh has been at the core of

Lerwick's community activities — in drama, music, photography, table tennis, committee meetings, junior clubs, and many more.

Continuation classes became increasingly popular. In 1949 there were 249 enrolments in a number of centres; in 1954 — 395; and in 1959 — 527. Courses included shorthand, typewriting, cookery, dress-making, physical training, Norwegian, building construction, country dancing.

In 1948 new legislation requiring skippers of fishing-boats over 25 tons to have at least a Second-Hand's (Special) Certificate created a demand for courses in navigation and seamanship. Classes were established in Lerwick, Scalloway, Whalsay and Skerries. Those in Whalsay and Skerries were well supported and in 1954 28 fishermen successfully completed courses, many of them young men destined to spearhead the dramatic development of Shetland's fishing fleet in the 60s and 70s.

A constant problem in organising courses for fishermen was their difficulty in attending block courses in a single centre. This was overcome in 1968 by a remarkable piece of pioneering work done by Whalsay teacher Mrs Jeanette Williamson who organised and prepared a radio/correspondence course in navigation. She broadcast on VHF a series of 20 lectures, each one supported by full notes. A one week's course in Lerwick enabled individual problems to be discussed and sorted out. Twenty-one Shetland students completed the course successfully.

In the post-war years it became increasingly obvious that the academically oriented curriculum of the secondary school was inappropriate for a considerable number of pupils. The Brunton Report, published by the Scottish Education Department in 1963 recommended that secondary courses should include provision for the less academically inclined pupils. Courses were to be designed with a "vocational impulse" in their make-up by being related to local industries. It appeared at a time when there was considerable debate in Shetland on the way ahead for indigenous industries. In 1959 Shetland Development Council declared in a formal motion that "The educational system in Shetland must be geared to the needs of a fishing community and that pre-sea training and vocational further education must be provided for Shetland boys and youths in a Shetland Fisheries and Sea Training School with practical training afloat". This radical statement got a positive reception from the Education Committee which set up in 1960 a study group on education and local industries.

Plans for Agricultural Training

New interest in local agricultural training was sparked off in 1964 by the council's acquisition of Voxter Farm, Delting as a possible Day

Further Education Centre. The initial proposal was ambitious: 20 places for students with the aim of equipping young people to be self-supporting on crofts in Shetland. There would be courses in animal and crop husbandry, rural handcrafts, building skills, farm machinery, poultry keeping, social studies, accounts. A hostel would be built to accommodate students. The project, largely the brainchild of Robert Innes, Further Education Officer, had to be trimmed as it encountered financial realities, the prospect of limited student numbers, and a lukewarm response from the Inspectorate. But the Education Committee, convinced that it had a role to fulfil in vocational or leisure education, continued to view it as an educational unit. Working in close liaison with the North of Scotland College of Education it began a programme of development. A grieve was appointed, cattle and sheep stocks upgraded, hill pastures regenerated, steading for animals built, and the old manse situated on the farm, began to be refurbished.

The Education Committee still hankered after some form of educational use for the farm. After the raising of the school leaving age to 16 in 1972 work-based courses were pioneered by Brae Junior Secondary but these did not progress much beyond basic building operations and paintwork. The mood was swinging more towards the development of the buildings as an outdoor centre. The farm land was leased to a private individual in 1977 and in the early 1980s the responsibility for developing Voxter as an outdoor centre was given to the Leisure and Recreation Department. A Voxter Centre Trust was established in 1981 to undertake the management of the centre. The house was refurbished and since then a variety of groups, including schools, have made good use of the facilities for outdoor activities.

The Education Committee's aspirations to develop Voxter as an agricultural training centre were bedevilled from the start by finance and the official perception that the limited number of agricultural students from Shetland could receive training at Weyland Farm in Orkney. The story of the Shetland Fisheries College at Scalloway, conceived and developed in the 80s, when finance was more readily available from the council's oil monies, illustrates how the fate of projects, however desirable, hinge ultimately on money.

Rapid Expansion

In 1965 the Education Committee, in anticipation of the opening of a new public library, decided to take over the previous hutted accommodation for classes in machine knitting and engineering.[19] Instructors were appointed and courses developed in engineering to cover Day Release students from local garages and secondary pupils from local schools, and in machine-knitting for secondary pupils and interested adults.

For a time local garages were reluctant to release apprentices on the grounds that small businesses could not afford to lose employees even for the one day, but eventually industrial training boards introduced a compulsory levy on all businesses employing apprentices and garages realised the only way to benefit from these levies was to send their apprentices for training. The courses followed the City and Guilds Certificate syllabuses, with two years for mechanical engineering and a further year for marine engineering.

The headmaster of Anderson High School was appointed part-time principal of Lerwick F. E. Centre and when the new High School extension was planned in the early 70s, purpose-built accommodation was included for engineering, machine knitting, business studies, and catering. On completion it was occupied in 1977.

Sullom Voe Terminal proved to be a generator of commercial and technical activities in the community with a resultant demand for further education courses in business studies; light engineering/electronics; building and construction; and health and care. Pressure on space necessitated expansion and in 1984 a new building opened on the High School site.

The scale of operations in the college now pointed towards a full-time principal and in 1987 Shetland College of Further Education was established. Still the rapid growth continued, spilling over on to six different sites. In 1984 the college was catering for 268 full-time equivalent students following courses in business studies, computer studies, general studies, health and caring, management studies, building construction, technology, textiles, and catering. There were 26 full-time and nine part-time lecturers, supported by three technicians and two clerical assistants. The majority of courses lead to National Certificate or to General Scottish Vocational Qualifications.[20]

Planning had again failed to keep pace with expansion and in 1995 new, permanent accommodation was built at Gremista. Shetland College now fulfils a key role in local industry and in the community in general.

Fisheries Training

The rapid expansion of Shetland's fishing fleet from the 1970s and the highly successful development of salmon farming from the 1980s brought Shetland sea fisheries into the heart of modern technology. Fishermen matched the moment with impressive skill. They adapted rapidly to the new situation but it became more and more obvious that modern training facilities were inadequate in equipping the local seafood industry to exploit fully the challenge ahead.

In 1984 a local fishing consultant, Dr Alistair Goodlad, in a report to Shetland Islands Council on the future of the Shetland fishing industry, recommended that a fisheries training college should be established. In the face of scepticism, both local and national, the council faced up to the challenge and, with its development department at the helm, launched into what they regarded as an ambitious but vital project.

The building, which cost over £6m, was opened at Port Arthur, Scalloway in 1992 and within a few years had demonstrated the wisdom of those responsible for its creation. It offers a wide range of courses from short one day practical training sessions to one year full time National and Higher National Certificate courses. There are courses in maritime studies, marine engineering, fisheries science, aquaculture, fish processing. College staff are also involved in research projects related to the fishing industry.

Within a remarkably short time the college has established itself at the forefront of North Atlantic fishing operations, attracting not only local students but several from as far away as Peru and the Seychelles. Its annual running costs of about £1m are met approximately one-third by Shetland Islands Council and two-thirds by outside sources, principally the European Union.

REFERENCES

1. Shetland News, 13/3/1897
2. Ibid. 27/3/1897
3. Ibid. 13/2/1897
4. Sandison, Tom, The New Shetlander, No. 118, 1976
5. 1861-1962, Anderson Educational Institute, John Johnston, pp 50-51
6. Ibid. Andrew T. Cluness, pp 40-41
7. Ibid. p.43
8. Ibid. William J. Tait, p.76
9. Baltasound Centenary Booklet, 1979
10. Record of Work, Haroldswick Primary School, Unst
11. Deyell, Annie, My Shetland, Thuleprint Ltd., 1975
12. SA, CO9/2/1/1
13. Mrs Johnson, Herrisdale, Tingwall, 14 Sept. 1969
14. Education in Zetland, Report by H.M.I., 1963
15. Education in Zetland, Report by H.M.I., 1971
16. Ibid. 1963
17. Ibid. 1971
18. Irvine, James W., Through Storm to Calm, A. Irvine, Printing, 1995
19. SA, CO5/2/30
20. H.M.I. Report on Shetland College of Further Education, 1994

Chapter 17

Retrospect

WHEN WE look back at the insanitary hovels in which children of the 18th and early 19th centuries struggled to learn to read, count and write, and follow the long, slow climb towards the conditions of today with modern, splendidly equipped buildings, professionally trained teachers and varied curricula, we can only marvel at the dramatic improvements in such a relatively short time.

From the early 18th century when the first scatter of SSPCK schools began to appear, there is a recognisable thread running through the process, and that is the strong commitment to education shown by local people: the commitment indicated by the Foula folk who in 1716 were described as having "a very vehement thirst and desire after knowledge"[1] or that made in 1768 by the folk of Walls in offering their services free to help build the school at Happyhansel; in 1803, by the young Andrew Dishington Mathewson, less than five years old, learning at his aunt's knee to read the Bible; in 1826 the evidence from the Inverness Society's research that 76 per cent of children over eight in Shetland could read; in 1855 the young men of Lerwick volunteering, after they had finished a long day's work, to help teach poor children in the evenings; and many more examples. That interest was driven, in the first instance, by the 18th century kirk's belief that a godly community could be created by educating the young to read the Bible and, secondly, by the feeling among Shetland folk that education provided an escape route from the economic and social poverty fettering them. The Nesting folk were displaying that conviction when they petitioned[2] the SSPCK in 1755. They stated that some years previously the Society had established a school in the district where the children had been taught the "principles of Christian religion" to the parents' "great Comfort and Satisfaction." The school had subsequently been removed "whereby our children are at an unspeakable loss; our own mean circumstances prevent us from employing a sufficient person to teach, but we will contribute to our utmost towards a Schoolmaster, his comfortable living among us."

And that same spirit that moved young Yell seamen to attend A. D. Mathewson's school in the 1820s is present in the young Shetland fishermen of the 1990s who attend the North Atlantic Fisheries College in Scalloway.

Now at the close of the 20th century educational horizons have expanded to an incredible extent. The modern curriculum, apart from developing the traditional skills, makes pupils more aware than ever of their place in "the global village" as well as their role in their own community. And still there remains that underlying community awareness of the value of education which creates that indispensable bond between home and school.

REFERENCES

1 SSPCK General Minutes, 7/6/1716, SRO
2 ZPM 4/6/1755, SA

APPENDIX A
Shetland Teachers

DETAILS OF schools and teachers in the Shetland parishes are given insofar as they could be traced. These were researched up to 1900 on the assumption that later records are more readily available

AITHSTING & SANDSTING
1741-1744	Robert Cumming (SSPCK School)

Twatt
1813	Parochial School established at Twatt
1813-1855	David Walterson
1856-1886	Gilbert Williamson – Board School after 1872 (Parochial School building enlarged and improved 1875)
1886-1892	Robert Fairbairn
1892-1893	Mrs Fairbairn
1894-1910	John McCullie

Clousta
1878	New Board School opened
1878-1880	Magnus Nicolson
1880-1880	William Hamilton
1880-1881	Elizabeth McQueen
1881-1883	Eliza Lamb
1883-1888	Isabella Morren
1888-1893	John S. Peterson
1894-1895	James A. Keith
1895-1896	George Henderson
1896-1901	Arch. Johnston

Gruting
1829	General Assembly School opened
1831-1843	Alexander Wallace
1843-1856	Gilbert Williamson
1856-	Hugh M. Rankine
1877	New Board School opened

1877-1882   Robert Cuddie (dismissed by School Board –
            reinstated after parents' petition)
1882-1885   Duncan Stewart
1885-1890   William Robertson (petition from 23 families opposing
            appointment)
1890-1893   John Hastie
1893-1929   John S. Peterson

Reawick
1805   SSPCK School established at Arg, Reawick
1805-1823   John Henry
1824-1872   George Henry (son of John)
1842-1862   James Stout – teacher of school at Wart, Reawick

Sand
1831   Subscription School established by parents at Sand
at 1835   Sinclair Coutts
1850s   SSPCK School established
1850s   Charles Moodie (later pastor of Baptist Church)
1875   New Board School opened
1875-1880   Mr R Wiseman
1880-1883   Roderick McLean
1883-1886   Robert S. Fairbairn
1887-1892   James McCullie
1893-1895   D. Angus
1896-1900   Mrs Lyell

Sandsound
1805   SSPCK School established
1806-   George Jamieson
1807-1811   Robert Law
1812-1834   Peter Dalziel
1835-1836   John Moodie
1836-1838   (School withdrawn because classroom was "ruinous")
1838-1853   John Moodie
1877   New Board School opened
1877-1882   Adam Arthur
1882-1883   Maggie D. Lees
1883-1885   Helen Polson
1886-1887   Margaret Sime
1888-1892   Isabella Kennedy
1892-1893   Miss Myles

1893-1894	Miss Hynd
1895-1896	Miss Sime
1896-1899	Miss Charleson
1900-1903	Miss Morrison

Skeld
1877	New Board School opened
1877-1885	William Robertson
1886-1894	Duncan Stewart
1895-1897	R. Gillies
1897-1902	William Merkin

West Burrafirth
1878	New Board School opened
1878-1886	Peter Henderson
1886-1887	Miss Hynd
at 1892-1895	Miss McInnes
1896-1897	Mrs Hutton
1897-1898	N. Matheson
1898-1900	Jeremiah Dalziel

Also Subscription School in Sand; and Private Adventure Schools in West Burrafirth, Berry Knowe, Culswick-Teacher, Mary Jamieson; Wart (above Cruganess, Clousta), Skeetaplootch, Clousta; Uphouse, Aith-Teacher, Mary Johnson of Ayres; Daek-end (Voehead), Aith-Teacher, Joan Manson; Aithsness-Teacher, James Johnson

BRESSAY, BURRA & QUARFF
Bressay
1728-1732	James Buchan (later Minister in Walls)
1765	Parochial School (East School) established
1766-1783	John Smith
1784-	James Leask
1794-1806	Thomas Jamieson
at 1809-1842	George Scott
1843-1878	John Ross
1879	New Board School opened
1879-1883	George Linklater
1883-1888	William Smith
1888-1895	George Wilson
1895-1902	Magnus Yates
c. 1802	SSPCK School established

c. 1802-	Robert Sinclair
at 1874-	Robert Anderson
1830s	Assembly School (West School) established at Hoversta
c. 1833-1835	James Beattie
1836-1837	A. McKay
1838-	Walter Russell
at 1878	Peter Henderson

Burra Isle

1793	SSPCK School established
1793-1801	Alexander Sutherland
1818-1841	Magnus Thomason
1851-1861	Gilbert Gray (SSPCK School closed)
1851	General Assembly School established at Bridgend
1858-1861	Gilbert Gray (became Teacher of General Assembly School)
1861-1906	William Edgar Morrison (Assembly then Board teacher)
1905	New Board School erected at Hamnavoe

Quarff

1802-	James Tyrie
1803-1805	Robert Gaudie (S.S.P.C.K. School)
1805-1806	William Henry do. (appointment opposed by heritors and people on moral grounds)
1841-1845	Magnus Thomason
c. 1850	Bourmeister Spence
c. 1860s/70s	Rev. William Fordyce (Blind after an accident in infancy – Free Church)
1878	New Board School opened
1879-1880	Miss Jane Stobo
1880-1882	Miss Bella Johnston
1888-1889	Mrs Kemp
1889-1890	Mrs Mathewson
at 1892-1901	Miss Mary A. McLeod

DELTING
Brae

1720s	Alex. Mitchell (tutor to Gifford of Busta — also taught local children)
1728-1730	Francis Beattie – SSPCK School.
at 1756	Andrew Gifford – do.
1759	Gifford dismissed and school moved to Laxobigging

APPENDIX A

1800	Parochial School established; vacant from 1803-1816; ambulatory until 1831
1800-1803	David Bissett
	Andrew Robertson
-1824	Rev. James Robertson (at Moorfield, Laxobigging)
1824-	William Pole do. do.
1830-at 1876	John Anderson
1877-1884	James Irvine
1828-1829	Charles Moodie, SSPCK, Sursetter, Voe
1830-1832	Robert Rennie do. do.
1832-c. 1854	John Sandison do. do. (son of Christopher Sandison, Society teacher at Eshaness)
c.1854-c.1874	James Louttit do. do.
1827	General Assembly School established at Brae
1827-1834	John Williamson – General Assembly
1835-	Donald Forbes – do.
at 1874	John S. White – do.
at 1876	James Louttit – do.
1882-1894	Peter Ferguson — Board School in operation
1894-1905	James Moodie
1867	General Assembly School established at Olnafirth — 1872 became Board School
at 1889-1894	Andrew Henry
1895-1900	Ann Alexander
1900-1901	Jeremiah Halcrow
at 1874-	John Johnson – Private Adventure School at Gonfirth
1877	New Board School opened at Gonfirth
1877-	James Hunter
at 1882-	E. Allison
at 1883-	Miss Fraser
1886-1892	Mrs McPherson
at 1861 & 1876	Peter Fraser – Free Church School at Scarvataing, Muckle Roe
1875	Board School opened at Muckle Roe
at 1882-	Anna Douglas
1886-1887	Mrs Waugh
1889-1901	Peter Henderson
1871-	(U.P. School built at Mossbank – Teacher, Miss Helen Johnson)
1879	New Board School opened at Firth
1882-1885	Thomas Douglas
1885-1887	Charles Wood

1887-1888	Mrs Waugh
1888-1908	Thomas Hanton (to Ollaberry)
at 1874-	John Johnson (Gonfirth Private Adventure)
1875	New Board School opened at Gonfirth
at 1892-1907	Mrs McPherson
	Garth/Collafirth Side School
1896-1899	James C Grindlay
1900-	Andrew Blance

DUNROSSNESS (Cunningsburgh and South)
Sandwick

1803	Parochial School established at Sandwick
1803-c. 1840	James Jameson – Parochial teacher
at 1840-	John Thomson – do.
1846-1850	James Johnston – do. (forced to resign by Kirk Session)
1851-1855	George Thomson (resigned after conflict with Minister – Rev. John Scarth)
1856-1862	James Russell
1863-1876	Laurence Johnstone
1876-1879	Donald McDonald
1879	New Board School opened
1879-1881	John Douglas
1881-1885	John McDougall
1885-1887	W. Reynolds
1887-1903	W. Richmond

Church School organised by minister
1720s	John Smith (102 children attended)

S.S.P.C.K. Schools
1729-1733	Alex Halcrow (Sandwick)
1733-	Andrew Balfour (Sandwick)
1730-1735	Francis Beattie (Scatness)
1747-1749	Alex. Halcrow
1749-1759	Robert McPherson (Bremer)
1750-1760	Alex. Halcrow (Laichness)
1780-1786	Robert Thomson (Quendale)
1786-1797	James Strong (Brew)
1799-1806	Robert Sinclair do.
1807-1853	William Henry do. (Small man – known locally as 'King of the Fairies')

1836-1837   Magnus Manson (Sumburgh)
1838-1850   Magnus Manson (Vatchley)
1850-1852   George Stewart   do. (Author of 'Shetland Fireside Tales')
1853-1859   James Laurenceson do.
1860-1872   William Laurence   do.

Free Church School (Skeoberry, Quendale):
1853-1883   John Burgess

Private Adventure Schools:
Scatness:
in 1860s-   Laurence Harper

Tolob:
1860s-   Robert Harper, Thomas Aitken, William Manson

Cloddy Knowe: William Henderson, John Moncrieff, John Henry

Ireland, Bigton:
1850s & 60s   Thomas Thompson, Robert Morrison, Robert Jamieson

Bigton

1735-1739	Francis Beattie SSPCK at Windhouse, Bigton
1741-	James Cheyne do.
1881	New Board School opened
1881-1885	Miss Mary M. Stephen
1885-1886	Miss Margaret Craib
1886-1889	M. Burgess
1889-1891	Miss Isa Bell
1891-1892	Miss Ellen Hay
1892-1893	Miss Jean Hunter
1894-1900	Miss M. B. Lyon

Boddam

1880	New Board School opened
1880-1882	George R. Gray
1882-1884	J. D. Mitchell
1885-1887	Joseph Strathern
1888-1900	Miss Maggie Turnbull

Cunningsburgh

SSPCK School – est. 1734
1809-1847   Robert Gaudie (at Greenfield)

1847-1854   John Thomson

Free Church School:
c.1850-c.1882   Malcolm Gaudy (building taken over by School Board c.1874) (Gaudy was a local man, largely self-educated, who attended Normal School[1] (for Teacher Training) in Edinburgh)
1874   New Board School opened
1882-1883   William Smith
1883-1887   William Richmond
1887-   David Menzies
at 1892-1899   Sam McKee
1900-1903   James B. Souter

Fair Isle

1730   SSPCK School established
1730-1732   William Strong
1732-1736   Thomas Stout
1736-1740   William Strong
1740-1750   Robert Arcus
1751-1756   Robert Omand
1766-   Robert Jamieson
1773-1780   Robert Thomson (transferred to Quendale)
1780-1793   John Irvine
1794-1814   John Irvine, jr.
1815-   Andrew Wilson
1818-1821   Andrew Henderson
1823-1853   James Cheyne (son James acted as assistant)
1861-1863   Laurence Johnston
1863-1864   Rev. J. Craig
1865-   Rev. Andrew McFarlane
1870-1874   Rev. Alex. Arthur
1874-1875   Andrew Wilson
1876   New Board School opened
1875-1887   William Laurence – from 1878 Board teacher (Was J.P., Catechist, Registrar, Lloyd's agent, responsible for Lifeboat and lifesaving apparatus)
1887-1887   William Manson
1888-1894   William Brown
1894-1922   Donald McLean

Levenwick

1882	New Board School opened
1882-	Mrs Goudie
1883-1888	Malcolm Gaudy
1889-	Miss Slater
1895-1905	Miss Susan Mutch

Quendale

1881	New Board School opened
1881-1882	Miss Anne Goodlad
1884-1887	Maggie Turnbull
1888-1889	Janet Lemon
1890-	M. Watson
at 1892-1894	Miss Jessie Smith
1895-1900	Miss E. Hay
1900-1902	Mrs Irvine

Virkie

1880	New Board School opened
1880 -1885	Miss Annie Sinclair
1885-1887	Miss Isabella Simpson
1887-1893	Miss Annie Park
1894-1901	James Shewan

After 1872 and before board schools built there were side schools at: Ireland, Bigton; Levenwick – Teacher, Adam Robertson; Vatchley; Scholland – Teacher, R. Harper; Cloddy Knowe; Channerwick; Brakes of Ness.

LERWICK

c. 1709-	David Pyot (Private School) Also Clerk to Presbytery
1724-1727	John Anderson (Sound and Gulberwick – SSPCK School)
1743	Grammar School in existence
-1765	Walter Robertson
1775-1778	Charles McNab – Private Subscription School
c.1808-	James Ross do. (Also Postmaster & Session Clerk)
1817-1823	John McMorine do.
1823-1828	James Robertson do.
1836-	Robert Burgess (a Dissenter)
1835-1838	John Hull (Moravian)
1839-	W. L. Wunsche do.

1842-   John G. Glass   do.
1840s   Catherine S. Spence (Private schools)
c. 1792   John Sutherland – SSPCK School
1818-   Robert Ridland   do.
1830-1848   Robert Ridland   do.
at 1799-   John Black, teacher of English

Private Teachers
c. 1850s/60s the Misses Duncan, Greenfield Place (Sheriff Duncan's sisters); John B. Lyall, Annsbrae Place; Mrs John Smith, Annsbrae Cottage; John Arthur, Subscription Rooms
1816   Parochial School established
1816-1832   James Ross
1832-1843   James Barclay (afterwards Minister of Mid & South Yell)
1844-1854   John G. Glass
1854-1879   James Hunter (Board teacher after 1872)
1879-1885   G. H. Drummond
1885-1889   Andrew Calderhead
1889-1902   Janet Gulland

Anderson Institute — Headmasters

	Lower School –	Higher School –
1862-1863	James Bryan	G. W. Ellaby
1863-1871	Robert Bryan	James Bryan
1871-		Alex. Clark
1872-1876	George Nicholson	Nathaniel Leask
1876-1879	D. M. Ireland	John Allardice (1876-1883)
1879-1881	F. P. Wellwood	
1881-1883	Daniel Stewart	
1883-1894	Alex. MacDonald Reid	Alex. MacDonald Reid
1894-1899	Robert Millar	Robert Young
1899-1924	Closed-1902	Joseph D. Kirton

Gulberwick
SSPCK School
1818-1829   Robert Ridland
1838-1872   Robert Laing

1877   New Board School opened

1877-1887	Peter Williamson
1887-1889	Mrs Margaret Johnstone
1889-1896	Miss Catherine S. Spence
1896-1897	Mrs George Barrack
1897-1898	Miss Hay
1898-1910	Miss Isabella Innes

NESTING & LUNNASTING
SSPCK Schools
at 1724-	William Laurenson (at Benston, Nesting)
1732-1735	John Campbell do.
1743-1749	William Laurenson do.
1793-1831	Michael Thomson (at Schoolton, Vidlin)
1831-1835	William Pole do.
	Alex. Sutherland do.
1860	Assembly School opened at Brettabister (Donation of £100 from Miss Inches)
	Mr Anderson
	Gilbert Gray
	Mr Forbes
at 1876 & 78	Andrew Gilbertson
	Miss Kirkness
at 1882-1885	Adam Arthur
1886-1923	William Pottinger

South Nesting
c. 1830	School at Garth but in 1840s laird took it over to house tenant; moved to barn at Skellister – Teacher, Miss Jean Brown. Gilbert Gray also had school in barn at Upper Catfirth. William Edgar Morrison taught at school in Garth
1876	New Board School opened at Vassa, South Nesting
1877-1904	John Spence

Laxfirth
1830s	Laurence Johnson and Miss Wishart taught in small 'faelly house'
1881-1895	School opened by William Pottinger (13 pupils) at Billister. W.P. also taught at a school at Grunafirth, week about with Billister. Pupils moved with teacher. Grunafirth closed 1886 and school fixed at Laxfirth.
1895-1896	Miss Gordon Gogel
1897-1902	Robert Cleland

Vidlin

1830-1857	Andrew Anderson (Parochial School – at Quiness, Vidlin)
1860-1885	John McGowan Anderson (1876 — New Board School opened at Quiness)
1885-1900	J. P. Tulloch

Lunna

1849-1856	James Smith (SSPCK)
1857-1861	Laurence Johnston do.
1864-1872	James Irvine do.
at 1892-1894	Gilbert Anderson

Whalsay

1800	Parochial School for Nesting, Lunnasting, Whalsay & Skerries established at Brough
1801-1805	Andrew Henderson (Par. School vacant for 25 years, then established at Vidlin)
1812-	John Scrymgeour (left soon after appointment for more lucrative job as factor for Bruce estate)
1831	Andrew Anderson – Private Adventure School at Marrister
	From c.1840 for about 20 years Whalsay had no recognised school. No children receiving education apart from Sunday School.
	Population 8-30 – c. 486
	Of those, can read – 181
	… can read & write – 78
	… read, write & count – 7
	Can neither read, write, or count – 220
c. 1864	General Assembly School established at Brough – teachers included Mr Macwhirter, Mr Campbell, Mr Forbes, Mr James B. Spence
c. 1840-	Andrew Hughson at Tripwell (was blind) Private Adventure School
at 1848-	James Smith – not effective and dismissed
c. 1850s-	James Poleson at Toft, nr. Isbister (called "Peerie Uncle") Do.
1873	Board School established at Livister
1873-	James Manson ("Peerie Manson")
at 1878-	Magnus Nicholson
1881-1882	James B. Spence

1883-1885	Miss Webster
1885-1899	Miss Duff
1900-1901	John Shaw
1914	New School built at Livister – old General Assembly school became schoolhouse
1873	Board School opened at Brough
1873-1885	James Louttit
1885-1888	T. Ferguson
1888-1898	Mrs Ferguson
1899-1903	John Lee

Skerries

1824-	John Thomson (young lad from Lunnasting; sent to A. D. Mathewson of East Yell for tuition before going to Skerries for six months as teacher)
1840s	Sinclair Thomson, Baptist pastor, established small school in an old hut which eventually fell down. He had a new building erected.
1845-1850	An Irvine man from Whalsay taught – presumably in the above building
1850	Arthur Anderson founded school in Skerries – raised money for schoolhouse.
c.1850-1881	William Peterson – acted also as catechist
1881-1891	James B. Spence
1891-1894	Donald McLean
1894-1910	George McKay

NORTHMAVINE

S.S.P.C.K. School established 1719

1719-	Charles Ross, Ollaberry
1724-	Charles Ross, Eshaness
at 1722-	Rev. Jas Buchan reports three local schools in parish with 180 children
at 1722-	William McIntosh, Nibon
at 1722 & 1724	John Clark, Hillswick
at 1722-	unnamed at Gluss
1773	Parochial School established
1773-1780	John Morison (poss. later minister of Delting)
1780-	James Fordyce
1792-1794	John Dick
1801-1823	John Clark (at Findlins)
at 1828-	Peter Sandison

1830-1842   Thomas Anderson (School first at Muir, Hillswick, then Urafirth)
1843-1879   James Bruce
1877   Parochial School rebuilt and enlarged
1880-1889   Robert Stewart
1889-1890   George Shearer
1890-1892   G. Y. Ferguson
1893-1894   Louis Martin
1895-1896   Barbara McPherson
1896-1903   Mrs Calderwood

Eshaness
1820-1864   Christopher Sandison (SSPCK)
1864-   Gilbert Anderson
1866-   Arthur Sandison (Christopher's grandson)
1869-at 1871   Andrew Gilbertson
1878   New Board School opened
1878-1888   J. Robison
1888-1903   James Manson
1904-   Elizabeth McNicoll

Collafirth
at 1830   Schoolhouse in existence – teacher paid by Kirk Session
c.1850-   Katie Leask – at Barnafield
at 1900-   Miss Inkster

Ennisfirth
c.1850-   Andrew and James Henderson (brothers from Clothister, Sullom) Private Adventure School
c.1850-   Mary Smith

Nibon, Gunnister
c. 1840s   Magnus Manson ("Cripple Magnie") Private Adventure School in converted fish booth
at 1900-   Miss Porteous

North Roe
at 1765-   Arthur Irvine
1860s   Private Adventure Schools: Robert Anderson — lived at Toam; School at Orwick
c.1860   Methodist School opened
1860-1875   Thomas Scott

1878	New Board School opened
at 1878-	William Sloan
1878-1923	Robert S Bremner

Ollaberry

1719-	Charles Ross (SSPCK School)
	Private Adventure Schools – mid 19th century) – Agnes Clark, Sunnyside; Tammie Lowrie Henderson, Gluss Ayre, Bardister
1869	School built by United Presbyterian Church
1870-1871	David J. B. Haxton
1871-1877	John Jack
1878	School taken over by School Board
1877-1888	James Manson
1888-1895	James T. Robison (from Eshaness)
1895-1897	James A. Keith
1897-1904	Gilbert Y. Ferguson

Sullom

c. 1850-	Hugh Robertson – Private Adventure School – at North end of Loch of Lunnister
1875	New Board School opened
at 1876 & 1898	Hugh Robertson

TINGWALL

at 1714-	Barbara Henry, Gott (Private Adventure School)
1718-1721	Francis Beattie (SSPCK School)
1727-	John Smith do. (Also Session Clerk and Precentor)
1758-	James Tulloch (School at Strand)
1769	Parochial School built
1769-1773	Thomas Stout (Previously Society teacher at Fair Isle)
1780-1790	John Tulloch (dismissed by Kirk Session)
1801-1837	Alex. Sutherland (at Saundersfield, Brake of Tingwall)
c.1835-	John Thomson taught at Swinister for some years during Alex. Sutherland's illness)
1837-1839	John Carmichael
1839	Assembly School opened at Laxfirth
1839-1843	John Ross (moved to Bressay)
1843-1887	Charles C. Beatton
1873	New Board School opened – Charles Beatton appointed head

1887-1892   Laurina Halcrow
1892-1897   Gilbert Y. Ferguson (to Ollaberry)
1897-1908   Eliza Peterson

Girlsta

1875   New Board School opened
1882-1884   Miss Dick
1886-1888   Miss Sangster
1889-1890   J. Ferguson
1890-   Mrs Craib
at 1892-1894 D. Duncan
1894-1898   Miss Reid
1899-1900   Miss Smith

Whiteness

1737-   John Smith (SSPCK)
1750-1756   James Tulloch (to Weisdale) (SSPCK)
1760-   William Henry (at Quoyness)
17766-1775   Gilbert Henry (SSPCK)
1810-1833   James Irvine (SSPCK) (Went to Papa Stour)
1834-1836   William Fea (SSPCK)
1837-1840   David Towers   do.
1841-1843   James Bruce   do.
1843-1844   Robert Tulloch do.
1846-1848   John Omand   do.
1848-1858   Robert Jamieson do. (at Brugarth)
1858-1861   James Irvine   do.
1862-1863   J. Peterson   do.
1863-1865   Hector Towers do.
1866-1872   David Hobart   do. (New Board School after 1877)
1897-1898   Charles Robertson
1898-1904   J. Cowie

Weisdale

1736-1774   Gilbert Henry (maintained week about in houses of parents – Fee – 5d p. quarter)
1754-1755   James Tulloch   (SSPCK) (from Whiteness)
1777-1778   W. Yorston   do.
1781-1810   George Clunies   do.
1811-1817   Simon Paton   do.
1818-1833   Robert Bain   do.
1834-1865   Laurence Henderson do.

1877	New Board School opened
1877-	Mr Campbell
	Miss Coghill
at 1882-1885	Mr S. McKee
1886-1894	Miss Cooper
1895-1896	Miss Mary A Low
1896-1903	Miss Middleton

Scalloway

at 1718-	James Gadie
1741-1743	John Smith
	Grammar School
1756-	William Brown

SSPCK School – built 1821 on land donated by John Scott, sited North of Castle

1821-1844	Robert Tulloch (Joined Free Kirk and left School)
1844-1856	Thomas G. Jamieson (Appointed Inspector of Poor, Lerwick)
1856-1872	James Turnbull Smith
1876	New Board School opened
1876-1882	Donald McInnes
1882-1888	J. Cleland
1888-1890	George Beale
1891-1912	William Robertson (from Skeld)

Trondra

in 1831-c.1835	Charles Moodie (General Assembly School)
at 1837	School in wooden hut which was blown over in storm – school transferred to Old Booth
at 1837-	Peter Thomson
	New Board School opened
1885-1886	James Hunter
1886-1901	Adam Arthur

UNST
Baltasound

1721-1725	Francis Beattie (SSPCK School)
at 1729	William Ogilvy do.
1744-1746	James Kelman do.
1805	Parochial School established
at 1805-1833	Magnus Winwick

1834-1836   John Ingram
1837-1867   George Robertson
1868-1902   D. J. White
1878   New Board School opened

Burrafirth

c.1856-1884   Charles Arthur (General Assembly School) Possibly first
              Shetland teacher to receive a Government Pension

Haroldswick

1829-   General Assembly School established at Norwick
c.1830-1860   James Smith
1864-1898   Robert Dowal
1880   School Board acquired Assembly School – Robert
              Dowal appointed Headmaster
1898-1902   Miss McKerrell

Uyeasound

1838-1846   John Bain (SSPCK School)
c.1850- 1865 Laurence Jamieson (Free Church School)
at 1876-   G. McWhirter   do.
1873-1877   Alex. Arthur (General Assembly School at Gritquoy)
1877   New Board School opened
1882-1885   T. Hanton
1885-1886   Miss Alston
1886-1888   Mrs Kemp
1888-1892   Miss Hardie
1892-1893   Miss Allan
1894-1897   Miss Foubister
1898-1899   William Rowan

Westing

1846 -1867   John Clark (Free Church School after 1843)
1867-1876   John Spence
1878   Free Church School acquired and enlarged by Board
at 1882-1901 A. D. Sinclair

WALLS

1713   First SSPCK School in Shetland
1713-   Adam Marjoribanks (died a few weeks after taking up
              post)
1714-1715   Charles Ross (SSPCK School)
1740-1754   James Cheyne - Sandness   do.

1754-	George Cheyne (son of James) do.
1730/40s	Private Adventure Schools at Mid Walls – Teacher, George Fea; Braebister – James Moncrieff; and Kurkigarth (woman teacher)
1746-1748	Private Adventure School at Mid Walls – Thomas Henry of Hivdigarth
1751	Mid Walls school revived – James Jacobson
1757	Mid Walls school moved to Stove – Teacher, Duncan Moncrieff
1769-1779	George Greig (SSPCK School) 1774 – Happyhansel School became Parochial School for Walls
1779-1831	Alexander Greig
1832-1862	Rev. John Rannie
1862-1878	James Russell
1878-1879	James D Robertson
	New Board School opened
1879-1897	George Andrew
1897-1903	Andrew McCullie (from Mid Walls)

Dale

at 1878-	Henry Tait
at 1882-1883	Miss E. Sheridan
1883-1888	Miss M. Middleton (to Foula)
1889-1895	Miss Alexander
1895-1906	James D. Robertson

Mid Walls

1877	New Board School opened
1878-	Hector McKenzie
1882-1885	T. Smith
1886-1887	Miss J. G. F. Adam
1887-1893	Miss A. L. Hynd
1893-1894	Robert Burd
1894-1897	Mrs Martha Andrew
at 1899-	D. McKenzie

Sandness

1740-1754	James Cheyne (SSPCK School)
1755-1792	George Cheyne do.
1771-	George Jameson (Private Adventure at Watsness)
1793-1829	Laurence Moncrieff (SSPCK School)
1831-1836	Alex. Sutherland do.

1836-1858   William Pole   do.
1858-1899   Robert Jamieson   do.

Papa Stour
1741-1745   John Greig (SSPCK School)
1747-1755   John Greig   do.
1764-1770   George Greig (went to Happyhansel in 1770)
1800-1829   William Henry (SSPCK School)
            Vacant for considerable time
1829-1832   John Anderson
1834-1853   James Irvine (SSPCK School)
1855-1867   Thomas Manson   do.
1869   William Pole   do.
1875-1915   Duncan Robertson
1877-   New Board School opened

Foula
1733-   Thomas Henry
1755-1800   William Henry (SSPCK School)
1802-1821   Thomas Henry
1823-1848   John Fraser
1850-1853   Thomas Manson
1853-   James Cheyne
at 1861   Thomas Manson
1872-   Robert Gear (SSPCK School)
1877-   New Board School opened
1879-1882   Peter McWhirter
1882-1883   Mary Dow Morrison
1883-1886   Elizabeth Ann Morrison
1886-1888   James Hunter
1888-1894   Mary Middleton
1894-1895   Mary MacKay
1895-1900   John Shaw

YELL
Burravoe
c.1810-   Margaret Laurenson (Private Adventure School) at Houlland
1876   New Board School opened
    -1882   John Tulloch
1882-1883   Jessie Calder
1883-1904   Alex. Robb

East Yell

1823	Parochial School established
1823-1878	Andrew D. Mathewson
1879	New Board School opened
1882-1885	Miss Muir
1885-1887	Miss Forbes
1887-1888	Miss Scott
1888-1892	Miss M. J. Barron
1893-1900	Miss Helen Lyon

Herra

1890	New Board School opened
at 1892-1916	Gilbert Scollay

Mid Yell

1725-1728	Francis Beattie (SSPCK School)
c. 1810-	Catherine .... of Reafirth (Private Adventure School)
at 1878-	James Smith
1879	New Board School opened
at 1882-1885	D. Ogilvie
1885-1886	Miss Kate Clark
1886-1911	Alex. Watson

Ulsta

1879	New Board School opened
at 1882-	Miss Davidson
1883-1885	Miss Budge
1886-1889	Mrs Robertson
1890-	Miss Esson
1893-1895	Alex Falconer
1896-1897	Norman Mathieson
	School vacant for much of 1890s

West Sandwick

1881	New Board School opened
1881-1886	Miss Maggie H. Tait
1887-1892	Miss Harriet McRae
1893-1922	Mrs M. H. Sinclair

West Yell

at 1878-	Basil Johnson and J. L. Thomason
1879	New Board School opened

1884-1885	Miss Barr
1886-1888	Miss Ann Johnston
1888-1889	Miss C. Spence
1889-1898	Miss Arkle
1898-1902	Miss Bella Innes

North Yell

1827	Parochial School established at Braeside
1827	William Craigie
at 1854-	William Levie
at 1861-	John S. Houston
at 1861-	John T. Paterson – General Assembly School at Sellafirth
at 1870 & 78	Rev. Telfer do.

Colvister

1879	New Board School opened
1883-1885	Miss Clark
1885-1888	Miss Brown
1888-	Miss Young
at 1893-1909	Miss Weir

Cullivoe

1879	New Board School opened
at 1882-1886	J. Watson
1887-1906	J. C. Clubb

Gutcher

1879	New Board School opened
1856-1882	John S. Houston
1884-1885	Miss Phimister
1885-1889	Miss McCombie
1889-	Mrs Henry
at 1892-1906	Mrs Hoseason

Fetlar

1796-1814	Magnus Hoseason (SSPCK School)	
1814-1826	William Craigie	do.
1833-1834	Laurence Henderson	do. (Transferred to Weisdale)
1834-1845	Robert Bain	do. (After 1835-at Still)
1847-1866	Peter Inkster	do.

1873-1877	Peter Williamson (Board School)
at 1882-1883	C. Wood
1883-1887	Miss McKay
1887-1894	Miss Bond
1894-1896	Miss J. Bell
1896-1898	Miss Hilloake
1899-1900	Miss McLean

REFERENCES

1 Normal meant pertaining to the norm or pattern (of teaching)

APPENDIX B
Country Act anent Parochial Schools

AT LERWICK, the 14th November, 1724, anent proposals for erecting parochial schools in Zetland, in presence of Thomas Gifford of Busta, stuart and justiciar depute of Zetland, sitting in judgment, the whole heritors in Zetland present by themselves or their proxies, of which proposals the tenor follows in these words: Proposals unto the Gentlemen heritors of Zetland, anent settling parochial schools there, as law provides. As it is not unknown to any of you, that there is no legal school settled in any parish of this country, so there is none can pretend ignorance of the laws and acts of parliament made thereanent, whereby it is ordered and strictly observed throughout the whole kingdom of Scotland, that a legal school be erected in each parish thereof, as particularly by act W. par. I. ses. 6th. cha. 26, ratifying all former acts anent schools and schoolmasters, by which act the heritors of each parish are obliged to settle a fund for maintaining a school not under 100 marks Scots money yearly, nor exceeding 200 marks said money: and although that good and necessary law has not yet obtained in this country, yet certainly we are no less bound to the observation thereof than any other place within the said kingdom, nor can the same be supposed less necessary here than any where else; nay, it is plainly obvious to any thinking person, that the gross ignorance and immorality that doth every where abound here, is chiefly if not solely, owing to the want of that early education and instruction of children, not only in the knowledge of letters, but also in the principles of our holy religion, which a school in each parish would in great measure supply; and to insist upon the usefulness and necessity of such parochial schools were superfluous, seeing it is not presumable that any good man will dispute that, or refuse to contribute his utmost reasonable endeavours to propagate a work so pious and beneficial to the country, for in whatever parish a legal school is once settled, beside the benefit of that school; if the parish is discontiguous so as one school cannot serve the whole parish, they are, upon a right representation thereof, intitled to a school from the Society for Propagating Christian Knowledge, whereas the parish where no legal school is settled has no title thereunto. Now the grand objection against erecting these legal schools in this country is, that the heritage, or land rent, in most parishes here, is so inconsiderable, that the small heritors are not able to support the charge thereof; for obviating of which difficulty, although it cannot be denied but the charge thereof will be a greater burden upon the small heritors of Zetland, than upon most places in Scotland, yet considering the great benefit that may thereby arise to the poor inhabitants, it can be demonstrate if the heritors are willing and unanimous, there is not a parish in Zetland but can afford one hundred marks yearly, without any great burden upon the heritors, according to this method, that seeing there is no certain valuation of land-rent here, let that fund for the school be laid on in the same manner the cess is upon the marks of land, and the tenants to be the first advancers thereof, and the one half of what they advance to be allowed them out of the land rent; and thus there are some parishes in Zetland that by an imposition of one shilling Scots upon the markland will amount to upwards of one hundred pounds Scots: other parts there are that are at the rate of one shilling and sixpence, said money will surely amount to 100 marks, so that it can be left to the discretion of the heritors in each parish to proportion it upon the land as they shall see cause, the quota not being under 100 marks yearly; and this being agreeable to the method proposed in the act of parliament, and common practice throughout the kingdom, it is expected it will take the better in this place, or if any better method can be offered by any person or persons for effectuating this pious and necessary design, let the same be produced to be considered of by all the gentlemen concerned, or any other needful amendments, and the fund being once settled, the direction thereof to be left to the heritors, minister, and kirk session in each parish, to be improven to the best advantage for promoting the end thereby designed. *T.G.*

Lerwick, November 13th, 1724, the above proposals were read in open court, the whole heritors present, who took the same to advise and on till to-morrow at ten of the clock in the forenoon, being the 14th day of the said month: the said day the heritors under subscribing having deliberately considered the above proposals, did unanimously go in thereunto, upon the conditions and under the restrictions following; viz. 'that the fund above proposed be levied out of these lands commonly called King's Land, as well as the Udell land, by an equal proportion upon the marks of land; and, 2dly, that the said fund should be under the direction of the heritors; and also the nomination of the schoolmaster and seat of the school in the respective parishes, shall be, with the special advice and consent of the heritors; and in case of any schoolmaster being placed in any parish without consent foresaid, the heritors to be liberate from the payment of the fund above proposed; the heritors also having power to present a fit person for collecting of the said fund as proportioned upon the land by them in each parish; and in testimony whereof they did subscribe the same with their hands, and craved an act of court thereupon; and that extracts thereof should be transmitted to the several baillies and principal heritors in each ministrie; subscribed by Robert Sinclair, Laurence Bruce, James Mitchell, William Dick, Magnus Henderson, Andrew Scott, George Pitcarne, Robert Cragie, Robert Bruce, William Bruce, Thomas Hendrie, Robert Sinclair, John Laurence Stuart, Hector Scott, James Dunbar.

The Judge having seen and considered the premises, and finding the gentlemen heritors above-mentioned had unanimously gone into the proposals and method above laid down, for raising an annual fund in each parish in Zetland, for the maintenance of a school under the restrictions foresaid; and that the said fund may be made effectual in manner and for the end above proposed, did interpose, and hereby interpose the authority of the Stuart Court of Zetland thereto, and ordains the same to be recorded in the books thereof, and extracts of the same to be transmitted to the baillies and principal heritors of each parish; and in regard the right honourable the earl of Morton's concurrence thereto is not yet obtained, that his lordship's tenants may not be distressed for payment of the said fund until his consent be procured; and that for each extract, the clerk extractor be paid a crown. (Signed) T.G. extracted J.G.

(Extracted from Thomas Gifford's "Historical Description of Zetland" pp81-83)

APPENDIX C

KIRK SESSION RECORDS OF WALLS AND SANDNESS.

LIST OF SCHOLARS AT THE CHARITY SCHOOL IN SANDNESS (JAMES CHYNE, MR) ATTESTED AT THE VISITATION OF SAID SCHOOL DECEMBER 13TH 1744.

Scholars Names.	Yr Ages	qr. read last visit	qr. reading now	Watts 1st sett	Watts 2d sett	Watts Ass.Cat.	Prooff Cat.	Mors Cat.	Plain Cat.	Prayers.	Graces.	Attendance.
1 Males.												
And: Keith P.	17	Ps.	Josh. p 3tio	3 P.	3 P.	—	—	Whole	Whole	2 M 2 E.	2 B 2 A	very seldom.
And: Aisbr	10	N.T.	Do. p 2do	—	—	—	—	2 P	Do.	—	2 B 1 A	frequent
And: Twatt P.	9	N.T.	Mat. p 2do	—	—	—	—	—	5 P.	—	Do.	Seldom.
Arth: Wmson	17	Ps.	Josh p 3tio	—	—	—	—	Whole	Whole	Do.	2 B 2 A	very seldom
Geo: Anderson P.	16	Josh	Isa.	Whole	—	—	—	Do.	Do.	Do.	Do	Seldom.
Geo: Anderson Jun P	16	Ps.	Do p 2do	Do.	—	—	—	Do.	Do.	Do.	Do	Do
Geo: Crottie P.	15	Ps.	Josh p 2do	Do	—	—	—	Do.	Do.	1 M 1 E.	Do	Do.
Geo: Greig P.	16	N.T.	N.T.	Do.	—	—	—	4 P.	Do.	—	1 B 1 A	Do.
Henry Cowtt P.	9	N.T.	Do p 3tio	—	—	—	—	2 P.	Do.	—	2 B 2 A	freq.
Henry Bartleson P.	10	Ps.	Jer.	Do	3 P.	—	—	Whole	Do.	2 M 2 E.	Do	seldom.
Ja: Frazer.	12	Isa.	Isa p 2do	—	12 P.	—	—	Do	Do.	1 M 1 E	Do	Do.
Ja: Johnson P.	9	Ps.	Josh p 2do	—	—	—	—	—	4 P.	—	1 B. 1 A.	freq.
Jas: Malcolmson P.	6	Spell.	N.T.	—	—	—	—	Do.	Whole	—	Do	seld.
Ja: Muffeat	13	Ps.	Josh p. 3tio	—	—	—	—	Do	Do	Do	Do	Do
Ja: Twatt.	12	Do.	Do.	—	—	—	—	4 P.	Do.	—	2 B 2 A.	Do
Jno: And:son P.	8	N.T.	N.T.	—	—	—	—	3 P.	Do	—	1 B 1 A.	Do
Jno: Frazer	8	Do.	Do.	Whole	—	—	—	—	Do	—	Do	Do
Jonath: Duncan P.	9	Do.	Do.	—	—	—	—	Do.	Do.	2 M 2 E.	2 B 2 A.	Do
Law: Abernathy	19	Ps.	Josh.	—	—	—	—	6 P	Do.	1 M 1 E.	Do	Do
Law: And:son P.	19	N.T.	N.T.	—	—	—	—	—	Do	Do	Do	Do
Law: Gilbson P.	10	Ps.	Josh. o 2do	—	—	—	—	2 P.	Do	—	Do	Do
Law: Frazen P.	12	N.T.	Do.	—	—	—	—	Whole	Do.	2 M 2 E	Do.	Do
Gab: Cowtt P.	14	Ps.	Josh. p 2do	—	—	—	—	Do	Do	Do	Do.	Do
Mal: Wmson	15	Do	Do p 3tio	—	—	—	—	—	—	—	1 B 1 A	Do
Pet: Aisbr P.	10	A.B.C	R. Cat.	—	—	—	—	Do	Do.	Do	2 B 2 A	Do
Tho: Frazer	14	N.T.	Josh.	Whole	—	—	—	3 P.	Do.	—	1 B 1 A.	Do
Tho: Aisbr P.	13	Do	N.T.	—	—	—	—	—	5 P	—	Do	Con.
Tho: Lesslie	7	Spell.	N.T.	—	—	—	—	1 P	Do	—	Do	freq.
Tho. Robertson	8	R Cat	Do.	—	—	—	—	1 P.	Do	—	Do	Seld.
Walter Frazer P.	10	Do.	Prov.	—	—	—	—	—	Do	—	Do.	V : seld.
Walter Leisk P	9	Do.	R. Cat.	—	—	—	—	—	—	—	Do.	Do
Willm. And:son P	7	Do.	N.T.	—	—	—	—	Do	Do	—	Do.	Do
Geo: Thosson. P	11	Ps.	Josh p 2 do.	Whole	—	Whole	—	—	Do	2 M 2 E	2 B 2 A.	freq.
2 Females.												
Ag: Abernathie Sen P	13	Prov.	Prov.	—	—	—	—	1 P	5 P.	—	1 B 1 A	seld.
Ag: Abernathie Junr.	6	R Cat	N.T.	—	—	—	—	Do	Do	—	Do	Do
Ag: Frazer P.	7	N.T.	N.T.	—	—	—	—	1 P.	whole	—	1 B 1 A.	Seld.
Ag: Henry P.	8	R. Cat	Prov.	—	—	—	—	Do.	5 P.	—	Do	Do
Ag: Peters dr P.	14	Josh.	Josh p 2do	—	—	—	—	whole	whole.	1 M 1 E	2 B 2 A.	Do
Chr: Cowtt P.	13	Do	N.T.	—	—	—	—	Do	Do	Do	Do	Do
Eliz: Frazer Sen.	9	N.T.	R. Cat.	—	—	—	—	5 P	Do.	—	1 B 1 A.	Do
Eliz: Frazer Jun.	6	R. Cat	Do.	—	—	—	—	—	1 P	—	Do.	V : seld
Eliz: Frazer 3td	6	Spell.	R. Cat	—	—	—	—	—	—	—	Do.	Do
Euph: Frazer.	6	A.B.C	R. Cat.	—	—	—	—	—	—	—	Do.	Seld.
Euph: Muffeat	9	N.T.	N.T.	—	—	—	—	1 P.	6 P.	—	2 B 2 A.	Con.
Jan: Anders. dr.	13	Isa.	Isa p 2do	—	—	—	—	whole	whole	2 M 2 E	1 B. 1 A.	Sold
Jan: Chyne.	8	N.T.	N.T.	—	—	—	—	1 P.	5 P.	—	2 B 2 A.	Con.
Jan: Wms dr Sen	9	Ps.	Josh p 2do	—	—	—	—	whole	whole	1 M 1 E	1 B 1 A.	Seld.
Jan: Wms dr Jun P	7	Spell.	Prov.	—	—	—	—	1 P.	5 P.	—	Do	Do.
Jacobina Keith P.	11	N.T.	N.T. p. 2do	—	—	—	—	whole	whole	—	Do.	Do.
Jean Chyne	7	Prov.	N.T.	—	—	—	—	1 P.	5 P.	—	Do	Do.
Jean Keith P.	7	R. Cat	Prov.	—	—	—	—	2 P.	Do.	—	Do	Con.
Kath: Frazer P.	9	Prov.	N.T.	—	—	—	—	2 P.	Do	—	Do	Seldom
Marg: Andr dr.	6	Ps.	Josh p 2do	—	—	—	—	whole	whole	1 M 1 E	2 B 2 A	Constant.
Marg: Henry P.	11	N.T.	N.T. p 3tio	—	—	—	—	1 P	Do.	—	1 B 1 A.	Seldom.
Marion Abernathie	14	Ps.	Josh p 2do	—	—	—	—	whole	whole	Do	Do	Do.
Marion Frazer P.	11	N.T.	Ex.	—	—	—	—	1 P	Do.	Do	Do.	frequent.
Marion Wms. dr P.	15	Josh.	Josh p 2do	—	—	—	—	whole	whole	Do.	2 B 2 A.	Seld.
Mary Keith P	11	N.T.	N.T p 3tio.	—	—	—	—	Do	Do	—	1 B 1 A	freq.
Mary Peters dr P	10	R. Cat	R. Cat.	—	—	—	—	1 P	5 P.	—	Do	Seldom.
Sinavoe Frazes P	9	N.T.	N.T. p 2do	—	—	—	—	Do	whole	—	Do	freq.

Aisbr – Isbister
N.T. – New Testament
qr – where
And: son – Anderson
P – poor
Thosson – Thomson
Anders. dr – Andersdochter
Prayers: M=Morning; E=Evening
Watts, Proof, Mors (Mothers) Plain – Various editions of the Catechism

APPENDIX D

Plan presented c.1775 to William Balfour of Trenaby by Rev. James Buchan, Minister of Walls regarding establishment of a Legal School at Happyhansel, Walls[1]

Plan for turning the School of Happyhansel into a Legal School to be as extensively useful as Possible both to the Parish and the Country

1mo. That the Master be a married man of a good religious and moral character or be willing to marry and settle in a family, and have a wife capable to wash and dress, and keep boarders clean and neat both in bed clothes and back-clothes, as well as to prepare and serve up their dyet, in a Genteel and Decent manner.

2mo. That the Master be capable to teach Latin so far as to fit some scholars for the Colledge.

3tio. That he be Capable to Teach his English Scholars not only to read, spell, write and Cypher, but also if possible to teach Book-keeping and Navigation, and especially to Instruct both his English and Latin Scholars to purpose in the Principles of Religion and Morality and to Maintain a proper Authority and Discipline among them.

4to. That he be bound to keep from six to twelve boarders in his house on as easy terms as possible if so many or even more offer.

5to. That he be bound to teach Twenty English Scholars within the Parish of Walls, (if so many attend) and that gratis i.e. without exacting quarter payments in Spelling, reading, Church Music, and the Principles of Religion, but no further branches of Education, unless he be paid for it. And that the Quarter Payments be adjusted by a majority of Votes by the Heritors and Session, both for the Scholars that learn Latin, and those that are taught Writing, Arithmetic, Book-keeping or Navigation.

6to. That the said Master be also Capable to Officiat as Session Clerk and Precentor and be bound to do so. As also to Sing, read and pray in the Latron[2] when there is no Sermon in the Parish of Walls.

7mo. As to the Masters Encouragement it is Humbly Proposed

(1) That the Minimum of a Legal Salarie (or an Hundred Mark Scots) be paid him Yearly by the Common Tennents or land labourers through the Ministry which amounts only to a penny half-penny upon each Mark of Land called Rentild land, and that the Outbreaks or Cotter

1 Orkney Archives, D2/18/13
2 Lectern

Rooms which are not rentild, be reckoned to pay as for a Mark of land for each Crown of Rent they pay to their Master.

(2) That the Heritors pay their half of the Minimum over and above (being only nine pennys Scots on the Mark land) for a further encouragement to the Master.

(3) That he have the Sole benefit of the Ministers Mortification[3] for Teaching the Children of the Commons as above Specified viz. The Principal House, office houses, yard and four and a half Acres of Uncultivated ground adjacent thereunto, with Priviledge of Moss and one Cows grass in the Hoga of Voe besides the four and a half Acres abovenamed all which may be valued to Three Pound Sterling per annum, besides forty shillings Sterling yearly to be paid him by the Person to whom the Minister is to Assign his House and nine mark land in the room of Voe.

(4) That he has Twenty Shillings of Salarie as Session Clerk and Precentor, the Perquisites of that ofice being also valued to twenty shillings more. Now if the above Articles be sumd up, they soill amount to fifteen Pound, six shillings and eightpence sterling of a fixed yearly income. And as for other more casual emoluments arising from the boarding Scholars, and the quarter payments of these that are taught Writing, Cyphering, bookkeeping, Navigation or Latin, it may very possibly rise to an equality of his settled encouragement, but cannot well be supposed less than the half thereof.

I shall now consider the Principal objections that may be Stated against this Plan, and endeavour to Answer them to satisfaction, and

(1) It may be objected that the present Master is not so fully qualified as proposed in the plan, and yet that it would not be fair to set him aside during life. To which it is answered 1) That I am perfectly of the mind that it would be both unjust and unnecessary to set aside the present Master from the Station he is now in provided he behaves as well in that Station as he has hitherto done since he Commenced a Schoolmaster.

(2) That though Mr Greig be not yet capable to teach Latin so far as to fit boys for the Colledge, yet he is daily making progress in that branch of Literature in Proportion as the boys he is now teaching are standing need and it is my intention Personally to assist him till his present Latin Scholars be fit for going to the Colledge by spending three hours a day with him and them, unless on Friday, Saturday and Sabbath. And though Mr Greig cannot teach Navigation, I will undertake for it, that such as want to have that Branch of Education shall have Access to be taught it at his School and Book-keeping also within three or four years hence. And as for Arithmetick and every other branch of an English Education

3 Bequest in perpetuity

mentioned in the Plan I have not known any Schoolmaster in this Country either more capable or more assiduous and succesful in teaching the same than he is.

(3) It may be objected as unreasonable to lay the whole minimum of a Legal Salarie upon the Tennents in this Ministry, since there are three United Parishes of it, viz. Sandness, Papa and Foula that can have no access to a school in Walls and therefore cannot be supposed willing to pay their quota of a legal salarie to it, though they may be in law compelled so to do. To this I answer, that for my own part I could not find in my heart to insist on these remote Parishes paying their quota of a Legal School to Walls on the supposition that they had no access to the means of a Christian Education by the erection of a Legal School in Walls, and I grant further that without their quota, even the minimum of a Legal Salarie could not be made out. But then I must add that in the event of getting a Legal School erected in Walls, and no otherwise, the Society for Propagating Christian Knowledge will undoubtedly bestow the four Pound ten shillings of salarie they now give to the Charity School in Walls, to be divided between two Charity Schoolmasters, one to teach in Sandness and the other in Papa and would also continue the Small Salarie they give to Foula whereby the common people in these three remote parishes would have the means of a Christian Education among themselves and books gratis from the Society to boot. And this could not miss to engage them Cheerfully to pay their small quota: For there are but three land labourers of the common people in the whole ministry that occupy nine mark land, only one that labours eight mark, and only two that labour seven, but a few that labour six, the far greater part not having above four, and a great many that have less, and those few that have six mark land and above are of the most substantial common people. In a word, the most part would not have above a sixpence a year, and none save three above a shilling to pay the Legal School Schoolmaster, so that a lispound of bear or one and a half Lispound of Potatoes or two pair of good (?coarse) Stockings would defray the whole charge of an English Christian Education to the Greatest Common tennent in the Ministry, and the half of that value would pay the Greatest of the quotas of others, if they do not aspire to Higher branches of Learning, than what I have abovementioned. And if they do, it is supposed they are able to pay for it.

(4) Another objection, and indeed very plausible, is the seeming improbability of getting a Master so qualified as above to undertake the task during life upon the encouragement proposed by the plan. But in answer to this Objection let it be considered that the Plan does not suppose that there is a Necessity of having a Schoolmaster who has cost

his Parents the expence of an Academical Education. Such a man might be found capable to teach all the branches of Learning proposed by the Plan who had never been at a University. Mr Barclay Minister of Delting has such a one just now and there is no doubt but several such might be found in the North of Scotland. But without going so far off I dont at all despair but a Succession of such Schoolmasters may arise out of the present school at Happyhansel and I doubt nothing but the present seeming difficulties of that kind will be superseded in a few years hence if the plan now proposed be agreed to and established.

A third objection may be that if you teach the children of the Commons Writing and Arithmetick they will make a bad use of it, they will grow Vain and Proud. Theill think themselves too wise and too good to be fishers and landlabourers in their own Country and go off to foreign parts in hopes of growing rich and great and men of renown etc. I answer (1) This objection seems to be obviate already by the Plan itself whereby the children of the Common People are provided in no other branches of Learning save that of Spelling, Reading, Church Music, and the Principles of Christian Religion unless their Parents be willing and able to pay for it, and I assure you there is little ground to expect the one or the other far less both among the Commons in this Ministry. (2) I can say by experience there are few young men who have voluntarily gone abroad from this Ministry, and these but Illiterate Persons, and who have gone off without their Parents consent, and against their will, a thing that is in itself unjust and unnatural, for I have always preached the same Doctrine to them that you did, when last here, and which every Divine and Moralist teaches, that it is as Incumbent on Children to Assist and Provide for their Parents when they need it, and cannot help themselves, as it is on Parents to Assist and Provide for their Children when they could not help themselves. And that no Son or Daughter have a power to leave Father or Mother, or Marry without their consent, unless they withhold their consent unreasonably and without a good Cause. (3) I think further, that the better Children are instructed in their Relative duties, (which is certainly the duty of Schoolmasters as well as of Ministers and Parents to do) the less will their Conscience allow them to break off from their Parents against their will. And surely a Schoolmasters authority joined to that of Parents would be more likely to prevail with them, than that of Parents, at least Ignorant Parents, alone. And I think this is a point in which Magistrates, Ministers, Parents and Schoolmasters should concur in their Respective Spheres to Establish in this, and in Every Country, unless Weighty reasons appear to determine any of them otherways.

A fourth objection may be Drawn from the Place and Situation of this School. It may be said, it is far off in a Corner; Lerwick is more centrical; has more accommodation for Boarders; more Polite Company and Converse, etc. Answer. No fear of Accommodation in this place in or near the Schoolhouse. No such Temptations here as in Lerwick, either to Idleness and Sauntering nor for the Corruption of Boys morals by ill company and bad example.

On the other hand how Considerable and extensive might the advantages of this Plan be if it could be brought into Execution.

(1) As to the Heritors of the Parish and other Gentlemen through the Country they would have the advantage (1) of Cheaper boarding (by the half I suppose) than by sending their Children abroad or to Lerwick (2) Cheaper teaching by half (3) Cheaper Clothes and Linnens by a good deal, and little or no demand on them for Pocket Money (4) no Expense for fire nor much for Light (5) no Expense for a house to the Master and Scholars, that being provided already, yea and a fund agreed upon by the Minister and Session for the future reparation and upholding of it (6) the Heritors share of the legal Salarie very small, being only the Minimum that law requires and no more but nine pennies Scots for each Mark of Land.

(2) As to the Scholars; the Boarders would (1) have their Education within the house where they are lodgd, and be always under the Masters eye and inspection, which would contribute much both to their Close attendance and learning and Morals. (2) Other Boarders not lodgd with the Master would at least be lodgd very near him. (3) None of the Children in Walls would have two miles to travel to the School, and most of them would be within one mile or half a mile or less distance, unless Eight families in a place called Watsness, which families join with a Contiguous place called Dail in Sandness for a small School among themselves; and as to the Charity Scholars in Sandness, Papa and Foula, scarce any of them will have a whole mile to their School and but few so much as half a mile.

(3) As to the Common People through the whole Ministry; Those would have the advantage of a Sufficient Christian Education for their Children, almost for nothing. It would be only from three pense to a shilling yearly. Prodigiously easy to the poorest householder that can or ought to keep house at all. Besides that in this case every family would have access to the Publick reading of Gods word and other good books with Publick Prayer and Singing and that in their own Parish Kirk, even on Sabbaths when there is no Preaching. And all this to be continued (under God) from Generation to Generation.

(4) As to the Master himself besides the pretty tolerable Encouragement abovementioned for one that has not had a Colledge Education he will have besides: (1) Some Emoluments from the land that will be always increasing in proportion to its improvement (2) Freedom from all Publick burdens, Scatt, Cess, Corn Teind, and, I suppose, of Casual tiends too (3) Freedome from the usual expence of free hospitality ....etc. which is no small saving in this Country to People of any fashion but is not to be expected nor ought to be allowed to a Schoolmaster especially one that keeps boarders.

(5) The Education of his own Children with little or no cost save a few books.

Now I do hope (however Visionary you may suppose that hope to be) that as my Plan is Sincerely meant for the Publick good, He whose Influence directs and Order the Hearts and Ways of Men will not make my well meant Scheme altogether abortive, and will furnish out a succession of Proper Masters to Carry it on, upon the funds his Providence has already, or may here after think fit to order for it. If he has otherwise Appointed, His Holy Will be done. It well becomes me to Submitt. Meantime, upon the small encouragement I am to give for myself, i.e. the money, the house, the land, and other Priviledges above mentioned, with the Salarie and Perquisites of the Session Clerk and Precentor I can obtain a Tolerable English Schoolmaster Sufficient for teaching the Children of the Commons <u>In Walls</u>. But indeed I do think the house rather too good for a Common Man, being so well accommodate for a better Masters family as well as for Scholars and Boarders. And Above all it would be a very mortifying disappointment to me to want the Societys help which Sandness, Papa and Foula might have if we had a Legal School in Walls. And which we cannot expect without it.

GLOSSARY

adventure school — private school run usually by an elderly woman in her home. Generally accepted fees in kind — potatoes, milk, fish, peats.
ad vitam aut culpam — till some misconduct be proved
catechism — questions and answers relating to the principles of Presbyterian belief
heritor — landowner of a Scottish parish
merk — two-thirds of a pound Scots or 13 1/3d sterling
pound Scots — one shilling and eight pence sterling (8p)
12d old money — 5p new money
reader — substitute for a minister in Church of Scotland
skeo — rough, stone-built shed for wind-drying fish
stent — quota of duty or tax payable by inhabitants of a parish

MAIN SOURCES CONSULTED

Manuscript

Anderson Educational Trust, Minutes, 1888-1932, SA
Commissioners of Supply for Shetland, Minutes, SA
Gifford, Thomas, Day Book 1708-1732, SA
Heritors of Lerwick and Gulberwick, Minutes, SA
Kirk Session Minutes for Shetland Parishes, SA
Log Books of Shetland Schools, SA
Mathewson, Andrew D., Papers, SA
Nicolson Papers, SA
Procurator-Fiscal Precognitions, SA
Record of Work, Haroldswick Public School, Unst
Register of Bonds, SA
Reid Tait Papers, SA
Shetland School Board Minutes, SA
Shetland Secondary Education Committee 1893-1894, SA
SSPCK, Minutes of General Meetings, SRO
SSPCK, Minutes of Committee Meetings, SRO
SSPCK, Returns by Parish Ministers 1755, SRO
SSPCK Records No 65 — Reports of visits to the schools of the SSPCK 1834-37, SRO
Zetland Presbytery Minutes, SA

Official Reports

Answers made by Schoolmasters in Scotland to Queries circulated in 1838, PP 1841, xix, 64, SRO
Digest of Parochial Returns made to the Select Committee appointed to enquire into the Education of the Poor, Session 1818, Vol. 3, 1819, SRO
Education Commission (Scotland) Second Report by Commissioners appointed to enquire into the Schools of Scotland, PP 1867, Nat. Lib. of Scotland
Education Enquiry: Abstract of the Answers and Returns made pursuant to an Address in the House of Commons dated 9th July, 1834
Education in Orkney and Shetland, Professor George G. Ramsay, 1876, Shetland Library

Education in Zetland, Reports by HMIs 1963, 1971, Shetland Library
Endowed Schools (Scotland) Commission, 1874, Nat. Lib. of Scotland
Moral Statistics of the Highlands and Islands of Scotland compiled by
 Inverness Society for the Education of the Poor in the Highlands
 and Islands, Inverness, 1826, SRO
Returns from the Sheriffs of the Several Counties of Scotland, relative
 to the Parochial Schools of 905 Parishes, PP 1826, xviii, 95, SRO
Statistics relative to Schools in Scotland collected by the Registrars of
 Births, Marriages and Deaths, 1865, SRO

Newspapers and Periodicals

John o Groat's Journal
Shetland Life
The Educational News
The New Shetlander
The Shetland Advertiser
The Shetland News
The Shetland Times

Books

Anderson Educational Institute 1862-1962, Lerwick 1962
Baltasound School Centenary, 1979
Brand, John, A New Description of Orkney, Zetland, Pightland-Firth
 and Caithness, Edinburgh 1703
Cowper, A. S., SSPCK Schoolmasters 1709-1872, Scottish Record
 Society, New Series 20, 1997
Deyell, Annie, My Shetland, Sandwick, 1975
Donaldson, Gordon, Shetland Life under Earl Patrick, Edinburgh 1958
Donaldson, Gordon, (Ed) Court Book of Shetland 1602-1604,
 Edinburgh 1954
Duncan, W. Rae, Directory of Shetland, Lerwick 1861
Fasti Ecclesiae Scoticanae, Vol 7, ed. Scott, Edinburgh 1928
Gifford, Thomas, Historical Description of Shetland 1733, Edinburgh
 1889
Hjaltland Miscellany, Vol 2, ed. Reid Tait, Lerwick 1937
Irvine, James W., Through Storm to Calm, Lerwick 1995
Knox, Henry M., Two Hundred and Fifty Years of Scottish Education,
 1696-1946, Edinburgh 1953
Low, Rev. George, A Tour through the Islands of Orkney and Shetland
 1774, Kirkwall 1879
Lewis, George, Scotland a Half-educated Nation, Glasgow 1834
Manson, Thomas, Lerwick in the Last Half Century. Lerwick 1923

Manson's Almanac 1892-1900
Memoirs of Arthur Laurenson, ed. Catherine Spence, London 1901
Mill, Rev. John, Diary, Scottish Historical Society, Edinburgh 1899
New Statistical Account of Shetland, Edinburgh 1841
Old Statistical Account of Shetland 1791-1799, ed Reid Tait, Lerwick 1925
Osborne, G. S., Scottish and English Schools, London 1966
Peace's Almanac and County Directory of Orkney and Shetland 1882-1892
Reid, John T., Art Rambles in Shetland, Edinburgh 1869
Saunders, Laurence J, Scottish Democracy 1815-1840, London 1950
Scotland, James, A History of Scottish Educàtion, 2 vols, London 1969
Simpson, Ian J., Education in Aberdeenshire before 1872, London 1947
Society in Scotland for the Propagation of Christian Knowledge, A Summary Account of the Rise and Progress, Edinburgh 1783

INDEX

A Friend to Zetland – 81
Aberdeen Journal – 160
Aberdeen – 9, 14, 43, 69, 118, 132, 160, 172, 193, 243
Aberdeenshire – 9, 43, 243
Act of 1803 – 106-107, 112-113
Act of the Head Court – 9
Act of the Lawting – 8
Address in the House of Commons, 1834 – 109, 117, 241
Advanced Divisions – 194
Adventure Schools – 17, 25, 50, 68-69, 109-110, 128, 136, 209, 213, 220-221, 225
AEI — prospectus 1888 – ill. 24
AEI, 1932 — Class Six with teachers – ill. 22
AEI staff and pupils c. 1880 – ill. 2
AEI with teachers and pupils c. 1880 – ill. 1
Aithsting – 5, 8, 12, 17-18, 20, 23, 25-27, 73, 81, 88, 101, 136, 156, 188, 194-195, 197, 207, 209, 242
Aitken, John M. – 184
Alford – 43
Allardice, John – 157, 171-173, 216, ill. 18
Ambulatory Schools – 34, 54-55, 67
America – 106
Anderson Bursary – 174
Anderson Educational Institute – 128, 132, 134, 146, 154, 157-158, 160, 164-176, 184-185, 192, 204, 216, 242
Anderson Education Trust, Governors of – 170
Anderson Endowment – 170, 172
Anderson High School – 195-197, 203
Anderson, Arthur – 99, 105, 110, 131, 134, 164-165, 167, 175, 178, 184, 219, ill. 16

Anderson, John – 32, 211, 215, 226
Andrew, George – 144
Anne, Queen – 20
Archibald, Rev. William – 74
Argyll Commission – 112, 138, 140
Argyll, Duke of – 139
Arthur, Adam – 137, 208, 217, 223
Articles of Agreement – 124
Assembly School – 122, 137-138, 152, 207, 210-211, 217-218, 221, 223-224, 228
Assembly school, Laxfirth, Tingwall – ill. 7
Astronomy – 83, 92, 94-95
Attainment tests – 191, 192
Auld Kirk – 126, 135, 166
Aywick, East Yell – 86
Bain, Captain George – 167-168, 172
Bain, Mr (of Burravoe) – 103
Balfour of Burleigh, Lord – 158, 160-162, 167, 170
Balfour of Trenaby – 65, 69, 234
Balfour, Andrew – 35, 37, 212
Baltasound – 187, 194, 204, 223, 242
Baptist Church – 183, 208
Baptist Manse on the Hillhead – 128
Baptist Manse – 128
Baptist – 110, 128, 183, 208, 219
Barclay, Rev. James – 102, 216
Barclay, Rev. John – 74
Bardister – 143, 221
Bayne, Robert – 120
Beattie, Francis – 25, 34, 39, 53, 210, 212-213, 221, 223, 227
Beatton, Charles C. – 148, 221, ill. 9
Bellevue – 197
Bendrie, Walls – 59-60
Bible – 7, 24-25, 30, 34, 38-39, 50-51, 66, 83, 91-94, 97-98, 103, 110, 131, 145, 169, 177, 193, 205
Bigton – 136, 189, 213, 215

INDEX

Billister – 137, 217
Binning, Rev. William – 14
Birsay – 48
Blair, Barbara – 110
Blance, George W. – 185
Block Release – 200
Board of Education – 139
Boddam – 145-146, 153-154, 189, 213
Boer War – 189
Bonar, Rev. John – 118
Booth of Urie – 85
Bothwell, Bishop Adam – 7
Brae – 58, 60, 122, 194-197, 202, 210-211, 216, 225, 228
Braebister – 58, 60, 225
Brand, Rev. John – 10, 15
Bressay Sound – 118
Bressay – 2, 8, 18, 24, 50, 75, 77-79, 82, 118, 122, 146, 154-155, 179, 209, 221
Brettabister – 188, 217
Britain – 141
British Linen Company – 41
Brough, Whalsay – 194, 218-219
Brougham, Lord – 108-109
Brown, William – 76, 214, 223
Bruce Hostel – 192
Bruce, Robert – 192, 232
Bruce, William – 68, 232
Brunton Report – 197, 201
Bryan, James – 165
Brydon, Rev. John – 101
Buchan, Rev. James Jnr – 38, 50-51, 53-54, 56-69, 72, 74, 83, 209, 234
Buchan, Rev. James Snr – 21, 30-32, 44, 50
Burgess, J. J. Haldane – 154, 172
Burn of Setter, Walls – 59
Burra Isle – 2, 210
Burrafirth – 188, 209, 224
Burraland, Walls – 58
Burravoe – 102-103, 122, 143, 226
Butter, Patrick – 81-82, 118
"Byre" school, Laxfirth, Nesting – ill. 23
Caesar's Commentaries – 124

Caithness – 12, 17, 26-27, 242
Campbell, John – 37, 217
Canada – 27
Canisbay – 26
Canongate – 80
Captain Parry's *Discoveries in Quest of a New Passage* – 99
Catechisms – 7, 15, 24-25, 34, 38-39, 51, 91-94, 97, 110, 119, 121, 145, 148, 233, 240
Cattanach, Rev. John – 24
Central School – 155, 184-185
Certificate of Merit – 152
Chaplain to the Episcopal Laird (of Lochend) – 23
Cheyne, George – 67, 225
Cheyne, James – 38, 54-56, 60, 181, 213-214, 224-226
Church collections – 28, 31, 53, 64, 72
Church Courts – 155
Church of Scotland – 20, 75, 110, 122, 136, 138, 240
Church schools – 16, 17, 139
City and Guilds Certificate – 203
Clark, John – 31, 219, 224
Classroom in Burra Public School, c.1910 – ill. 27
Cluness, Andrew T. – 174, 176, 186-187, 204
Code, New, 1875 – 142
Collafirth – 188, 212, 220
Collector of Customs – 63
Colvaster – 142
Commercial Course – 191, 196
Commission of Inquiry – 109
Commissioners of Police, Lerwick Burgh – 170
Commissioners of Supply – 10, 43-44, 61, 74-77, 80, 170, 241
Committee of Council on Education – 168
Committee of Established Schoolmasters – 97
Common Course – 195-196
Commons, House of – 109, 117, 241
Company of Linen Manufacturers of Zetland – 41

Conditions of Service – 152
Confession of Faith – 18, 20, 23, 88
Conservative government – 199
Consultative Council on the Curriculum – 195
Control Examination – 191
Copenhagen – 13
Corn Laws – 126
Country Acts – 9, 14, 47
County Council – 190
County Rooms – 166
Court and Commissary Records – 8
Court of Session – 74, 78
Cowan, Rev. Charles – 100, 113
Craig, Rev. Alexander – 14
Craigie, William – 113, 228
Craik, Sir Henry – 173, 184
Crawford, Dr John – 189
Cruisdale, Sandness – 179
Cullivoe – 113, 142-143, 228
Cunningsburgh – 8, 37, 72-73, 118, 136, 154, 197, 212-213
Curkigarth, Walls – 58
Dale – 23, 33, 59, 71-73, 76, 96, 118, 121-122, 154-155, 179-180, 188-189, 204, 212-215, 222, 225, 228
Davis Straits – 107
Day Release – 200, 202
Delting – 18-19, 23-24, 32, 34-35, 45-48, 50, 57-58, 60, 74, 81, 87, 100, 112, 122, 136, 188, 197, 201, 210, 219, 237
Deyell, Annie – 188
Director of Education – 192
Disraeli, Benjamin – 181
Donaldson, Prof. Gordon – 3, 8, 242
Douglas of Spynie – 44
Doura Voe – 2
Down-Walls – 58, 60
Dunbar, Rev. Alexander – 24
Duncan, Andrew – 124
Duncan, Gilbert – 86, 88, 90, 104
Duncan, Rev. George – 21, 44, 50-51
Duncan, Rev. John – 24, 51
Dundas, Sir Laurence – 65
Dunn and Raby, missionaries – 98

Dunrossness – 8, 18-19, 23, 33-35, 37, 48, 55-56, 72, 81-82, 140-141, 143, 145, 152-153, 163, 181, 189, 197, 212
Durham, W. Robertson – 185
Dury Voe – 143
Dutch – 33, 45, 107
E.I.S. – 142, 154, 161-162
Earldom – 4, 11, 45
Earlston Presbytery – 22
Early Closing Movement – 130
East Burrafirth – 188
East Yell schools – ill. 6
Edinburgh – 4, 10, 12-13, 17, 19, 20-22, 24-25, 29, 37, 42, 51, 53, 79-82, 86-87, 97, 103-104, 110, 118, 135, 139, 154, 180, 182, 214, 242-243
Education (Scotland) Act, 1872 – 139, 173
Education (Scotland) Act, 1901 – 184
Education Act, 1918 – 190
Education Act, 1946 – 192-193, 200
Education Authority – 190
Education Bill, 1869 – 106, 134, 139, 164
Education Committee of the Church of Scotland – 110
Education Committee – 110, 174, 176, 191, 193-196, 200-202, 241
Education Endowments (Scotland) Act – 170
Education of Pupils with learning Difficulties – 198
Educational Institute of Scotland – 160, 162-163
Education (Scotland) Act, 1901 – 173
Educational News – 149, 163, 242
Ellaby, Rev. G. W. – 134, 165-167, 216
Elvista, Walls – 59
Endowed Schools (Scotland) Commission – 168, 176, 242
England – 147, 154, 187, 190, 196
English Education Act, 1870 – 139
Episcopal – 23, 44, 47, 138, 168, 182
Erfurt, University of – 13

INDEX

Eshaness – 25, 31, 118, 188, 190, 211, 219-221
Established Church – 99, 181
European Union – 204
Fair Isle – 1-2, 8, 35-37, 72, 77, 136, 177, 181, 214, 221
Fairbairn, Robert – 151, 207
Fetlar – 19, 28, 34, 81, 84-86, 89, 96-97, 100-101, 104, 107, 111-113, 115-118, 120-121, 136, 228
Feuars and Heritors – 184
Fidelity – 118
"Fifteen" Rebellion – 39
Fifth Book of Euclid – 171
Finlayson, Rev. John – 90
First Book of Discipline – 11
First Lerwick Public School – 183-184
First World War – 145, 154, 186
Firth – 12, 17, 87, 137-138, 143, 146, 148, 188, 194-195, 209, 211-212, 217, 220-221, 224, 227-228, 242
Fisken, Rev. Andrew – 45, 47
Fordyce, Dorothy – 83
"Forty-five" Rebellion – 41
Foula – 1-2, 27, 35-38, 42, 53, 56, 58, 60, 68, 118, 180-181, 205, 225-226, 236, 238-239
Fraser, Alex – 23
Fraser, John – 118, 226
Free Church – 110, 150, 157, 210-211, 213-214, 224
Free Kirk – 122, 138, 223
Freemasons – 124
French Revolution – 106
Gaddie, William – 33
Garth Estate – 140
Garth Estate – 140
Gaudy, Malcolm – 214, 215, ill. 15
General Assembly Commission – 10, 18
General Assembly Report – 7
General Scottish Vocational Qualifications – 203
Gifford, Arthur, of Busta – 88
Gifford, Thomas (of Busta) – 3, 4, 44-46, 48, 50-51, 53, 123, 230, 232, ill. 10

Gifford, Rev. William – 31
Girlsta – 51, 188, 222
Glasgow – 172, 242
Glass, John G. – 126-128, 216
Gluss, Ollaberry – 31, 143, 219, 221
Godly Commonwealth – 28
Goodlad, Dr Alistair – 204
Gordon, Rev. James – 116
Gossabrough – 86, 95, 102, 188
Gott – 55, 148, 221
Grammar School in Lerwick – 123
Gray, Gilbert – 137, 210, 217
Gray, Rev. Robert – 24, 37
Great Circle Sailing – 95
Greek – 185
Greenland – 61, 66, 85, 89-90, 107-108, 130
Greig, Archibald – 68
Greig, George – 61, 63, 67-68, 225-226
Greig, James – 115
Greig, John – 54, 56, 226
Gremista – 203
Grierson, Rev. James – 45
Griffen, El Gran – 8
Grott, Katherine – 72
Group Certificate – 1-86
Grunafirth – 138, 217
Gruting – 122, 147, 207
Gulberwick – 32, 122, 135, 149, 151, 163, 170, 183, 215-216, 241
Gunnister – 188, 220
Gutcher – 142, 228
Guttorm, Foula – 36
H.O.R.S.A. Classrooms – 194
Hamburgh – 4
Hamnavoe – 197, 210
Hanseatic merchants – 3
Happyhansel – 62-65, 67-68, 77, 144, 194-195, 205, 225-226, 234, 237
Happyhansel School — ruins – ill. 11
Haroldswick – 187, 204, 224, 241
Harray – 27
Hascosay – 84
Havera – 188
Hay & Ogilvy – 126
Hay, James – 41, 126

Hay, William – 118
Henderson, Andrew James – 78
Henderson, Laurence – 121-222, 228
Henderson, M. J. – 193
Henry, Archibald – 62
Henry, George Jnr – 119
Henry, George Snr – 119
Henry, James – 50-51
Henry, Thomas – 36, 59, 226
Henry, William – 68, 210, 212, 222, 226
Higher Class Public School – 171
Higher Leaving Certificate – 157, 174, 199
"Higher Still" – 199
Highland Society of Scotland – 80
Highlands and Islands Educational Trust – 174
Hildasay – 188
Hillswick – 31, 52, 143, 219, 220
Hivdigarth – 59, 225
HMI – 103, 105, 118, 142, 144-145, 147-152, 155, 157-158, 160-161, 168-169, 171, 180, 184, 186, 194, 196, 199, 202, 223, 242
Holy Communion – 11
Homer – 124
Hoseason, Horatio – 85
Hoseason, James – 90, 104
Hoseason, Magnus – 85, 228
Houll, North-a-voe, Mid Yell – 83
Howll – 58
Hudson Bay Company – 27
Hugens, Walter – 23
Hull, Mr – 126
Hunter, James – 148, 211, 216, 223, 226
Illustrated London News – 180
Ingram, Rev. James – 85
Innes, Robert – 202
Innes, Walter – 15
Inspector – 117-122
Intelligence and Attainment Tests – 191-192
Intermediate Certificate – 186
Inverness Society for Education of Poor in Highlands – 98

Inverness – 98, 110, 117, 141, 205, 242
Irvine, James W. – 200
Irvine, James – 118, 121, 211, 218, 222, 226
Isabella – 39, 207-208, 215, 217
Islesburgh House, Lerwick – 200
Jacobitism – 41
Jacobson, James – 60, 225
James III – 13
Jamieson, Christina – 180
Jamieson, Edward – 180
Jamieson, Frank – 180
Jamieson, Dr James – 180
Jamieson, Professor John – 104
Jamieson, Mrs – 180
Jamieson, Robert – 179-180, 213-214, 222, 226, ill. 5
Janet Courtney Hostel – 192
Johnson, Laurence – 137, 217
Johnston, Arthur Anderson – 175
Johnston, James Halcro – 156
Junior Student system – 155
Jutland – 13
Kemp, Dr John – 79-82, 118
Kerr, John – 151
King Harald Street – 197
King James VI and I – 9
Kirk Session – 9, 10, 17-19, 28, 32-33, 46, 53, 55, 58, 60, 90-91, 95, 98, 155-156, 220-221, 231, 241
Kirkwall Grammar School – 13, 124
Kirkwall – 11-13, 15, 29, 42, 124, 242
Kirton, Joseph D. – 162, 216
Knox, John – 11
Labour Government – 195
Latin – 15, 20, 64-65, 67, 74, 84, 86, 88, 92-93, 102, 110, 123-125, 127, 144, 147, 152, 158, 171-174, 180, 185, 234-235, 240
Laurence, William T. – 181
Laurenson, Arthur – 127, 135, 243
Law, James, Bishop of Orkney and Shetland – 9
Lawting Act – 9
Laxfirth, Nesting – 137-138, 217
Laxfirth, Tingwall – 148, 221

INDEX

Leask, Belle – 137
Leaving Certificate – 157, 159, 161, 173-174, 186, 197, 199
Legal School – 11, 21, 30, 32, 39, 43-45, 47-49, 54, 57, 60-61, 64-65, 67, 69-77, 79-81, 87, 230, 234, 236, 239
Leisk, John – 159
Leisure and Recreation Department – 202
Leith – 122
Leon, Ollaberry – 107, 141, 143
Lerwick Central School – 183-185
Lerwick F. E. Centre – 203
Lerwick Harbour – 164
Lerwick Infant school – 144
Lerwick Instruction Society – 128, 129, 131, 165
Lerwick Parochial School – 127, 148, 165, 168
Lerwick Parochial School c.1872 — pupils with headteacher – ill. 20
Lerwick Subscription School – 86-87, 123, 164
Lerwick – 13-15, 17-19, 23, 32, 34, 36, 39, 47, 51-52, 61, 63, 69, 71, 75, 77, 81, 86-87, 90, 97, 100-102, 107, 110, 114-118, 122, 123-129, 131-135, 140, 143-144, 148-149, 154, 156-157, 159-165, 168, 170-176, 178, 181, 183-185, 190-192, 194-197, 200-201, 203, 205, 215, 223, 230-231, 238, 241-243
Leslie, David – 8
Letters of Horning – 78
Letters Patent – 20, 40
Levenwick – 189, 214-215
Lewis, Rev. George – 136
Light out of Darkness – 131
Lighthouse Commissioners – 110
Linga – 188
Liverpool – 85, 165
Livy – 171
Local Government – 7, 14
Lochend – 23, 188
Log Book – 162, 168, 241
London – 17, 28, 37, 79, 110, 131, 139, 168, 175-176, 180, 243
Lords of Session – 43
Lords, House of – 139
Lordship Estate – 65
Low, Rev. George – 27
Lunars and Chronometers – 95
Lunnasting – 2, 41, 101, 117-120, 137, 217-219
Lyell, Sir Leonard – 141
Macfarlane, Rev. Andrew – 129
MacGowan, Rev. John – 100
Macnab, Charles – 123
MacPherson, Robert – 37
Madras School – 180
Mainland (Shetland) – 1, 30, 36, 52, 77, 119, 150, 174
Mair, Rev. Patrick – 77-78
Malcolmson, James – 123
Manpower Services Commission – 198
Manson, Thomas – 129, 135, 226
Marjoribanks, Adam – 22, 224
Marshall, Alexander – 86, 88-89, 96, 104
Mathewson, Andrew D. – 83-105, 113, 205, 227, ill. 4
Mathewson, Arthur – 85
Mathewson, Laurence – 103
McMorine, John – 86, 104, 124, 215
McNicoll, Elizabeth – 190
Meal Roads – 143
Medical Officer of Health – 189
Melby – 24, 51, 61, 70, 180
Member of Parliament – 95
Menzies, Rev. John – 81
Merchant Marine – 175
Merit Certificate – 173
Mid Walls – 58-60, 225
Mid Yell – 83, 86-87, 97-98, 162, 194, 227
Mill, Rev. John – 71-72, 82, 182
Millar, Robert – 158, 171, 216
Minister for Education – 158, 160
Mitchell, Alexander – 46
Mitchell, Lady – 41
Mitchell, Rev. James – 232
Mitchell, Sir Andrew – 40-41, 76
Mitchell, Sir John – 41, 63

Mitchell, Rev. William – 76, 155
Moderator, Church of Scotland – 23, 87-88
Moncrieff, Duncan – 58
Moncrieff, James – 50, 225
Moncrieff, Laurence – 41, 225
Moneypenny, David – 16
Mongersdale, Fetlar – 96
Moravian – 124-126, 215
Morton, Earl of – 4, 44-45, 47-48, 71, 232
Mossbank – 143, 197, 211
Mouat, Thomas (of Gardie) – 68, 70, 80-81
Muir, Robert J., HMI – 145, 149-151, 171
Munn and Dunning Reports – 198
Napoleonic Wars – 107
National and Higher National Certificate – 204
National Certificate – 203-204
Natural History Society – 81
Neill, Patrick – 81-82
Nesting – 2, 8, 15, 18, 24, 32, 36-37, 55-57, 120, 136-138, 188, 205, 217-218
Netherdaill – 60
New Statistical Account – 116, 122, 243
New Testament – 34, 51, 83, 93-94, 233
New Zealand – 156, 173, 180
Newton, Sir Isaac – 83
Nicolson, Sir Arthur – 113, 115, 117
Night School – 130, 200
Nordern Lichts – 193
Norn – 27
Norse – 9, 17, 27, 43, 180
North Atlantic Fisheries College – 205
North Isles – 174
North Mainland – 174
North of Scotland College of Education – 202
North of Scotland – 167, 170, 202, 237
North Roe – 122, 188, 220
North Sea oil – 197

North Sea – 13, 197
North Unst – 122
Northmavine – 8, 21-22, 25, 30-32, 44, 50, 55, 57, 79, 111, 136, 143, 145-146, 219
Norway – 27
Norwegian – 27, 201
Norwick – 188, 224
Noss, Scousburgh – 153
Occaness (Eshaness?) – 31
Ogilvy, Charles – 126
Old Testament – 38, 94
Old Vidlin schools – ill. 25
Ollaberry – 31, 143, 188, 212, 219, 221-222
Olnafirth, Delting – 87, 143, 211
Omand, Gilbert – 46
Orcadians – 27
Organiser of Further Education – 200
Orkney and Shetland Association – 174
Orkney – 7, 9, 11-15, 17, 26-30, 34, 41-42, 44- 45, 48-49, 65, 79-82, 99, 105, 110, 123-124, 136, 140-141, 162, 170, 172, 174, 202, 234, 241-243
Oxna – 188
P&O Shipping Co – 131
Pack Report on Discipline in Schools – 198
Papa Stour – 2, 38, 51, 53-54, 56-58, 60-62, 67-68, 118, 121, 136, 222, 226, 236, 238-239
Papa – 188
Parochial Board – 146
Parochial School – 3-4, 19, 24, 26, 32, 43-44, 51, 54, 56, 58, 60, 63, 71-72, 74, 77-81, 86-87, 89-91, 94, 97, 100-102, 104, 106, 109, 111-113, 115, 117-118, 120, 127- 128, 131, 137-139, 142, 148, 164-165, 168, 183, 187, 207, 209, 211-212, 216, 218-221, 223, 225, 227-228, 230, 242
Parochial Schools (Scotland) Act, 1803 – 89
Pauper Olaus – 13

Peterhead – 118, 122, 158
Peterson, William – 110, 178-179, 219
Petition – 2, 21, 23-24, 30, 34-35, 40, 45-46, 52-55, 57, 61, 67, 73, 78, 88, 95, 103, 106, 114-115, 134, 143, 147, 149, 156, 160, 174, 181, 187, 205, 208
Pettister, Unst – 188
Pitcairn, Rev. James – 8
Pole, William – 120, 211, 217, 226
Polson, Samuel – 187
Poor Box or Sacrament Collections – 32
Poor Law Board – 181
Port Arthur – 204
Porteous, A. A. – 159, 184
Pottinger, Rev. James – 138
Pottinger, William – 138, 217
Press Gang – 66, 83
Prime Minister – 181
Prince Alfred Street – 183
Privy Council – 8-10, 12
Procurator of the Church of Scotland – 75
Promotion Scheme – 191
Protestant – 8
Proverbs – 34, 38, 51, 83, 92-94
Provost of Lerwick – 159
Public School – 138, 148-149, 151, 153-154, 171, 183-184, 187, 241
Punch – 180
Pupils and teacher in new school, Vidlin – ill. 28
Quarff – 2, 8, 77-78, 136, 209-210
Quarff bairns c. 1903 – ill. 17
Quarter Sessions of the Justices of the Peace – 114
Quendale – 23, 72-73, 122, 154, 189, 212-215
Quiness, Vidlin – 120, 137, 218
Rampini, Sheriff – 146
Ramsay, Prof. George G. – 140, 241
Ramsay, Rev. Robert – 14
Readers – 15-16, 92, 99, 184
Reawick – 177, 208
Rechabite Hall – 183

Reformation – 7, 13, 20, 39, 179
Reformed Church – 7
Reid, Alex McDonald –157-158, 171
Returns from Sheriffs of the Scottish Counties – 109
Rhind, William – 187
Richmond, Duke of – 139
Riskaness, Walls – 58
Robertson, Hugh – 95, 104, 221
Robertson, J. J. – 193
Robertson, Rev. James – 87, 100-101, 211, 215
Robertson, Tom – 95
Robertson, William – 146, 208-209, 223
Roman Catholic Church – 11
Ross, Captain George, RN – 74
Ross, Charles – 22, 31, 219, 221, 224
Ross, John (of Westsandwick) – 99
Ross, John – 146, 209, 221, ill. 8
Royal Burgh – 13
Royal Engineers – 143
Royal Navy – 107, 125
Sabbath School – 87, 97-99, 103, 179
Sabbath Schools Union – 97
Sallust – 124
Salt Tax – 3, 18
Sandness – 2, 21-22, 32, 38, 41, 50-60, 67-68, 70, 118, 136, 179-180, 224-225, 236, 238-239
Sandness School — Appeal Letter – ill. 3
Sandsound – 118, 208
Sandsting – 5, 8, 18, 55, 73, 81, 101, 119, 122, 136, 188, 207
Sandwick – 23, 35, 37, 73, 99, 136, 152, 154, 156, 194, 197, 212, 227, 242
Savile, Rev. David – 80
Saxony, Germany – 125
Scalloway Grammar school – 71
Scalloway – 8-9, 13-15, 33, 40, 63, 71, 76, 78, 118, 123, 143, 146, 194, 201-202, 204-205, 223
Scandinavia – 9, 27, 44
Schneider – 171

School Board (various) – 103-104, 138-143, 147-149, 152, 154, 156-163, 168-176, 183, 189-190, 200, 208, 214, 221, 224, 241
School Board letter – ill. 14
School Dues – 95
School Log – 143, 148, 154, 162
School Management Committees – 190
School Medical Officer – 189
Scotch Education Code – 169
Scotch Education Department – 139-140, 152, 159, 162, 171
Scotland a Half Educated Nation – 136
Scotland – 1, 9, 11, 13, 15, 17, 19-21, 24, 28, 42, 47, 70, 75, 80, 82, 89, 91, 98, 110, 117, 122-123, 128, 135-136, 138-140, 160-163, 167-168, 170, 173-174, 176, 184-185, 187, 190, 196, 198, 202, 230-231, 237, 240-243
Scotsman – 180-181
Scott, Dr R. T. C., RN – 180
Scott, James – 78
Scott, John – 2, 24, 51, 55, 57-61, 71, 223
Scott, Mrs (of Vaila) – 62
Scottish Advisory Council on Primary (1946) and Secondary Education (1947) – 193
Scottish Certificate of Education – 196
Scottish Certificate of Education Ordinary Grade – 197
Scottish Education Act, 1872 – 173
Scottish Education Department – 163, 173, 184, 191-193, 195, 201
Scottish Office Education Department – 199
Scottish Office, Education and Industry Department – 199
Scottish Reformation – 7
Scottish School Book Association – 97
Scotts of Melby – 180
Scriptures – 7, 16, 20, 98, 179
Seafield – 84

Second Letters Patent – 40
Second World War – 192
Secondary Education Minute – 171
Sellafirth – 188, 228
Senior Chief Inspector of Schools – 180
Session Clerk – 16, 32-33, 54, 61, 63, 71, 76-77, 103, 155, 181, 221, 234-235, 239
Session Register – 54
Shennan, Sheriff Hay – 174
Sheriff Court – 8, 146
Sheriff of the Counties of Orkney and Shetland – 170
Shetland Advertiser – 128, 134-135, 162, 165-167, 175-176, 182, 242
Shetland College of Further Education – 203-204
Shetland Development Council – 201
Shetland Fisheries and Sea Training School – 201
Shetland Islands Council – 197, 204
Shetland Literary and Scientific Society – 132, 166
Shetland News – 129, 159, 163, 176, 182, 204, 242
Shetland Presbytery – 9, 79
Shetland Times Printing Works – 183
Shetland Times – 117, 135, 140, 147, 151, 162-163, 176, 183, 242
Side schools – 188, 212, 215
Sinclair, Laurence, of Brugh – 12, 14
Sinclair, Rev. Malcolm – 8
Skallowaybankis – 14
Skeld – 118-120, 146-147, 209, 223
Skellister – 137, 217
Skerries – 1-2, 35-37, 109-110, 117, 137, 178-179, 201, 218-219
Smiles, Samuel – 108
Smith, Elizabeth J. – 155
Smith, John – 33, 35, 48, 77-78, 209, 212, 221-223
Smith, Mr (the tacksman) – 85-86
Smith, William – 132, 209, 214
Sneddon Report on Learning to Teach – 198

INDEX

Soc. in S. for Pr. Chr. Know. – 19-20, 24, 28-29, 39, 41-42, 45, 48-49, 51, 53-54, 60-61, 64, 69-72, 78-79, 81-82, 85, 110, 138, 141, 162, 172, 181-182, 205-211, 213-218, 220-228, 241-242
SOED – 199
SOED Report – 199
Sound, Lerwick – 2, 64, 88, 117-118, 122, 168, 187, 194, 197-198, 204, 208, 215, 223-224, 242
South Mainland – 52, 174
South Nesting – 138, 217
South Ronaldsay – 26
South-the-Voe – 188
Spence, Catherine Stafford – 124
Spence, Dr G. W. – 167
Spence, Dr William – 124
Spinning Mistress – 41
Spinning School, Lunnasting – 41
SSPCK School, Tangwick, Eshaness – ill. 12
St Andrews House – 198
St Helens – 134
St Kilda – 21
St Magnus Church – 168
St Magnus Episcopal schoolroom – 183
Standard Grade Examination – 198-199
Statistical Account – 6, 106, 116, 122, 135, 243
Stenness – 15
Stephen, William – 97
Stewart Court – 46-47
Stewart, George – 141, 213
Stewart-depute – 45, 47-48
Still, Fetlar – 120
Stirlingshire – 11
Stout, James – 177-178, 208
Stout, Thomas – 76-77, 214, 221
Stove, Walls – 58, 225
Strong, William – 36, 214
Subscription Rooms – 126, 128, 130
Subscription School – 86-87, 123-124, 127-128, 164, 208-209, 215
Sullom Voe Terminal – 197, 203

Sumburgh – 192, 213
Sutherland, Alexander – 156, 210
Sutherland, Walter – 137
Swinister – 156, 221
Swinton, Rev. Robert – 8
Symbister – 42, 68
Tait, Lowrie – 107
Tawse, John – 118
Taylor, Chaplain James – 23
Technical, Vocational and Educational Initiative – 198
Telemaque – 171
Thatcher Government – 198
The "Fivepenny Book" – 145
The God of Glory – 131
The Graphic – 180
The Methodist Magazine – 99
The Old Infant School – 183
The Philosophical Journal – 99
The Schoolmaster – 10, 14, 32, 62, 65, 68, 70, 78, 108, 172, 231
The Shetland Bank – 126
The Shetland Book – 193
Thomason, Magnus – 119, 210
Thomson, John – 156, 212, 214, 219, 221
Thomson, Robert – 177, 212, 214
Thomson, Sinclair – 110, 219
Three Rs – 2, 21, 83, 91, 120, 142, 144, 152, 175, 178, 184, 187, 236
Tingon – 188
Tingwall – 8, 14-17, 19, 25, 27, 32-34, 42, 45, 50, 55, 63, 71, 75-80, 82, 122, 155-156, 188, 204, 221
Tingwall, Archdeacon of – 8
Town Council – 174
Trondra – 122, 188, 223
Tulloch, John – 155, 221, 226
Turdaill, Walls – 59
Twageos – 164
Twatt – 151, 207
Umfra, William – 14
Union Bank – 134
United Brethern – 125
United Presbyterian Church – 129, 221
University Bursary – 174

University Preliminary Examinations – 157
Unst – 1, 8, 14, 24, 27, 32, 34, 74, 80-81, 85, 89, 111, 117, 122, 136, 141, 174, 187-188, 204, 223, 241
Up Helly Aa – 169
Upper Catfirth – 137
Urafirth – 194-195, 220
Uyea – 188
Uyeasound – 117, 122, 224
Vaila – 17, 28, 33, 35, 41, 61-62, 65, 75, 77, 88, 112-113, 120, 130, 138, 174, 180, 183, 186, 188, 190, 202, 207
Vassa, Nesting – 138, 217
Vatchley, Dunrossness – 181, 213, 215
Verbal reasoning tests – 191
Vidlin – 120, 137, 217-218
Vidlin Primary School, 1996 – ill. 26
Vindicator – 80-82
Virgil – 124, 127
Virkie – 153, 189, 215
Visitation Report – 10, 18, 22, 34, 35, 37, 42, 45, 54, 72, 78, 81, 118
Voe – 1-2, 52, 62, 83, 102-103, 113, 119, 122, 137-138, 142-143, 188, 197, 203, 209-211, 226, 228, 235
Voxter Centre – 202
Voxter Farm – 201
Waldie, Rev. – 32
Walker, John – 103, 140
Walls – 2, 8, 21-22, 24-25, 31-32, 38, 42, 44, 50-53, 55-65, 67-74, 78-79, 83, 97, 119, 140, 143, 148, 188, 200, 205, 209, 224-225, 234, 236, 238-239
Warnock Report on the Education of Pupils with Special Educational Needs – 198
Wart School, Reawick – 177
Weisdale – 33, 71, 76, 118, 121, 155, 222, 228
Weisdale Public School c.1895 — pupils with headteacher – ill. 21

West Burrafirth – 188, 209
Westminster – 141
Westray – 26
Westsandwick – 99
Westshore, Scalloway – 40
Westside – 174
Weyland Farm, Orkney – 202
Whalsay – 2, 68, 120, 136-137, 194-195, 201, 218-219
White, David J. – 187
Whiteford, Robert – 168-169
Whitehall – 139
Whiteness – 33, 42, 76, 118, 121, 155, 162, 197, 222
Wightman, W. M. – 184
Williamson, Gilbert – 207, ill. 13
Williamson, James – 2, 35
Williamson, Jeanette – 201
Williamson, Laurence – 95-96
Williamson, Peter – 149, 151, 217, 229
Windhouse, Dunrossness – 35
Wishart, Miss – 137, 217
Wünsche, W. L. – 126
Yeat, Rev. John – 14
Yell – 18, 32, 34, 55-56, 81, 83-91, 93-103, 105, 111-113, 115-117, 122, 136, 141-142, 149, 162, 188, 194, 204-205, 208, 216, 219, 226-228, 242
Young, Robert – 157, 159-161, 173, 184, 216, ill. 19
Zetland Commissioners of Supply – 170
Zetland Education Committee – 193
Zetland Presbytery – 16, 21-22, 24, 26, 28, 31, 34, 36, 44, 52-53, 156, 241
Zetland – 6-9, 11-12, 16-17, 21-22, 24, 26, 28-29, 31, 34, 36, 40-41, 44-45, 49, 52-53, 69, 81, 156, 170, 193, 204, 230-232, 241-242
Zetland, Archedeacon of – 8